THE TRAVELERS' GUIDE TO
EUROPEAN CUSTOMS & MANNERS

How to converse, dine, tip, drive, bargain, dress, make friends & conduct business while in Europe

Nancy L. Braganti and Elizabeth Devine

Meadowbrook
Distributed by Simon and Schuster
New York

Library of Congress Cataloging in Publication Data

Devine, Elizabeth, 1938- The travelers' guide to
European customs and manners.

1. Europe—Description and travel—1971-—Guidebooks. 2. Etiquette—Europe. 3. Europe—Social
life and customs. I. Braganti, Nancy, 1941- II. Title.
D909.D48 1984
914'.0455   83-23700
ISBN 0-88166-009-4
S & S Ordering #: 0-671-54493-4

Published by Meadowbrook, Inc., Deephaven,
MN 55391.

BOOK TRADE DISTRIBUTION by Simon and
Schuster, a division of Simon & Schuster, Inc.,
1230 Avenue of the Americas, New York, NY 10020

10
Printed in the United States of America

Editor: Louise Delagran
Design: Anne Brownfield
Cover Illustration: Leland Klanderman
Interior Illustration: Bob Doeg, Jim Olson
Production: Pam Barnard, Don Nicholes, Gloria Otremba,
Vicki Revsbech, Lynn Rusch, Sharon Stanton, John Ware

To Fausto, who cooked lots of pasta and offered his support and encouragement; to Tanya, who learned to be self-sufficient; and to M.E.F., who was always there.

N.B.

To La, Patrick, and Caitlin who give more joy than they will ever know.

E.D.

ACKNOWLEDGEMENTS

We wish to thank the following people for their assistance in this project: Luis Abiega, Beatia Ahmad, Birgitta Amsler, Helle Andersen, Angela Anderson, Sandra Anitua, Carol Antonsson, Belma and Sam Baskett, Dorothy W. Bennett, Eleanor and Nancy Benson, Fatima Brazâo, Jan Buechting, Pamela Cabell-Whiting, Joseph Callewaert, Joan Campagne, Maria Grazia Caporali, Maureen and Michael Carey, Hans Cedarblad, Jonathan and Beverly Cohen, Benjamin Crocker, Monique, Brigitte, and Arsen Darnay, Mari Delagran, Eeve de Felice, Natalio Diaz, Sila Dikici, Ivan Dimov, John and Georgiana Dolejsi, Nicola Dyde, Victor Eugene Dyer III, Barbara Eachus, Aline Egger, Milagros Emmart, Mary Farrell, Kevin Featherstone, Nancy Ferguson, Bernardo and Christine Fernandes, Martha and Richard Forsyth, Loreto and Trudi Forti, Graham Frear, Slawomir Fryska, Üstün Germen, Kari Hamre, Socrates Heracleous, Gail Pike Hercher, Andreas Iacovides, Anne-Marie Jouglarisse, Jane Lakatos, Bistra Lankova, Cybèle Léger, Kelley Leveque, Hanibal Lopez-Molne, Liv Lyons, Shelley Madson, Paivi Manner, Margaret Mariani, Hanna Matousek, Lillian Maury, Patricia McGurdy, Lois and Ole Meerwald, Elaine Metzler, Genevieve Moloney, Ira Alexandra Nopola, Marie Nappi, Costantino and Johanne Negulescu, Lennart Nielsen, Christine Oprecht, Alexandra Papazoglou, Patricia Parker, Bert and Anne-Lise Paulsen, Seija Peterson, Ray Phillips, Mary Pierce, Hervé Pierre, Marie Jose Pierrot, Anna and Piotrunio Przytula, Alex, Beatriz, and Marcel Quiroga, Michael Radovanovic, Susan Raskin, Mark and Ghyslaine Renn, Barbro Roehrdanz, Victoria Vargas Rosello, Irving Rubin, Anelise Sawkins, Rosemary Schneider, Karen Bachant Sellars, Jan Smith, Marie Luise Smith, Karen Solstad, Jose Sousa, Gerd Steckel, Henry Steiner, Eva Ström, Mark Szajner, Helen Szakacs, Argie Tiliakos, Monica Tucker, Dincer and Priscilla Ulutaş, Rose-Marie VanOtterloo, Mijke VanOtterloo, Anna Vojtech, Peter Wanka, Laura Warren, Trautel Wiechman, Elsa Wiersma, Birthe Winer, Peter Wishnock, Karen Wylie, Jane Wyman, Margaret Young, Katerina Zencuch.

Contents

INTRODUCTION

Finally, here's the book that gives you the "how to" of European travel, not just the "where to." The guidebooks all tell you where to find the monuments, museums and cathedrals that you want to see, and the restaurants and wines that you want to sample. But this is the only book that tells you how to understand and enjoy one of the most important parts of foreign travel: the people and their customs.

Customs and manners in other countries vary widely from those in the U.S., and these differences can make you feel awkward, uncertain and embarrassed when you travel. That's why we decided to write *The Travelers' Guide to European Customs and Manners*—so that even first-time visitors to Europe can understand European customs and feel at home.

With this book we hope to help you by indicating what you can expect of Europeans and what they expect of you. We tell you what to do in a variety of settings—from public places, such as shops or restaurants, to private homes and business meetings. In all of these situations, *The Travelers' Guide* shows you how to fit in, and how to avoid being rude inadvertently and embarrassing yourself or others. With this knowledge you'll be comfort-able meeting Europeans in any situation, and you are sure to get the most out of your trip, whether you travel for business or pleasure.

For easy reference, the book is arranged in chapters alphabetically by country. The chapters are divided into sections, each of which deals with a major concern of travelers. Below we discuss what you will find in each section and give examples of how this information can help you deal with unfamiliar situations.

Greetings: Since first impressions are crucial, we begin each chapter with information on the customary ways to greet people. We suggest when you should shake hands and how you should address people. In Portugal, for instance, it is important to address professionals by their occupational titles (i.e., "Hello, Engineer Sousa").

Conversation: In this section, we suggest good topics of conversation and list topics you should avoid, so that your friendly attempt at small talk doesn't result in a major *faux pas*. For example, a sure way to make the French write you off is to use the classic American conversation opener, "What do you do for a living?" To the French, this is a very personal question.

Telephones: Most of us end up having to rely on public telephones at some point, and there's little that's more frustrating than standing in line for a phone and not having the foggiest idea what to do once it's your turn. We give explicit instructions for using the phone in each country.

Public Manners: In this section, we consider customs that affect behavior in public places, so you won't embarrass yourself in front of a crowd. Toss away your gum wrapper on a street in Switzerland, for example, and people may reproach you for being rude and inconsiderate.

Dress: You can rarely offend by dressing conservatively. But you can upset people if you enter a Turkish mosque in shoes, or dress too casually for a dinner party in Austria. We provide dress "codes" for most of the situations you will encounter.

Meals: This section begins with the customary times and foods for each meal, so you know what to expect. Don't try, for instance, to go to a restaurant in Spain at 5:00 or 6:00 p.m. expecting to order dinner—all restaurants will be closed at that time.

We continue this section with table manners, so you don't unintentionally offend your hosts. In Poland, for instance, you should take small portions the first time food is offered, because you're sure to be pressured to have seconds and even thirds. If you fill up on the first round and refuse a second helping, you could insult your hostess by implying that the food wasn't good.

Also in this section, we discuss the variety of places where you can get food and drink. Many times, reading the sign outside a place offering food doesn't really tell you what to expect. We explain what kind of food and atmosphere you'll find. We also list some of the country's special dishes you will want to try.

Hotels and Private Homes: In these sections we consider what you should know about staying in hotels and visiting private homes. (Information for private homes also applies to bed-and-breakfast accommodations.) In Greece, for example, you could be unwittingly rude by filling the tub for a bath, because water tanks in Greek homes tend to be very small, and you would be depriving others in the house of hot water.

Tipping: This subject seems to distress travelers more than almost any other. We tell you when and how much to tip.

Business Practices: It is increasingly important to know the correct behavior for business situations, as America becomes ever more involved in world markets for its products and services. We tell you the proper way to act and what to expect in business affairs. A Spaniard who makes arrangements for American business people told us that he has trouble convincing them that they should not do business at the first meeting—that the Spanish want to know business associates as people first. At least one American flew home after his first meeting at a Spanish firm, complaining that people just kept asking him questions about himself and didn't want to get down to business. A little understanding could have meant a big sale.

Holidays: We list the holidays in each country, so you can plan your trip to include a special holiday celebration or arrange a business itinerary to avoid a holiday lull.

Transportation: Unless you are on a package tour, you will need to arrange to get from one place to another. We discuss both public transportation and what to do (and not do) if you drive. Note the important advice concerning seat belts which are mandatory in most European countries, and alcohol and driving. In Ireland, for example, failing a breathalyzer test can bring a fine of 500 pounds and/or six months in jail.

Legal Matters and Safety: We include information on major legal obligations you might have when traveling. This section is especially important for anyone traveling to Eastern Europe. For instance, if you are traveling to East Germany, you should know that you must register with the police if you plan to stay more than 24 hours.

Key Phrases: We end each chapter with a few useful phrases and their phonetic pronunciations. You'll find that the small effort spent in learning a few words and phrases in the country's language will be richly repaid. And you'll find magic in the simple words "Please" and "Thank you."

Note: As you read through the sections in each country, you may sometimes detect what seems to be sexism in our advice. It isn't really sexism, but a reflection of the country we're describing. Much as we might wish that standards of behavior for men and women were the same, they aren't, especially in the more traditional European countries.

We have also given advice based on the most conservative behavior you will be likely to encounter. You can't err by being too polite, but you can by being too informal. In any situation, if you notice that standards of behavior are more casual than we have suggested, by all means take your cue from the people around you.

General Tips for European Travel

You'll find some customs true wherever you go in Europe: people shake hands a lot more than in the U.S.; they eat with fork in left hand and knife in right; and they never put their hands in their laps at the table. Note also that the toilet and tub or shower are usually in separate rooms; public toilets are often unisex; hotels often keep your passport overnight; and the streets are far safer after dark than the streets in U.S. cities.

You'll also find that the following advice will help you get along with people everywhere in Europe.

• Don't judge. Enjoy each country on its own terms, for what it is and for what it has to offer. Try not to compare it with the U.S., especially when you're speaking to natives of the country. Don't consider American customs the standard against which all others must be measured. How many times have you heard of the American who asks a European shopkeeper, "How much is that in real money?" or says that the English drive on the "wrong" side of the road. There is no "real" money, no right or wrong side of the road. People simply do things differently.

• Be informed. Before you go, read about the countries you will visit. Any good encyclopedia will give you a capsule history. The Michelin Green Guides and the Companion Guides both offer excellent histories. And pay special attention to the news from Europe in the weeks before you leave. You will be stunned—and perhaps embarrassed—at how much Europeans know about American history and politics and how ignorant we are about other countries.

• Ask questions and listen. A good technique in conversation is to interview people. Don't appear pushy or prying, but show a genuine interest in the subject. When bringing up one of the topics we suggest, try to use questions to draw your new acquaintance out—and then really listen to the answer. The best route to charming people is to be a good audience.

• Be sincere. Don't flatter people so obsequiously that "insincere" lights up all over. If you genuinely like something, say so, but be low-keyed and understated. As you'll read in several chapters, people in some countries feel awkward rather than pleased when they are complimented.

• Learn a few foreign words. Try to learn a few phrases in the language of the country you are visiting, but don't worry too much about the language barrier. It's there, all right, but it's not so formidable as some people think.

If you are going as a tourist, or on a short business trip, you can probably get along with a phrase book and a slight flair for the dramatic. Sign language can be amazingly effective, as Nancy Braganti's experience shows: "My sister and I went to Greece, not knowing a syllable of the language. We were in a cafe, trying to order hard-boiled eggs, and getting nowhere with attempts at verbal communication. My sister made a noise like a chicken, flexed her arm muscle and made it hard, and made an egg shape with her fingers. We got hard-boiled eggs." Also try pointing to words in a small pocket dictionary or to items that you want in shops and restaurants.

If you're going to a country for an extended stay, however, you would be well-advised to study the language. There are adult education programs all over the country offering courses in a variety of languages. You can also buy or borrow library copies of language records that will help you pick up some basic phrases and vocabulary. Keep in mind, however, that native speakers will talk to you much more rapidly than the people on the recordings.

• Maintain a sense of humor. This is perhaps the most important advice of all for a traveler. If you're in a situation that is becoming increasingly irksome, try to look at it from the outside. Chances are it will be a funny moment to treasure when you return home.

About the Authors

We both brought to this book a love of travel and a curiosity about the ways in which people in different countries behave. Elizabeth Devine has written travel articles, and Nancy Braganti has taught languages, both in America and abroad. Between us, we have lived in or visited 15 of the countries covered in the book.

Our research for this book included months of bookwork and many personal interviews. We talked to 65 people who were either natives of the countries or Americans who had lived there: people from all 25 countries and from all walks of life—secretaries to screenwriters, engineers to folklorists, architects to homemakers, and tennis teachers to business people. We also conducted countless telephone interviews with travel agents and with people at various embassies and consulates. After we finished the manuscript, more than 50 native and non-native reviewers went over it to be sure we hadn't missed anything.

One of our favorite phone interviews was the one we had with an American woman at the Polish Consulate in Boston. We explained our project to her and asked if she knew the Polish word for eels, since they are so commonly eaten in Poland. The American protested, "I've just come from living in Poland for six months, and I never heard of eels being served." We persisted, and the woman finally looked up the word in her Polish dictionary. When she came back with the answer, she wailed, "Do you mean *that's* what I was eating all that time?" (Of course, if she had read this book, she would have known.)

We hope this book will help you do as the Romans do when in Rome, as the Parisians do when in Paris, as the Czechs do when in Prague, and. . . .

Bon voyage.

Nancy Braganti
Elizabeth Devine

CHAPTER ONE

AUSTRIA

LINZ •

★ VIENNA

• INNSBRUCK

• KLAGENFURT

For Austrians, the good life is filled with comfort and the pleasures of food and friends. They enjoy spending hours in a cafe having coffee and pastries and visiting with friends.

Austrians also value good manners, and they have made graciousness a way of life. When Austrians enter a shop, for example, they greet each person there. To Americans, this may seem unnecessary and almost silly. To Austrians, it is only common politeness to acknowledge that the people aren't part of the shop scenery.

This graciousness may make the Austrians seem more formal than Americans, but they are never rigid or stiff.

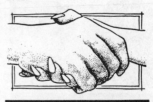

GREETINGS

• Shake hands when you're introduced, or when you greet someone, and when you leave. Be aware that Austrian men often kiss women's hands when they meet them. American men may simply shake hands with Austrian women.

• A man should wait for a woman to extend her hand before offering his.

• Don't introduce yourself to people in a group. Wait for your host or hostess to introduce you.

• Use occupational titles with or without the last name when you're speaking to male professionals (for example, *Rechtsanwalt Schaenzer,* Lawyer Schaenzer).

• Use *"Frau"* plus the occupational title when addressing female professionals, or the wives of professionals (for example, *Frau Rechtsanwalt,* Mrs. Lawyer).

• Address all women over 20 as *"Frau,"* which means "Mrs.," even if they're not married.

CONVERSATION

• Only address very close friends by their first names. Austrians are quite formal in this respect—many business colleagues address each other by last names throughout their careers.

• Good topics of conversation: what you like about Austria, American technology (Austrians are interested in and impressed by it), professions, families, cars, music (Austrians are very knowledgeable about classical music), hiking and skiing (people will be impressed if you know something about the Austrian skiing champions).

• Topics to avoid: money, religion, divorce or separation.

• Never call an Austrian a German. Although they speak the same language, Austrians and Germans have different customs, values and histories.

• Don't tease anyone playfully. Austrians won't understand what you're doing and may be offended.

• Don't offer casual compliments such as "I like your dress," or "That's an attractive hair style." An Austrian will likely demur and may be very embarrassed.

• Be cautious about making promises of any kind, as Austrians take them very seriously.

TELEPHONES

• To make a local call from a public telephone, insert a one-schilling coin. When your party answers, push the button to complete the connection. At the end of three minutes you will hear a tone, after which you have 20 seconds to deposit more money.

• Make long-distance calls from either the post office, where you pay at the end of the call, or from a public phone, where you must have a sufficient amount of change.

• Note that long-distance operators speak English.

• When answering the phone, say *"Hallo"* or *"Ja."*

PUBLIC MANNERS

• Men should stand when a woman enters a room and when they're talking to a woman who is standing.

• To attract someone's attention, hold up your hand with the index finger extended.

• When you enter a shop, always greet the salespeople.

• If you go to the theater, opera or ballet, don't try to wear or take your coat into the auditorium with you. Check it at the cloakroom. In fact, an usher will probably prevent you from entering until you have checked your coat.

DRESS

• Note that men usually wear pants and shirts for casual wear; women wear pants, skirts or dresses. Jeans are acceptable, but don't wear shorts in towns or cities.

• For business, men should always wear dark, conservative suits and ties, though in summer they can wear lighter colors. Women should wear suits or dresses.

• For dinner parties, men should wear suits, and women, dresses.

• For theater, opera and concert openings, dress formally:

tuxedos for men and cocktail dresses for women. At other times, men wear suits, and women wear dresses.

• Don't be surprised to see Austrians in native dress on special occasions—men in *loden* jackets (loden is a thick wool that comes in olive green, grey or black) and women in *dirndls* (full gathered skirts).

MEALS

Hours and Foods

Breakfast *(frühstück):* 8:00 a.m. The morning meal is usually rolls with butter and jam, cheese and sometimes cold cuts, a soft-boiled egg, and *melange* (coffee with hot milk).

Lunch *(mittagessen):* 1:00 p.m. The meal starts with soup, often a beef broth with dumplings or noodles. A meat dish, such as roast pork or broiled chicken follows, along with vegetables, and potatoes, rice or noodles. A salad is often served with the meal, and fruit, cheese, or dessert, and black coffee follow. Drinks are beer, wine or mineral water.

Dinner *(abendessen):*

7:00 to 9:00 p.m. The Austrian dinner is a substantial, hot meal, much like lunch. At a dinner party, wine or beer may be served before the meal, with an appetizer such as smoked salmon or caviar on bread. The meal will be much like the noon meal. Expect to be served an after-dinner brandy: *kirschwasser* (cherry), *himbeerbrandy* (raspberry) or *slivovitz* (plum).

Breaks: Many Austrians have *jause* (a coffee break) at 4:00 p.m. Sandwiches and pastries accompany the coffee.

Table Manners

• Serve yourself if platters of food are passed around the table. In some homes, you may be handed a plate with food already on it.

• Don't begin eating until your hostess does.

• Keep both hands on the table while eating.

• Eat as the Austrians do with the fork in your left hand and the knife in your right, and use the knife to push food onto the back of your fork.

• Don't cut fish or potatoes with a knife; it implies that they are not tender enough.

• Never bite into a whole roll. Break it apart with your fingers first.

• When you finish eating, put

your utensils side-by-side on the plate.

• Don't feel obliged to drink alcoholic beverages. People will not press you to, especially if you are driving, since laws prohibiting drunken driving are very strict.

• Leave by 11:00 p.m. from a dinner party, especially if this is the first time you've been to your hosts' house for a meal.

Places to Eat

• Try the following alternatives to traditional restaurants.

Beises are similar to British pubs. Guests can eat and drink, and play chess or cards.

A *heuriger* offers wine and food.

A *kaffeehaus* is a cafe that offers several different types of coffee. You can also order wine, although it's not what most people drink there. If you go to a cafe, don't feel that you have to leave or reorder after one cup. Austrians often spend a long time chatting, reading newspapers (often available in English) and playing cards in cafes.

A *keller* is a restaurant with a lively, noisy, convivial atmosphere. There is often live entertainment.

A *kellerlokal,* a cellar restaurant, offers inexpensive meals.

A *konditorei* serves pastries, coffee, tea and cold drinks. Some also offer souffles and sandwiches.

A *stube* serves wine and appetizers and offers a lively, friendly atmosphere. There is often live music.

• Don't expect menus to be posted in restaurant windows. However, the exterior often indicates how fancy the decor—and prices—will be.

• Look for a shield at the entrance to the restaurant with a "G" on it. This signifies that government inspectors have checked the quality of food and service.

• To call a waiter, say *"Herr Ober."* To call a waitress, say *"Fraulein."*

• Note that most large restaurants serve meals until midnight.

• Don't expect the waiter to bring a bill. Instead when you're ready to pay, tell the waiter what you've ordered, and he will calculate what you owe on the spot.

Specialties

• Austria is famous for its elaborate cream-filled pastries. Also try *Serbische bohnensuppe* (Serbian bean soup); *goulasch* (stew); *tafelspitz* (boiled beef with horseradish or chive sauce); *schnitzel cordon bleu* (veal, ham, and cheese dipped in batter and deep-fried); *spanferkel* (roast suckling pig); *bauernschmaus* (ham, salt pork, sausage, sauerkraut and dumplings); *rehrücken* (venison); *rotkraut* (sweet and sour red cabbage, with caraway seeds); *knödel* (a dumpling, more popular than potatoes or rice, used in soups, as a side dish with meat, or with jam as a dessert).

• For dessert, try *palatschinken* (pancakes filled with jam); *Salzburger nockerl* (oven pancake); *sachertorte* (chocolate cake); and *strudel* (pastry with apples, cherries, or cheese).

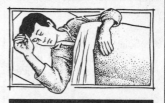

HOTELS

• If you want a room with a bath and toilet, ask for bath and "W.C." The two don't necessarily go together.

• If you are told that a room is *"garni,"* it means that bed and breakfast are included.

• In hotels, as in other buildings, remember that what the Austrians call the "first floor" is the American second floor.

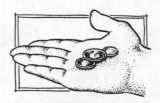

TIPPING

• Restaurants: The tip will be included, but round the bill up to the nearest schilling, or if it's a large bill, to the nearest 10 schilling. For example, if the bill is 285 schilling, leave 290 or 300.

  If there are musicians playing, place any amount you choose on the donations plate.

- Taxis: Tip 15% of the fare.

- Porters: Give 10 schilling per bag.

- Cloakroom attendants: Tip 5 to 10 schilling.

- Washroom attendants: Leave 5 schilling.

PRIVATE HOMES

- Plan to visit around 3:00 p.m., the customary visiting hour. Always call in advance; don't simply drop in. When you visit, expect to be served coffee and cake.

- If you're staying for a few days or more, offer to help with the cleaning up. Your hosts will probably welcome your offer.

- Don't ask to use the bathroom if you want the toilet, as they are separate rooms. Ask for the "W.C."

- Feel free to take a daily bath or shower, as there is generally no shortage of hot water.

- If you make a call in a private home, offer to pay for it.

Gifts: When invited to someone's home for a meal, bring flowers. Unwrap them before you present them to your hostess. Don't give red roses, a symbol of romantic love, and don't give red carnations, which are usually reserved for May Day. Another welcome gift is a bottle of wine.

If you're staying with a family, bring gifts from the U.S. such as records, calculators, portable cassette players with headphones, and flannel shirts for men to wear while hiking. If you'll be giving the gift shortly after you get off the plane, consider bringing lobsters or steak. Get them packed securely in dry ice, and check them through as baggage, so that they will be in the coldest part of the plane.

BUSINESS

Hours

Government office hours: 8:00 a.m. to 4:00 p.m., Monday through Friday.

Business office hours: 8:00 a.m. to 12:30 p.m. and 1:30 to 5:30 p.m., Monday through Friday.

Bank hours: 8:00 a.m. to 12:30 p.m. and 1:30 to 3:30

p.m., Monday through Friday. On Thursday, banks are open until 5:30 p.m.

Store hours: 8:00 a.m. to 6:00 p.m., Monday through Friday, and 8:00 a.m. to noon on Saturday. Be aware that many stores close for two hours around lunchtime.

Business Practices

• Be sure to arrange your appointments beforehand. Phone or use the telex when possible.

• Don't try to schedule appointments for the Austrian vacation periods: August, the Christmas-New Year period and Easter.

• Try to be on time, but keep in mind that your business colleagues won't be offended if you're less than 15 minutes late.

• Bring business cards. Give them to secretaries, receptionists and any business people you meet.

• If an Austrian gives you a business card with several titles, ask which one you should use.

• Don't worry about language problems. Most business people speak English.

• Prepare for some small talk before the business discussion. Expect to discuss general topics, such as the weather and what you have liked about Austria.

• Expect business to be conducted at a much slower pace than in the U.S. Be patient, as each detail of a business deal will be carefully scrutinized.

• If your Austrian colleagues take you out to lunch, be sure to reciprocate before you leave Austria.

Gifts: Give electronic calculator watches or a bottle of an unusual brand of bourbon. If you know the family, give the children hand-held electronic games.

HOLIDAYS AND SPECIAL OCCASIONS

Holidays: New Year's Day (January 1), Epiphany (January 6), Easter Monday, Labor Day (May 1), Ascension (five weeks after Easter), Whit Monday (eight weeks after Easter), Corpus Christi (approximately eight weeks after Easter), Assumption Day (August 15), National Day (October 26), All Saints' Day (November 1), Immaculate Conception (December 8), Christmas (December 25) and St. Stephen's Day (December 26).

• If you want to follow Austrian tradition on National Day (October 26), go mountain climbing. For the less agile, there are parades everywhere.

TRANSPORTATION

Public Transportation

• Note that Vienna subways cost 15 schilling. Buy your ticket at the booth near the entrance. You don't need exact change.

• In Vienna, save money by buying a book of tickets for use on the bus, streetcar or subway. The books are for sale at all tobacconist shops.

• Buy your ticket from the conductor when you ride on the streetcar or bus. In Vienna, the fare is 15 schilling, no matter how far you travel. You don't need exact change, but don't ask the conductor to change a large bill.

• Don't try to hail a taxi on the street. Go to a taxi stand, or ask the desk clerk at your hotel to call for you.

Driving

• Everyone should wear seat belts.

• At an intersection, give priority to cars coming from the right. Always give way to streetcars.

• Be sure to obey parking laws. The parking zones, which are clearly marked, are constantly patrolled by police.

• Don't have even one drink if you expect to be driving. The penalties are severe and are strictly enforced.

LEGAL MATTERS AND SAFETY

• Note that the drinking age in a bar or restaurant is 16 (14 if accompanied by a parent). There are no age restrictions on buying liquor in a store.

• If you buy a valuable art object, ask where you can get the export license you'll need to take it out of the country.

• If you spend 2,000 schilling or more on merchandise that you plan to take out of Austria, ask for a receipt. Show this at the airport before you leave Austria, and you can get the value-added tax, which is included in the price of the goods, refunded.

KEY PHRASES

See Germany

CHAPTER TWO

BELGIUM

LUXEMBOURG

In Belgium, you won't find one language but three, with legal borders between them. A majority of the people are Flemings, who speak a dialect similar to Dutch, while a sizeable minority, the Walloons, speak a dialect of French. There is also a German-speaking population of less than 100,000. All public signs are in the language of the region, except in Brussels, where signs are in both Flemish and French.

Brussels is the center for branches of the European Economic Community, and is consequently very international. It's also a bit "pricey," as is the country as a whole, since Belgium has one of the highest standards of living in Europe.

The small country of Luxembourg is very similar to Belgium in customs and manners, so we've included it here, noting only those times when Luxembourgish customs differ from the Belgian.

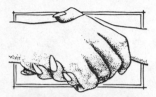

GREETINGS

• When you're first introduced to someone, shake hands quickly, with a light pressure, and repeat your name. Also shake hands when greeting or leaving someone.

• When you arrive at an office or a business meeting, shake hands with everyone there, including the secretaries. Do the same when you leave.

• If you haven't met someone in the group, introduce yourself and shake hands.

• At a large party, rely on the host or hostess to introduce you to the entire group. It's not necessary to shake hands with each person.

CONVERSATION

• Using professional titles is not important in conversation, but do use "Mr.," "Mrs." or "Miss." Never use a person's first name.

• Good topics of conversation: sports, such as soccer and bicycle racing; recent and popular books; political events (but don't take sides on political issues); the town you're visiting; Belgian cultural heritage.

• If you wish to make a favorable impression, read about the area you're visiting. Belgians will be pleased if you know something about the history and attractions of their area and ask questions about it.

• Topics to avoid: language differences in Belgium, very controversial political issues, and religion.

• Realize that the French Flemish situation can be uncomfortable. You can inquire about the two regions, but it's very rude to make fun of one area while in the other or to praise one group extravagantly to the other.

• If you don't speak Dutch, you may want to speak English in Flemish Belgium, rather than French. Also remember that Belgian cities often have different names in Flemish and French.

TELEPHONES

• When calling from a public telephone, insert a 20-franc piece, then dial. You'll hear a beep when your time is up, and you must insert more money. Note that public phone booths have instructions in English.

• In French Belgium, say *"Allô"* when you answer the phone. In Flemish Belgium, give your last name (without "Mr." or "Mrs.").

PUBLIC MANNERS

• On public transportation, men should stand until the women present are seated. Men should also let women precede them when boarding.

• Never snap your fingers or put your hands in your pockets while talking to someone.

• Keep in mind that backslapping and being loud or noisy are considered especially rude.

DRESS

• For a business meeting, men generally wear suits and well-polished shoes. Women typically wear dresses or skirts and blouses.

• As a dinner guest in someone's home, men are expected to wear suits, and women dresses.

• When an invitation to a meal or other social gathering calls for formal dress, men should wear tuxedos or dark suits, and women long dresses.

• At theaters and concerts, men wear dark suits and ties, and women wear cocktail dresses.

• Sunday is a "dress up" day in Belgium. People wear their best finery to go walking or visiting relatives.

MEALS

Hours and Foods

• For the Belgian names of these meals, see France and The Netherlands.

Breakfast: (French, *petit déjeuner;* Flemish, *het ont bijt*): 7:30 a.m. In French Belgium, you'll have croissants, bread, butter, jam, and coffee with milk. In Flemish Belgium, it will be bread and rolls, a variety of cold cuts and cheeses (sometimes eggs and bacon), butter, jam and coffee.

Lunch: (French, *déjeuner;* Flemish, *de lunch):* About noon. In the countryside, it's the main meal of the day, consisting of soup, followed by meat, potatoes and vegetables, then dessert. In cities, lunch is a light meal of cold cuts, with rolls and bread, or sandwiches (always made with butter, never mayonnaise), followed by fruit and a dessert of cake, pudding or ice cream. Beer sometimes accompanies lunch.

Dinner (French, *dîner;* Flemish, *het dîner*): 7:00 or 8:00 p.m. At a dinner party, the meal begins with soup, followed by a fish dish, such as stuffed flounder or *croquettes* (deep-fried fish balls). A light sherbet may come next to cleanse the palate, then meat, potatoes and vegetables. In the summer, salad follows this course.

Wine accompanies the whole meal. In Flemish Belgium, bread isn't served if there are potatoes. In French Belgium, there will be bread but no butter.

Dessert may be cake, fruit or pudding. Very dark, strong coffee and liqueurs will be served at the table after an informal meal, in the living room after a formal one.

Table Manners

• If your host offers a before-dinner drink, wait for him to name a selection of drinks and don't ask for other than what is offered. He will probably offer aperitifs, such as vermouth or Cinzano, rather than mixed drinks. Nuts, chips or hot cheese croquettes often accompany before-dinner drinks.

• Realize that the host or hostess will seat everyone, and that husbands and wives are never seated together. Expect the host and hostess to sit at either end of the table at a dinner party, with the male guest of honor to the right of the hostess and the female guest of honor to the right of the host.

• Don't be surprised if groups are seated at separate tables in more than one room at a large dinner party. Most Belgian dining rooms are small.

• Be aware that at a formal meal including a fish course, the table setting will include a fish fork and knife. The fish fork, to the left of the plate, looks like a salad fork, while the fish knife, to the right, looks like a butter knife.

• Look for the dessert spoon above the plate.

• Note that the Belgians eat with the fork held in the left hand and the knife in the right. They don't ever switch the fork to the right hand.

• Keep wrists on the table; don't put your hands in your lap.

• Don't expect to see bread and butter plates; the bread is put on the table next to the dinner plate.

• Serve yourself from dishes that are passed around the table.

• Place your fork and knife horizontally across the top of the plate, with the tines of the fork and the point of the knife facing left, to indicate that you've finished. Remember, it's impolite to cross your knife and fork.

• If you don't want an alcoholic drink, ask for water.

Mineral water is usually served at both lunch and dinner.

• After dinner in a home, you'll often be invited to the living room for liqueurs and cigars. Stay until cigars have been finished—about 30 minutes to an hour after the meal. If you move to leave and your hosts press you to stay, you can stay another half hour.

Places to Eat

• For variety, try these types of eating places:

Bistros are small restaurants that offer hot meals and alcoholic beverages. There is often live music featured in the evenings.

Cafés serve beer, wine and other alcoholic drinks as well as coffee and some snacks, such as *croque monsieur*, a grilled ham and cheese sandwich made with French bread.

Kafetarias are attached to supermarkets or located on highways in big cities. They offer hot dishes and cold cuts, sandwiches, and beer and wine.

Pâtisseries serve coffee, tea, pastries and ice cream.

• In downtown areas, you'll find stands on the streets selling herring, meatballs and French fries. It's okay to eat these snacks as you're walking on the street.

• Note that mussels are a favorite food; there are restaurants serving nothing else. On Fridays, most restaurants feature mussels steamed in white wine, garlic and parsley, with french fries.

• Be aware that many restaurants are very expensive. If you're a guest, ask your host or hostess to recommend some choices and order in that price range, or select one of the fixed-price meals, usually less expensive than ordering a la carte.

• To get scotch whiskey, ask for "whiskey." "Scotch" is a brand of beer.

• Never order tea or coffee with a meal. Wait till you've finished eating.

• Be aware that Belgian beer has a much higher alcohol content than American beer.

LUXEMBOURG

• Note that expensive restaurants offer international cuisine, but most restaurants have German-style cooking.

• Expect to find menus usually written in both French and German.

Specialties

• Try these Belgian specialties; *anguilles* (eels); *hochepot* (a stew of pork and mutton); *carbonnades flamandes* (beef cooked in beer); *civet de lièvre à la flamandes* (rabbit cooked in wine with carrots, mushrooms and onions); *waterzooi* (stewed chicken in a broth thickened with eggs and cream); and *endive* (a delicate-tasting vegetable that looks like a small, elongated lettuce.

• Be sure not to miss mussels when you're in Belgium. There are restaurants that serve nothing else, and on Fridays, most restaurants feature *moules marinière,* (mussels steamed in white wine, garlic and parsley) served with French fries.

LUXEMBOURG

• Don't miss these special foods when you're in Luxembourg: *quenelles* (dumplings of calves' liver served with sauerkraut and potatoes); *civet de lièvre* (hare stew); *liewerkniddellen* (meat and suet dumplings); *tartes aux quetsches* (plum tarts); *geheck* (a soup of pork and veal lungs with plums).

HOTELS

• Don't be alarmed if the clerk asks to keep your passport for a while to fill out forms. It will usually be returned at once if you need it right away.

• Never go out without leaving your key at the desk.

• In some hotels, you can leave your shoes outside your door to be shined. Some rooms have double doors, both of which lock. In the space between you can leave shoes to be shined and clothes to be pressed.

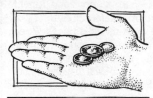

TIPPING

• Restaurants: If a restaurant service charge is not included, leave 15% of the check. If the service is especially good, leave another 3-5% on the table. In an elegant restaurant tip the *sommelier* (wine steward) 10% of the wine bill if he assists you in selecting the wine.

• Taxis: Don't tip in Belgium as the tip is included in the fare. In Luxembourg, tip 10-20%.

• Cloakroom attendants: Tip 5 francs in Belgium. In Luxembourg, there's usually an obligatory 20-franc charge.

• Ushers in cinemas and theaters: Give a 5-franc tip.

PRIVATE HOMES

• Always be on time for any prearranged visit.

• Avoid making telephone calls from a private home if at all possible, as phone calls are extremely expensive. If you must use the phone, find out how much the call costs and pay for it.

• Don't call people before 10:00 a.m. or after 10:00 p.m.

Gifts: If you're invited to dinner, bring flowers other than chrysanthemums, or fancy chocolates. If there are children, bring them candy or cookies as well.

If you're staying with a family, bring a book about your hometown or area, or phonograph records, which are very expensive in Belgium.

BUSINESS

Hours

Brussels business hours: 8:30 a.m. until noon, and 2:00 to 6:00 p.m., Monday through Friday.

Brussels bank hours: 9:00 a.m. until 12:30 p.m., and from 2:30 p.m. to 3:30 or 4:00 p.m., Monday through Friday.

Brussels shop hours: 9:00 a.m. until noon, and 2:00 to 6:00 p.m., Monday through Saturday.

Antwerp business hours: 9:00 a.m. until noon, and from 1:00 to 5:00 or 5:30 p.m., or from 2:00 to 6:00 p.m., Monday through Friday.

Antwerp bank hours: Same as Brussels.

Antwerp shop hours: Same as business hours, Monday through Saturday.

• The work day usually lasts from 8:30 a.m. to 6:00 p.m., with a lunch break of one and one-half to two hours at noon.

Business Practices

• Avoid business trips during July and August, during Holy Week and during the Christmas-New Year period.

• Don't attempt to schedule an appointment on a Saturday, even though some companies may be open. The day is reserved for sales meetings and conferences.

• Secure a prior appointment before calling on business or government offices. When you write or phone to make the arrangements, the Belgian firm will usually select the time. If they make the appointment for 11:30 a.m., presume you will be invited to lunch.

• Be aware that it's sometimes difficult to get appointments on Bourse Days, which are Mondays in Antwerp and Wednesdays in Brussels. This is the day when business people meet with colleagues in the same profession for lunch.

• Bring business cards, as they are widely used.

• Realize that the first meeting with a Belgian business person is for getting acquainted. You should exchange business cards and answer questions about yourself. Belgians must trust you in order to have confidence in your company. Don't try to do business immediately, or you will be thought pushy.

• Don't use the same person as a business contact in both French and Flemish Belgium.

• Realize that business people prefer to spend evenings with their families. To entertain a Belgian business person, it's best to arrange a lunch date. The typical business lunch lasts from 1:00 to 3:00 p.m., with one drink before lunch, and wine during the meal. If you do invite a business person to dinner, however, be sure to include the spouse in the invitation.

• Don't expect your French-Belgian business colleague to invite you home for dinner. Business entertaining at home has enjoyed increased popularity, as Belgians have traveled to the U.S. and enjoyed being invited to eat with American families. But a spouse who does not speak English might prefer that the entertaining be done in a restaurant. Flemish-Belgian business people are more likely to invite you home.

• When American business-women entertain Belgian businessmen, they should make arrangements to pay in advance, or they should indicate that their company is paying. Under any other condition a Belgian businessman won't allow a woman to pay.

Gifts: Choose a recent book related to the type of business you're in if you want to give a business gift.

LUXEMBOURG

Business Hours

Business hours: Same as Brussels.

Government office hours: 9:00 a.m. to noon, and 2:00 to 5:00 p.m., Monday through Friday.

Bank hours: 8:30 a.m. to noon, and 1:30 to 4:30 or 5:00 p.m., Monday through Friday.

Store hours: 8:00 a.m. to noon, and 2:00 to 6:00 p.m., Monday through Saturday.

Business Practices

• Don't try to schedule after-noon meetings before 2:30 p.m. Many business people go home to lunch.

• Don't worry about language problems. English is widely spoken and understood. The everyday spoken language is Luxembourgish, a German dialect, but almost everyone speaks both French and German. People will be impressed and grateful if you take the trouble to learn a few phrases in the local dialect.

• If you entertain business colleagues at a restaurant, they will appreciate a French wine.

HOLIDAYS AND SPECIAL OCCASIONS

Holidays: New Year's Day (January 1), Easter Monday, Ascension Day (five weeks after Easter), Whit Monday (eight weeks after Easter), Labor Day (May 1), National Day (July 21), The Assumption (August 15), All Saints' Day (November 1), Armistice Day (November 11), Christmas (December 25) and December 26.

• If one of the holidays above falls on a Sunday, it is celebrated the following Monday.

• On All Saints' Day and All Souls' Day, people go to church, visit cemeteries and stay at home. Don't send dinner or party invitations during that time.

LUXEMBOURG

• Holidays are the same as in Belgium with the addition of Shrove Tuesday, National Day (June 23—the birthday of H.R.H., the Grand Duke), and All Souls' Day (November 2). (July 21 and November 11 are not public holidays in Luxembourg.)

• *Schobermess*, the Luxembourg Fair, is held annually in the spring and fall and is also a public holiday.

• If you have a chance, go see the "Jumping Procession" in Echternach on the Tuesday after Whit Sunday. Thousands of ordinary people form rows and weave their way around the cathedral with a jumping, kicking step. The procession is a tradition dating back to the early 16th century, when local people danced and prayed to get rid of the plague.

TRANSPORTATION

Public Transportation

• Buy your ticket when you get on the bus. Pay at the entrance for the Métro (subway).

• When traveling a long distance by train, find out if there will be a dining car. If not, bring food and drink with you.

• Keep in mind that taxis are hard to find on the street. Go to a taxi stand or telephone for one. Be aware that taxis are very expensive.

Driving

• Remember seat belts are mandatory for all occupants of a car.

• Note that traffic coming from the right has the right of way, and streetcars have priority at all times.

• Use special telephones located along highways in case of emergency.

• Don't drink and drive. There are no spot checks for breathalyzer tests, as there are in some other countries, but if you are involved in an accident because of drunken driving, it is a very serious offense. As a non-citizen, you will be fined, put in jail and your license taken away if you're found guilty.

• Keep in mind that police are very strict in enforcing traffic laws, even with foreigners. Never argue with the police, even if you believe you have done nothing wrong.

LUXEMBOURG

• For traffic violations, police can issue on-the-spot fines for up to 600 Luxembourg francs. You are supposed to carry this amount with you at all times when you drive.

LEGAL MATTERS AND SAFETY

• Be assured that an international driver's license is not necessary to drive.

• Note that the price of goods includes a value-added tax. Some stores are authorized to refund this to foreigners; ask at each store about their policy. If they are authorized, they'll give you a form to fill out. Mail this before you leave Belgium.

KEY PHRASES

See France and The Netherlands

CHAPTER THREE

![BULGARIA]

VARNA •

• PLEVEN

SOFIA ★

• PLOVDIV

Westerners tend to envision Communist countries as bleak, grayish places populated by sad, depressed people. Visiting Bulgaria, you will perhaps be surprised at how "normal" everyday life is. Unemployment is virtually unknown, as is severe poverty. And you may be surprised at how inexpensive housing, bread and public transportation are. Costs on these items are kept low by government subsidies.

As a traveler in Bulgaria, you will be the object of great curiosity, since Bulgarians rarely receive permission to travel to the West. Most of their information about America comes from the official press (which stresses the negative aspects of the country) and from movies. You and Gary Cooper may be the impression of America your Bulgarian acquaintances carry with them.

GREETINGS

• Always shake hands when introduced.

• At a party, wait for the host or hostess to introduce you. You need not shake hands with each person in the room; simply nod to the entire group.

• Address a man or woman as "Comrade" with the last name, unless he or she is a professional.

• Use a person's professional title before his or her last name if you're speaking to a doctor, professor, architect, engineer or priest.

CONVERSATION

• Use first names only after your Bulgarian friends do so, as that form of address is generally reserved for close friends.

• Good topics of conversation: family and home life, and your profession. Expect people everywhere in Bulgaria to be curious about American life. Bring photos of your family and home, and photos or postcards of your town. Try not to suggest that life

in America is superior to that in Bulgaria.

• Topics to avoid: politics and social conditions in Bulgaria.

• Don't be surprised if people ask how much money you earn. If you prefer not to answer, a tactful response would be "Our life style is so different that it doesn't make sense to compare."

• Be aware that the gestures for "yes" and "no" in Bulgaria are the opposite of those in the U.S. To indicate "yes," shake your head horizontally; signal "no" with a vertical nod of the head. Be alert to catch these expressions because Bulgarians make them very subtly.

TELEPHONES

• Make phone calls from public telephone booths or from larger restaurants and cafes. Deposit a 2-stotinki coin before you pick up the receiver. You can talk for an unlimited amount of time on a local call.

• Say *"Allo"* when you answer the phone.

PUBLIC MANNERS

• Don't try to bargain in shops or markets.

• Be prepared to use toilet facilities which are very different from what you're accustomed to. You may find a regular toilet, or there may simply be a hole in the floor with places on either side for your feet. Bring toilet paper or facial tissue with you; toilet paper is not commonly available.

• Don't photograph soldiers, government installations, military zones or the Black Sea Coast from offshore.

DRESS

• Be aware that only children wear shorts in the city.

• For casual wear, men should wear pants and shirts, adding jackets or sweaters in winter. Women should wear sundresses, skirts or pants.

• When invited to someone's home for dinner, men should wear suits and ties in winter, and dress pants and shirts in summer. Women should wear dresses or skirts. Dress is less formal when the hosts are friends (pants and shirts for both men and women).

• Leave your tuxedo at home or in your suitcase. Formal dress for official parties and weddings is dark suits for men and short cocktail dresses for women.

• When visiting churches, women may wear sundresses, but they should not wear shorts. They don't have to cover their heads.

MEALS

Hours and Foods

Breakfast (zakuska): 7:00 a.m. or earlier (most people begin work at 8:00 a.m.). The typical breakfast is bread and butter, sometimes with cheese and fruit, or yogurt. Tea, including herb tea, is the most common beverage, because coffee is very expensive.

Lunch *(obet):* 1:00 p.m. Expect salad or soup, then a meat or fish dish with vegetables, followed by fruit and yogurt or a sweet. Wine usually accompanies the meal. In the winter, when there aren't many fresh vegetables available, pickled vegetables (peppers, green tomatoes and cucumbers) are common.

Supper *(vecherya):* 8:00 p.m. Enjoy a light, hot meal of soup, bread and pickled vegetables. If it's a dinner party, the meal will be similar to *obet,* the meal described above. You will be offered *rakija,* a plum or grape brandy, usually served in shot glasses, before the meal. With the *rakija* you'll probably have *shopska salata,* a salad of tomato, peppers, onions and feta cheese.

Table Manners

• As the guest of honor, sit at the middle of the table so that everyone can converse with you easily.

• Note that the table setting is the same as in the U.S., with forks to the left and knives and soup spoon to the right. Use the spoon above the plate for coffee.

• Never put your elbows on the table.

• Drink wine and/or mineral water with the meal.

• Take as much bread as you wish. A Bulgarian will eat bread with every meal and may consume as much as an entire loaf each day.

• Sop up gravy with bread if you wish. Break the bread into pieces and put them on the plate. Use your fork to pull the bread through the gravy.

• Take very small portions the first time food is served, and be prepared to have several helpings. In being hospitable to foreign guests, people often serve much more than they normally would. Don't offend them by nibbling or taking just a small bite of everything.

• Don't try to keep a conversation going during the meal. Enjoy the food as the Bulgarians do and reserve serious discussions for dessert or later.

• After the meal, you may be offered either European-style instant coffee or espresso. Bear in mind that Bulgarians serve coffee black. Your host may provide sugar, but probably won't offer milk or cream.

• Don't expect your hosts to signal when it's time for you to leave. If you try to end the evening, they will insist that you stay longer. However, plan to leave by 11:00 p.m., since public transportation closes down at midnight, and it's often difficult to find taxis.

Places to Eat

• Look for these types of eating places:

Mehahnah are taverns, much like British pubs. You can order both drinks and meals.

A *restorahnt* is a full-service restaurant.

A *skahra beera* offers quick meals. Specialties are grilled meats, sausages, cheese and bread.

A *slatkarneetsa* serves ice cream, pastries, sandwiches, coffee and tea, but not alcoholic beverages.

• Note that there are two types of self-service restaurants. In one kind, you tell the cashier what you want, and pay for it before you receive the food. In the other, you choose your own food as you go through a cafeteria line, and pay at the end.

• Make reservations more than a few days in advance for Saturday or Sunday dinners. Many restaurants are completely booked with wedding parties on those days.

• In most restaurants, you must seat yourself. If there are no empty tables, join others. As a courtesy, ask if you may sit down, but be assured that it's a common thing to do.

• Don't expect everything listed on the menu to be available. Ask the waiter what the choices are.

• To call the waiter, extend your hand palm down, and bring the fingers towards you, which means "Come here."

Specialties

• Bulgarian food features Balkan specialties such as lamb, sheep, cheese and yogurt.

Try these special foods: *tarator* (a cold soup of sour milk, chopped cucumbers, walnuts, dill and olive oil); *panagyurishte* (poached eggs with whipped yogurt, butter and paprika); *gjuvéch* (a stew of onion, eggplant, beans, peas and peppers); *tchorba* (a meat and vegetable stew); *sarmi* (cabbage or grape leaves filled with rice, ground pork and veal); *meshana skara* (mixed grill); *shishcheta* (pork roasted on a spit); *shopska* (a salad of peppers, onions, tomatoes, cucumbers and white goat's cheese); *imam bavaldá* (cold eggplant stuffed with onions, carrots, tomatoes and celery); *haiduchi kebab* (lamb grilled with onion); *bánitsa* (flaky pastry filled with cheese); and *kebabches* (chopped meat rolls made of spicy veal and pork and grilled on skewers).

• For dessert, try *kisselo mlekó* (a thick, creamy yogurt that also appears in many dishes) and *revane* (sponge cake).

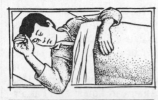

HOTELS

• Leave your passport overnight if the clerk asks for it.

• Leave your key at the desk when you go out.

• Don't expect around-the-clock hot water. Look for a notice telling the times when water will be available.

• Bring a plug for the sink with you, as many sinks don't have them.

• If you're going to a resort area and would like to have an opportunity to live in a private home (and to pay only about one-third the cost of a hotel room), book rooms in private lodgings through the Bulgarian Tourist Office. This national tourist agency has a branch in the U.S.

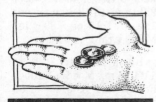

TIPPING

• Restaurants: Be aware that a service charge is included in the check. If you wish, leave 50 stotinki or 1 lev on the table.

• Taxis: Give 50 stotinki or 1 lev. Knowing that you are a foreigner, the driver may ask for more money. It isn't necessary to give it.

• Porters: Pay a fee of 1 to 3 leva.

• Washroom attendants: Give 10 stotinki for toilet paper.

• Ushers or cloakroom attendants: Don't tip.

PRIVATE HOMES

• Always call before visiting someone. Only very good friends would be welcome to drop in.

• Plan to accept refreshments, probably preserved fruits or nuts, when visiting. Each guest is served a table-spoonful on a glass saucer. For beverage expect coffee, tea or *rakija* (plum or grape brandy).

• *Rakija* is very potent, so be cautious in drinking it. When your hosts press you to drink, be very firm (to the point of being unpleasant) if you don't want to drink a great deal.

• Don't ask for an iced drink in a private home. Most people don't have refrigerators.

• If you're staying with a family, give them your passport so that they can register you with the police. Be aware that if they don't do this immediately, they can get into serious trouble.

• Feel free to go sightseeing on your own. In fact it's unlikely that a family member will have time to go with you, since most people work during the day. However, if you would like to have someone show you around, ask your hosts; they may be able to find someone to accompany you.

• Ask before taking a bath. The water may have to be heated, or the hot water system may be turned off for repairs.

• Offer to help with cleaning up if you wish, but expect your offer to be refused. As a guest, you'll hold a special place of honor.

Gifts: If you're invited to a meal, bring flowers, candy or wine. The flowers should be wrapped. Don't bring gladioli or calla lilies; those are reserved for solemn events such as weddings and funerals. And don't bring yellow flowers—yellow signifies hatred.

From the U.S., bring postcards of your town to give to people you meet casually.

If you're staying with a family, bring magic markers in unusual colors (such as silver or copper), coffee beans, blue jeans, cassettes of American music, cigarettes, American liquor and Parker ball-point pens (the brand is important). For a woman you know very well, bring lingerie or stockings.

If you haven't brought gifts from abroad, go to a *Corecom,* a dollar shop. With Western currency you can buy many items that Bulgarians can't.

BUSINESS

Hours

Government and business office hours: 8:45 or 9:00 a.m. to 12:30 p.m., and 1:00 to 5:15 or 5:30 p.m., Monday through Friday.

Bank hours: 8:00 to 11:45 a.m., Monday through Friday, and 8:00 to 11:00 a.m. on Saturday.

Shop hours: 8:30 a.m. to 7:00 p.m., Monday through Saturday.

Business Practices

• If you want to set up an appointment from overseas, start making the arrangements three months in advance. Make appointments through the company's protocol department, which is responsible for insuring "proper" relations with Western business people. You can also tell the Bulgarian company that you will need an interpreter, and they will arrange for one.

• Try to schedule your appointments around 10:00 or 11:00 a.m., or around 2:00 or 3:00 p.m. You could also suggest a business lunch or dinner.

• Don't suggest a lunch or dinner on the spur of the moment. Any meeting outside the office requires approval by the company's protocol department.

• Be on time for appointments.

• Don't expect people—other than those in the travel business—to speak English. German is the most frequently used foreign language, and Russian is spoken by those between the ages of 15 and 30.

• Expect to be offered an aperitif: *slivova* (plum brandy), *mastika* (an anise drink) or vodka. Accept this show of hospitality unless you don't or can't drink.

• Don't expect to be entertained in a home. Business entertaining takes place in restaurants and spouses are not included. If you are entertaining, take your guest to one of the best restaurants, rather than to one of the smaller, ethnic restaurants.

• If you want to continue a business relationship with a Bulgarian firm, prepare to go to Bulgaria fairly often, since personal contact is very important.

Gifts: Parker pens are popular business gifts.

HOLIDAYS AND SPECIAL OCCASIONS

Holidays: New Year's Day (January 1), Women's Day (March 8), Labor Days (May 1 and 2), Day of Bulgarian Culture (May 24), National Day (September 9 and 10) and Day of the Russian Revolution (November 7).

• Bear in mind that Christmas is very subdued, since no religious holidays are officially celebrated. An invitation to celebrate Christmas means Christmas Eve.

• Expect livelier festivities on New Year's Eve and New Year's Day. People have Christmas trees and exchange gifts. At 8:00 or 9:00 p.m. on New Year's Eve, join a family in a feast of roast suckling pig or turkey. At midnight, expect everyone to drink wine or champagne, and kiss.

• On March 1, as a springtime ritual, people give each other good luck charms. Buy the red and white string or silk charms at kiosks.

TRANSPORTATION

Public Transportation

• In Sofia, buy interchangeable tickets for buses, streetcars and trolleys. They cost 6 stotinki and can be bought at kiosks near the stops. At the kiosks you can also buy passes good for a month, or packets of 10 or 20 tickets. When you get on, cancel your ticket in the machine. Keep your ticket since there are frequent inspections.

• To get a taxi, phone for one, hail one on the street, or go to a taxi stand.

Driving

• Obtain an international driver's license before driving in Bulgaria, and carry it with you when you're driving.

• Highways are generally good, but be very cautious when driving at night. There are many unlit farm vehicles on the roads.

• For traffic violations, expect to pay fines of at least 5 to 10 leva when you're stopped.

• Don't drive if you've been drinking. You will be charged with drunk driving if you have any alcohol at all in your blood. The law is strictly enforced.

• Study the Cyrillic alphabet, in which Bulgarian is written, so that you will be able to read signs.

LEGAL MATTERS AND SAFETY

• Be sure to obtain a visa from the Bulgarian Embassy before you travel to Bulgaria unless you are going on a package tour. You won't be able to get a visa at the border when you enter Bulgaria.

• When you arrive, fill out a

special yellow card, giving information about yourself and the purpose of your trip. Keep this card; you must produce it when you are leaving the country. There will be a very long delay in departing if you don't have it.

• You cannot bring in or take out Bulgarian currency. Keep receipts from money exchanges, and be prepared to show them when you leave the country. Exchange money at the Bulgarian National Bank, *Balkantourist* offices or hotels.

• If you bring in costly objects, such as a camera or a tape recorder, a note will be made on your passport. Have these items with you when you leave the country. Otherwise, you will have to pay duty on them.

• Remember that it is illegal to take items of significant folkloric value, such as costumes or old musical instruments, out of the country.

• Be very cooperative with the police. Their authority is absolute. Don't ask them for directions to a person's home, since it might cast suspicion on the person for entertaining a foreigner.

• Don't agree to change money with people you meet on the street.

• Note that it's safe to go out alone, even at night.

• Note that there is no drinking age, nor are there any restrictions on when you can drink.

KEY PHRASES

English	Bulgarian	Pronunciation
Good morning	Dobro outro	Dó-bro oo-tro
Good evening	Dobur vecher	Dó-bur véh-cher
Please	Molya	Mól-yah
Thank you	Blagodarya	Blah-go-dahr-yáh
You're welcome	Molya	Mól-yah
Yes	Da	Dah
No	Ne	Neh
Comrade (man)	Drugaryu	Droo-gáhr-you
Comrade (woman)	Drugarkako	Droo-gáhr-kah-ko
Excuse me	Izvinete	Eez-vee-náy-tay
Good-bye	Dovizhdane	Do-veézh-dah-nay
I don't understand.	Ne razbiram.	Nay rahz-bee-ráhm
I don't speak Bulgarian.	Ne govorya bulgarski.	Nay go-vór-yah bool-gáhr-skee
Does anyone speak English?	Govori li nyakoi angliiski?	Go-vó-ree lee nyáh-koi ahn-glée-skee

CHAPTER FOUR

CZECHOSLOVAKIA

Shakespeare, who often took liberties with historical fact, once set a scene on "the seacoast of Bohemia," a province in modern Czechoslovakia. A traveler in search of that seacoast is in for a disappointment, because Bohemia—indeed the whole of Czechoslovakia—has no seacoast. It does, however, have abundant and beautiful mountains and countryside awash with fruit trees.

Travelers to Czechoslovakia may not realize initially that the country consists of two republics, the Czech Socialist Republic and the Slovak Socialist Republic, each with its own government and language. But this won't make much difference because the languages and customs in the two republics are so similar. When we talk about Czech customs in this book, we also mean Slovak customs and when we give a word in Czech, we do so knowing that anyone who speaks Slovak would understand it.

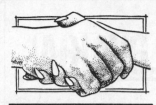

GREETINGS

• Shake hands with everyone on arrival or departure from any meeting—formal or informal, social or business.

• Note that women extend their hands first when greeting men, and older people extend their hands first to young people.

• At formal parties, don't talk to someone unless you've been introduced. At informal parties, go ahead and introduce yourself if the hostess seems busy.

• Use professional titles (without last names) when speaking to architects, doctors, engineers and lawyers (for example, *Pane inženýre*, Mr. Engineer, *Paní inženýrko*, Mrs. Engineer).

CONVERSATION

• Don't use first names until you know someone very well.

• Good topics of conversation: sports, especially soccer and ice hockey; traveling; music (including Czech composers Dvořák and Janáček); your impressions of Czechoslovakia.

• Topics to avoid: politics, especially socialism and the Soviet Union. Your hosts may bring up political matters in the privacy of their home. Feel free to participate, but don't criticize Czech government policies or structure.

• Feel free to ask personal questions about someone's job or family, even if you've just met the person.

TELEPHONES

• Look for public telephone booths in train and subway stations, in stores, and on streets everywhere. To make a call, dial the number, and when someone answers, deposit one koruna. Be aware that public telephones are often out of order.

• Expect people to answer the phone by stating their name.

• Don't telephone someone after 9:00 p.m.

PUBLIC MANNERS

• Don't try to bargain in shops, stores or markets anywhere in Czechoslovakia.

• Never applaud in a church, even if a concert is held there.

• Note that gambling is forbidden, except in card games in private homes.

• Don't take photographs in museums or galleries. Also avoid photographing Russian policemen, military installations, frontier zones, airports and railroad stations.

• Be aware that customs officials might destroy your film as you are leaving the country. You may want to protect your film by taking it out of your camera and putting it in an inconspicuous place in your suitcase.

DRESS

• Be assured that jeans and shorts are acceptable casual dress, even in cities.

• For business, men should wear suits and ties, and women suits or dresses.

• When dining at a home or in a small restaurant, men should wear pants, shirts and sweaters, and women should wear dresses or skirts and blouses. In better restaurants, men should wear suits and ties.

• For formal balls, men should wear tuxedos or dark suits, and women long dresses. (In February, all the country's institutions, such as libraries, have a ball. This tradition comes from Mardi Gras, which is no longer officially celebrated.)

• Wear the same formal attire for openings of plays, operas or ballets.

MEALS

Hours and Foods

Breakfast *(snidane):* 6:00 a.m. (since many people begin work at 7:00 a.m.). Rolls, butter, jam, and tea or coffee are standard fare. For a special treat there may be eggs, which are expensive in Czechoslovakia.

Lunch *(obed):* 12:00 to 1:00 p.m. Usually the main meal of the day, lunch begins with soup and follows with meat, potatoes or dumplings, a vegetable (usually canned; fresh green vegetables are rare and expensive) and ends with dessert, usually pudding. Beer, mineral water, and, occasionally, wine are the usual drinks.

Supper *(vecere):* 5:30 to 6:30 p.m. If lunch was a full meal, supper will be lighter—cheese or meat sandwiches and milk. If it's a dinner party, *slivovitz* (plum brandy) or *becherovka* (herb brandy) may be served before the meal. The meal will begin with soup, then follow with a main course such as roast pork, sauerkraut and dumplings. Dessert could be apple strudel, fruit cake or cookies. Turkish coffee follows the meal.

Snacks: 10:00 a.m. People break for sandwiches or hot sausages and yogurt. At 4:00 p.m. Czechs eat sandwiches and Turkish coffee.

Table Manners

• Keep in mind that Czechs prefer a hot meal to a cold meal, such as a salad, even in hot weather.

• Wait until everyone has been served a drink before picking up your glass. If it is a special occasion, toasts will probably be proposed. Feel free to offer a toast in honor of the celebration.

• Note that guests are usually served first, although the oldest woman at the table is sometimes served first.

• Don't be surprised if your plate appears with food already on it. Serving is usually done in the kitchen.

• Before you eat, say "Have a good appetite."

• Don't put your knife and fork down between bites.

• Keep in mind that the Czechs are very hospitable and will press you to eat more. However, it's polite to say "No, thank you" the first time you are offered a second helping. Your hostess will then say "Please do," and you are then expected to accept.

• To show that you're finished, place the utensils together at one side of the plate. To signal that you're just taking a break, cross your knife and fork on the plate.

• If you drink coffee at someone's house, expect that it will already be sweetened. Watch out for the thick grounds from the bottom of your coffee cup. In restaurants you'll need to add sugar. Stir the coffee, then wait for the grounds to settle before drinking.

• Don't put your elbows on

the table, even if you've finished eating and are simply sitting around the table chatting.

Places to Eat

• Try different types of eating places for a variety of foods and atmospheres.

A *bufet* serves fast meals and snacks. It usually doesn't have any place to sit.

Cukrárny offer pastries, ice cream and coffee.

Kavárny offer alcoholic drinks, coffee, sandwiches and pastries, but no warm meals.

Koliby are special restaurants serving regional specialties.

A *restaurace* is a regular restaurant that serves full meals.

Vinárny are wine cellars, where you'll be served a glass of wine from a barrel. You can get snacks or full meals there. They usually open in the late afternoon.

A *zahradna restauracia* is a beer garden, where you can also get a snack or a meal.

• If you are on business at a factory and are invited to eat lunch there, accept—the food is usually both good and inexpensive.

• Realize that no meat is served in restaurants on Thursdays. This is a government regulation due to meat shortages.

• Before you make your meal plans, check with the restaurant you want to go to, to make sure they are open. Some restaurants close for all or part of the weekend.

• Look for the rating of each restaurant, which you will find written in Roman numerals on the menu posted near the entrance to the restaurant. The best class of restaurants are represented by a one, and the lowest by a four.

• Expect to stand to eat your meal or snack at fourth-class restaurants.

• If a restaurant is crowded, look for an empty seat at an occupied table, ask if it is free and sit down. No one will be surprised or upset. In fact, someone may strike up a conversation with you.

• Be aware that some restaurants do not permit smoking at lunch or dinner time.

Specialties

• Roast pork and dumplings are very popular in Czechoslovakia (in fact, roast pork is the national dish of the Czech Republic). Also try *franecek* (herring); *sardinky* (sardines); *zavináč* (stuffed, rolled herring); *husa* (roast goose); *svíčková na smetaně* (filet of beef with sour cream); *párky* (long, thin sausages eaten in pairs); *jelita* (sausages made of blood, rice and liver); and *houskové knedlíky* (bread dumplings—with almost every dish: soups, stews, and even dessert).

• For dessert, try *koláč* (rolls filled with jam, poppyseeds, nuts or cottage cheese); *bryndzove halusky* (potato pancakes—the Slovak national dish); *palacinky* (crepe-like pancakes served with jam or chocolate on top); and *pischinger torte* (a cake made of wafers, chocolate meringue and chocolate frosting).

HOTELS

• Make reservations several months in advance, especially during times when festivals or congresses are being held, as hotel rooms are in short supply.

• If hotel rooms aren't available, contact CEDOK, the national travel agency, which may be able to find you a room in a private home.

• When you check in, leave your passport at the desk overnight.

• Be sure to leave your keys at the desk when you go out.

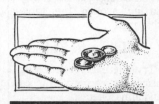

TIPPING

• Tip discreetly because tipping is officially discouraged. However, you won't have any trouble with the authorities if you tip.

• Restaurants: If the tip is included in your bill, round it off by 1 or 2 koruna. If the tip isn't included, leave 5-10%.

• Taxis: Give 5-10% of the bill.

Be aware that there is a coat-checking charge in restaurants, theaters and other public places. It's customary to leave some small change as well.

PRIVATE HOMES

• Set aside Sunday as the day for visiting. You may feel free to drop in any time of day, as long as you avoid calling near mealtimes (2:00 to 5:00 p.m. is good). People must plan far in advance before having someone over for a meal, because food is very difficult to obtain.

• Expect to be offered homemade cakes, sweets and Turkish coffee when you pay a visit to someone's home.

• Realize that Czechs will go out of their way to welcome you. They may insist that you take their beds (while they sleep on the floor) or prepare special foods not available everyday because of the cost. Be sure to reciprocate such kindness by taking your hosts out to a nice restaurant or giving them a special gift. Food would be most welcome, particularly fruit or chocolates, but any scarce item will do.

• If you're a guest in someone's home for several days, offer to do some of the food shopping. Since both men and women usually work, shopping must be done in the evening when there are long lines at each shop. Czechs will be grateful if you help with this chore.

Gifts: If you're invited to a home to dinner, bring flowers (if you can obtain them) or a bottle of wine, whiskey or cognac.

If you stay with a family, bring toys of any kind for kids, and blue jeans for teenagers. Bring cosmetics or clothing for women you know well. Other suitable gifts include ballpoint pens, cigarette lighters, pocket calculators, fancy tea, cocoa, popular records, chewing gum and T-shirts.

If you're complimented on a particular article of clothing while staying with a Czech family, it would be appropriate to leave it as a gift (if you wish).

BUSINESS

Hours

Business and government office hours: 8:30 a.m. until 5:15 p.m., Monday through Friday.

Bank hours: 8:00 a.m. until 2:00 p.m., Monday through Friday, and from 8:00 a.m. until noon on Saturday.

Shop hours: 9:00 a.m. to 6:00 p.m., Monday through Friday. Some shops are open until noon on Saturday; others are closed all day. Some small shops close from 12:00 to 2:00 p.m. for lunch.

Business Practices

• Avoid planning business

trips from mid-July to mid-August, as most people take vacations then.

• If you're making appointments from the U.S., allow a month by letter and two weeks by telephone or telex. Once you're in the country, try to arrange appointments at least a week to 10 days in advance.

• If you're writing a business letter to a company, address the letter to the firm, not to an individual there.

• To make an extremely good impression, have business letters translated into Czech (although you can write them in English).

• Consider hiring an interpreter. English is understood by people working in hotels, at airports and in tourist bureaus, but usually not elsewhere. It may help if you speak German, the most widely spoken foreign language.

• Bring and use business cards.

• Men should present flowers to a businesswoman when they first meet.

• Expect your hosts to offer you drinks and coffee at a business meeting. Accept something. If a toast is offered, you should return it.

• Don't be distressed if Czech business people seem overly cautious. They must be absolutely certain that they are not violating any of their country's laws.

• Don't expect to have much contact with your business associates outside of the office. They must prepare far in advance for a meeting in a restaurant or hotel, so you won't get any spontaneous invitations (i.e., "Let's have dinner tonight"), nor should you extend a last-minute invitation.

• If there is enough time for all the appropriate clearances necessary, take your Czech colleague to a small restaurant, not to a hotel restaurant. You may include his or her spouse in the invitation, but it's not necessary.

HOLIDAYS AND SPECIAL OCCASIONS

Holidays: New Year's Day (January 1), Easter Monday, Labor Day (May 1), National Day (May 9), Christmas (December 25) and St. Stephen's Day (December 26).

• Don't take photographs of the military parades that take place on May 9, the anniversary of the end of World War II.

• People celebrate the feast of their name saint with parties and dancing. If you know someone who is celebrating her or his name saint's day, bring a small gift. (All of the saints' days are listed on calendars.)

TRANSPORTATION

Public Transportation

• Note that public transportation is widely used, as only a small percentage of the population own cars.

• Buy tickets for streetcars, buses and trolleys in hotels, restaurants or at tobacconists. Each ticket costs one koruna.

• Deposit one koruna in subway machines to open the turnstile.

• Note that taxis are hard to find. It's a good idea to have your hotel call one for you, especially at night.

Driving

• Be sure to have an international driver's license as well as your U.S. license on you at all times.

• Wear seat belts if you drive.

• Never leave valuables in your car.

• Be cooperative if you are stopped; show your passport. Police frequently check drivers leaving Prague early in the afternoon to learn if they have permission to leave work.

• Do not drink even one beer if you are going to drive. The law in this case is strictly enforced.

• Be conscious that parking is limited to one side of the street on certain days and at certain hours.

• Don't smoke while driving a car or riding on a motorcycle; it's illegal.

• If you are stopped for a traffic violation, pay your fine immediately. The fine could range from 20 to 100 korunas, depending on the infraction and the leniency of the police. If you don't have enough money with you at the time, you must pay the fine before leaving the country.

LEGAL MATTERS AND SAFETY

• Obtain your visa at the Czech embassy before you leave, as you can't get one at the border.

• Don't try to bring Czech currency into the country or take it out. At your point of entry, you must exchange a set amount of money for each day of your stay (ask how much when you apply for a visa). If you don't do this, your visa becomes invalid. You must spend this amount during your stay.

• Change additional money at state banks and at officially designated exchanges found in hotels, train stations and CEDOK offices (the national travel agency). Don't change money anywhere else. You could cause yourself considerable trouble.

Save your proofs of exchange. If you have any Czech money left from exchanges, other than the one made at your point of entry, you can change the money back at the border when you leave.

• Bring food or clothing for gifts, as these won't cause problems at customs when you enter the country. (Customs officers will note items such as cameras and tape recorders on your passport when you enter and inspect your luggage when you leave to see that you are taking those items out with you.)

• Remember that you will have to pay a tax when you leave the country on all goods you take out except for those bought at a government store.

• Note that importing electrical equipment is forbidden.

• If you're staying more than 24 hours, register with the police. If you're staying at a hotel, the staff will take care of this; otherwise you must register in person at the police station within 48 hours.

• Don't try to swap American goods for Czech goods; it's illegal.

• To buy art works or antiques, visit one of the many branches of the Tuzex Shops or Artia Publishing House. Keep your sales slip to show at customs when you leave.

• Women can generally walk safely alone after dark.

KEY PHRASES

English	Czech	Pronunciation
Good morning	Dobré ráno	Dó-bray ráh-no
Good evening	Dobrý večer	Dó-bree véh-cher
Please	Prosím	Pró-seem
Thank you	Děkuji	Dye-kú-yee
You're welcome	Rádo se stalo	Ráh-do say stáh-lo
Yes	Ano	Ahno
No	Ne	Neh
Sir, Mr.	Pan	Pahn
Madam, Mrs.	Paní	Páh-nee
Miss	Slečna	Sléh-chnah
Excuse me	Promiňte	Pro-méen-tay
Good-bye	Nashledanou	Nah-shlay-dáh-nu
I don't understand.	Nerozumím.	Ne-ro-zúm-eem
I don't speak Czech.	Nemluvim česky.	Ném-loo-veem chés-kee
Does anyone here speak English?	Mluvíte někdo anglicky?	Mloo-vée-teh nek-dóe aln-glít-skee

CHAPTER FIVE

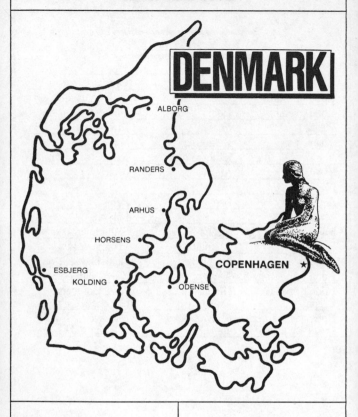

If any people have mastered the art of living in simple comfort and beauty, it is the Danes. Consider Danish furniture or porcelain; their beauty emerges from their very simplicity.

Danes have also mastered the art of being efficient without being cold, of being good managers without ever seeming to be in a hurry.

Since the country relies on imported goods more than the other Scandinavian countries, you will probably find it more cosmopolitan than Sweden or Norway.

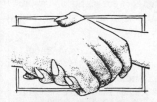

GREETINGS

• Rise when you are introduced and shake hands, whether the occasion is business or social.

• When introduced, look at the other person, nod and say "Hello" or "Good day."

• Feel free to introduce yourself if necessary.

• Shake hands heartily when you meet someone you know and when you leave.

• If you wish to be very polite, use professional titles (e.g., "Hello Professor Andersen") when speaking to someone, especially if he or she is older.

CONVERSATION

• If your Danish colleague uses first names, feel free to do the same; otherwise use last names.

• Good topics of conversation: food, what you like about the city you're staying in; your own hometown or area; current issues in the news.

• Topics to avoid: income and religion or any other personal subject, such as a divorce.

• Don't comment on someone's clothes, even with a compliment, as personal remarks such as this are considered odd.

TELEPHONES

• You'll find public phones in cafes, bars and train stations. Deposit 50 ore or 1 krone for a local call.

• Expect the person answering the phone to say "Hallo" or give their name or their phone number.

PUBLIC MANNERS

• Visit a restaurant that features dancing if you want to

meet members of the opposite sex. (This applies to women as well as men.)

• Don't look for a non-Lutheran church except in large towns. The vast majority of the Danish population belongs to the Lutheran Church (which is the state church), although only 5% of the population attend church weekly.

• Expect to see people changing into their bathing suits on the beach, using a towel as a cover.

• Note that Danes commonly go to public baths. If you decide to try one, be aware that you can take a sauna before your bath and have a massage after it, if you like. When you enter the building, buy tickets for the facilities you want to use. You can get towels and soap too.

The baths themselves will be in rows of private compartments, while the saunas will be communal by sex.

DRESS

• Prepare for a cool, rainy climate and bring a coat with you.

• For casual occasions, men

should wear slacks and sport shirts; women slacks and sweaters.

• For business, men should wear sports jackets or suits and ties. Check to be sure pants are neatly pressed and shoes polished. Women should wear suits or dresses, and heels.

• If you're invited to a casual dinner, feel free to wear clean jeans.

• At a more formal dinner party, men wear jackets and ties, and women wear dresses, blouses, and skirts or dressy pants.

• Don't be surprised to see many women wearing topless bathing suits at the beach.

MEALS

Hours and Foods

Breakfast *(morgenmad):* 8:00 a.m. Typical fare is cereal, *ymer* (a type of yogurt), bread or hard rolls, cheese, soft-boiled eggs, butter, marmalade, and tea, coffee or milk.

Lunch *(frokost):* 12:00 to 2:00 p.m. Open-faced sandwiches on thin rye bread with a variety of toppings (cheese, herring) are standard at lunch. The usual drinks are beer, soft drinks or milk, followed by coffee after the meal.

Dinner *(middag):* 6:00 to 8:00 p.m. A formal meal begins with soup, followed by a fish dish, then meat, potatoes (usually boiled) and cooked vegetables. Don't expect a salad at dinner, but if there is one, it comes after the meat course.

The meal ends with cheese and fruit, followed by dessert. After dessert, coffee and sometimes brandy and cognac are served. Then your hostess may offer you after-dinner drinks, such as scotch and soda, or gin and tonic.

A less formal dinner may start with sandwiches and beer, or consist only of a main course and dessert. Sometimes *akvavit*, an alcohol made from potatoes and served ice cold with a beer chaser, accompanies the sandwiches.

Snacks: Danes take a coffee break at 9:00 or 10:00 a.m., a tea break at 3:00 p.m. and, often, an evening snack of pastries or fruit at 10:00 p.m.

Table Manners

• If you're invited to dinner in a home, be punctual. There is usually no pre-dinner cocktail hour, so don't be surprised if you are seated in the dining room immediately.

• Expect the host and hostess to sit at either end of the table. The guest of honor is seated next to the host.

• Don't taste the wine (or other alcohol) until the host makes the first toast.

• Before you take the first sip of wine, lift your glass and look around at everyone. After you've tasted the wine, look around at everyone again.

• Note that the guests can propose subsequent toasts. If you're the guest of honor, propose a toast by tapping your glass with a spoon. Say "Thank you for having the dinner in my honor."

• Remember that, during dessert, the man seated to the left of the hostess should propose a toast to her.

• Follow the Danish custom of holding fork in the left hand and the knife in the right if you really want to fit in.

• Serve yourself from platters of food as they go around the table. It is important to try everything, but take small portions the first time around. The platters will be passed around more than once, and it is an insult not to take seconds of at least some dishes.

• Don't leave food on your plate. However, if you didn't

care for a particular dish, you don't have to take seconds of it.

• To show you've finished eating, place the knife and fork (tines up) side-by-side vertically on the plate. If you place the tines down, you are indicating that you would like more food.

• Expect a long, slow dinner with lots of conversation. The Danes will also stay at the table talking long after they have finished the meal.

• Don't get up from the table until the hostess does. Before leaving the table, thank her for the meal.

• Move to the living room for after-dinner cocktails.

• Guests often stay as late as 1:00 a.m. after a dinner party. Your host may serve coffee, soup or sandwiches between 11:00 p.m. and 3:00 a.m.

Places to Eat

• Look for these types of eating places:

Bars serve drinks only.

Cafes offer snacks with drinks.

Cafeterias serve American-style meals.

Pølsevogne are trucks on the streets that sell long, skinny pork sausages and beer and soda.

Smørrebrødsforretning

offer open-faced sandwiches to take out.

• If you're invited to *koldtbord* (cold buffet) or a *højt smørrebrød* (sandwich buffet), begin with the herring course. This can include 6 to 15 different kinds of pickled herring in various sauces. Sometimes salmon, tuna or shrimp are also served with this course. Drink *akvavit* and beer with the herring.

Follow the herring with a hot fish course, such as a fried fish fillet, then choose from different warm and cold lunch meats and pâtés. Finish with cheese, fruit and *akvavit*.

Don't be surprised if this meal lasts four or five hours.

• Women can feel comfortable going into a bar alone and can even initiate a conversation there.

Specialties

• Try these Danish specialties: *bøf tartare* (raw ground sirloin on white bread with a raw onion ring and raw egg yolk on top); *flaeskesteg* (roast pork, usually served with red cabbage); *frikadeller* (meatballs); *øllebrød* (rye bread mixed with black beer, sugar and lemon and cooked until it has a souplike texture); *rødspaetter* (sole); and *sild* (herring).

• For dessert, try *lagkage* (layers of sponge cake with

custard, strawberries and whipped cream) and *rødgrød* (fruit compote).

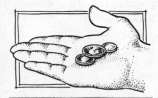

TIPPING

• Restaurants: Don't leave a tip, as a service charge will be added to your check.

• Taxis: Do not tip.

• Ushers: Do not tip.

• Porters: Tip 2 kroner per bag.

• Washroom attendants: Leave 1 or 2 kroner in the dish.

PRIVATE HOMES

• Don't ever drop in unexpectedly.

• If you're invited to a Danish home for the evening, don't assume dinner is included unless your host makes that clear. A family meal may be over as early as 7:00 p.m.

• Don't jump up after a meal to do the dishes; the Danes prefer to sit and chat. You can offer to help with the dishes later, but your offer will usually be refused.

• If you're spending a week or so with a family, offer to cook one entire meal. Your hosts will probably accept your offer and be pleased by it.

• If there is no maid, clean your room and make your bed.

• If you have special interests, let your hosts know, and they'll try to cater to them. Don't, however, expect to be entertained constantly. Be independent enough to go off on your own part of the time.

• If you're staying in a Danish home, don't use the family bath facilities every day because your hosts must supply towels, soap and hot water. If you want a daily bath, go to a *badeanstalt,* a public bath (see Public Manners).

• If you make a telephone call in a private home, ask the operator to find out the cost of the call. Note that even local calls cost money. If the operator does not speak English, he or she will connect you to someone who does. Have the correct amount ready and give it to your hostess.

Gifts: If you're invited to dinner, bring liquor or flowers. (Liquor is appreciated because taxes on it are very high.) For flowers bring tiny roses, anemones or the flowers of the season. Flowers should be wrapped.

If you know a Danish family well, bring them gifts from the U.S.: blue jeans, T-shirts, records, towels or even makeup, which is very expensive in Denmark.

BUSINESS

Hours

• **Business hours:** 8:00 or 9:00 a.m. until 5:00 p.m., Monday through Friday.

Bank hours: 9:30 a.m. to 4:00 p.m., Monday through Friday, and until 6:00 p.m. on Thursday.

• **Shop hours:** 9:00 a.m. to 5:30 p.m. during the week. Some close at 1:00 p.m. on Saturday, and some stay open until 7:00 p.m. on Friday.

Business Practices

• Avoid business trips to Denmark from June 20 to August 15 (the July Industrial Vacation) and around national holidays. Most non-retail businesses are closed between Christmas and New Year's Day, and many business people take vacations around Easter.

• Be on time for all business appointments. This is very important.

• Don't suggest a business meeting on the weekend. Danes spend weekends with their families.

• The Danes respect tradition, so be sure to mention if you represent a very old firm.

Gifts: Bring liquor, a product typical of your hometown, or a book describing your hometown or area. Don't give American cigarettes, as Danes generally don't like them.

HOLIDAYS AND SPECIAL OCCASIONS

Holidays: New Year's Day (January 1), Maundy Thursday, Good Friday, Easter Sunday and Monday, Whit Monday (eight weeks after Easter) Constitution Day (June 5), St. Han's Eve (June 23), Christmas Eve and Day (December 24 and 25) and December 26.

• On St. Han's Eve, Danes get together with friends and

family; they sing, play musical instruments and drink *akvavit* and beer. People clean out their houses and make a big pile outdoors of things they want to get rid of (or the pile can be made of driftwood). A witch made out of straw and old clothes, and filled with firecrackers, is placed on top of the pile. (In the past few years, pressure has decreed that the witch be sexless, not a woman!) At night the pile is burned, and everyone stands around and sings. The witch is supposed to take sorrows on her broom to Bloksberg, Germany.

• St. Martin's Eve (November 10) is also celebrated, although businesses and schools don't close. Goose or duck is traditionally eaten on this day.

TRANSPORTATION

Public Transportation

• Prepare yourself with exact change and buy your ticket in advance for subways (S-Bane). The trains work on the honor system, so don't expect a conductor to collect the ticket. However, anticipate spot checks by inspectors.

• Reserve a seat if you travel by train on a Friday night, as they are usually very crowded.

Driving

• If possible, avoid driving in cities such as Copenhagen, where the streets are narrow and there is little parking.

• Reserve a space for any ferry crossing well in advance. Otherwise, you'll have to wait for hours. (At holiday times you could wait for days.)

• Always ask car occupants to fasten their seat belts. If you're caught without them fastened, you must pay a fine immediately.

• If you are stopped for a traffic violation, pay the fine immediately, or your car will be confiscated until you can pay.

• Don't drink and drive. If you are found with excessive alcohol in your blood, you will lose your license, pay a heavy fine, or go to jail—or all three!

• If you're going to a party where there will be drinking, go by taxi or in a carpool, with the driver passing up drinking for that night. If you plan to drive, don't have more than one drink per hour.

LEGAL MATTERS

• Don't plan to stay in Denmark for more than three months. If you must prolong your stay, visit the passport police and offer a very good reason. They will then decide whether you can remain.

• Realize that it is extremely difficult to obtain a work permit. Even people who marry Danish citizens are not guaranteed work permits!

• Bear in mind that the drinking age is 18 and that it is possible to order liquor in a bar or restaurant 24 hours a day, unlike in other Scandinavian countries.

• If you buy a gift for under $100 and have it shipped out of the country, you don't have to pay the value-added tax.

KEY PHRASES

English	Danish	Pronunciation
Good morning	God morgen	go-móhrn
Good evening	God aften	go áhf-tehn
Please	Vaer så venlig at	váhr so ven-lee aht
Thank you	Tak	tahk
You're welcome	Velbekomme	vél-beh-kom-meh
Yes	Ja	yah
No	Nej	nigh
Sir, Mr.	Hr.	hair
Mrs., Madam	Fru	froo
Miss	Frøken	frúh-ken
Excuse me	Undskyld mig	oón-shkewl my
Good-bye	Farvel	far-víll
I don't speak Danish.	Jeg kan ikke tale Dansk.	Yáy ken ée-keh téh-leh dansk
Does anyone here speak English?	Hvem kan tale Engelsk her?	Véhm kan téh-leh éhn-gelsk háir

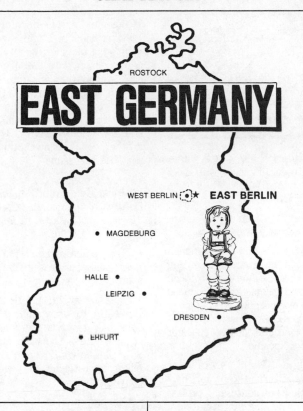

CHAPTER SIX

EAST GERMANY

ROSTOCK

WEST BERLIN ★ EAST BERLIN

MAGDEBURG

HALLE

LEIPZIG

DRESDEN

ERFURT

Ever since August, 1961, when the barrier of barbed wire known as the Berlin Wall was erected, travelers have been curious to visit East Berlin for at least a day—to catch a glimpse of life behind the Iron Curtain.

If you decide to make a trip into East Germany, whether out of curiosity or to see relatives or friends, you should have no problems if you follow the rules and don't do anything the government would regard as unusual for a tourist—like spending a lot of time watching the military police.

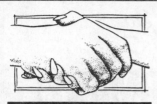

GREETINGS

• Shake hands when you're introduced, when you greet someone and when you depart.

• Always wait to be introduced at parties.

• Whether you are being introduced or are introducing others, be aware of protocol: young people are introduced to older people, and people of inferior social position are introduced to those of superior social position.

• Use "Mr.," "Mrs." or "Miss" plus the professional title when addressing professors, engineers, architects, pastors, lawyers or anyone with a Ph.D. For example, a male professor is *Herr Professor*, a female professor is *Frau* or *Fräulein Professor*.

When two people become good friends in East Germany, the older of the two, or the person with the highest social position, might propose a sort of ritual drink. The two friends intertwine right arms, drinks in hand, and say *"bruderschaft"* "to brotherhood." Following this they use first names.

• Refer to the country as the "German Democratic Republic" in all conversations. Use "Berlin" for the city, rather than "East Berlin."

• Good topics of conversation: families, professions and sports.

• Topic to avoid: politics. Don't try to draw political opinions out of East German acquaintances. You have no way of knowing who else might be listening to your conversation.

• Although people are extremely interested in information about the West, don't brag about the benefits of life in Western countries as opposed to Eastern Europe.

CONVERSATION

• Use last names until you're invited to use first names.

TELEPHONES

• To call from a public phone, deposit 20 pfennig and dial.

That amount pays for a local call lasting three minutes. When the time is up, a beep sounds. If you wish to continue the call, deposit more money.

• Phone also from cafes, where you pay when the call is finished. For long-distance calls within the country, the operator gives you notice of the amount due when the call is completed.

• Make long-distance calls to other countries from a post office.

• When answering the phone, give your last name or say *"Halo."*

PUBLIC MANNERS

• Don't litter, as East Germans are shocked by people who do

• Keep your hands out of your pockets while talking to someone.

• Stand up when talking to women or social superiors.

• Never try to bargain, as it's considered impolite.

• Consider leaving your camera behind. Keep in mind that photographing police, bridges, railroads or military installations may result in having your film and camera confiscated. You may also be held for questioning or have to pay a fine.

DRESS

• Be assured that jeans are acceptable casual streetwear, but don't wear shorts.

• Avoid flashy clothing for business. Men wear suits, and women wear tailored suits or dresses.

• When invited for dinner in a home, men should wear shirts and trousers (jackets are not necessary), and women should wear dresses or skirts and blouses.

• Be conscious of how others are dressed. A man wearing a jacket and tie to someone's home will remove them to make the others feel comfortable if they are dressed casually.

• For dinner in a restaurant, men wear shirts and trousers but bring jackets along in case others are wearing them; women wear dresses or skirts and blouses.

• Wear formal clothing for

weddings, funerals, operas or the theater. Men wear dark suits and women wear short, fancy dresses. For operas, however, women wear long dresses.

MEALS

Hours and Foods

Breakfast *(frühstück):* 8:00 to 9:00 a.m. Usual fare is a roll, butter, marmalade and coffee. Sometimes there's a slice of sausage or cheese, and a really luxurious breakfast may include a boiled egg.

Lunch *(mittagessen):* 12:00 to 1:00 p.m. This is the main meal of the day, consisting of meat, potatoes, vegetables, a bean or vegetable salad (rarely with lettuce) and, usually, a pudding for dessert. Coffee is not usually taken till the afternoon snack.

Dinner *(abendessen):* 6:00 to 7:00 p.m. This fairly light meal might include fried potatoes with eggs, a fish dish, or sliced cold meats and mayonnaise with a variety of breads.

If it's a dinner party, you will probably be offered ver-

mouth, sherry or wine before the meal. The meal will begin with a clear soup, and the main course will probably be meat, such as a pot roast, with cabbage and potatoes or dumplings and gravy. Dessert could be a layer cake with whipped cream or custard. Wine often accompanies the meal. *Schnapps* (brandy), but not usually coffee, follows the meal.

Breaks: About 4:00 p.m., people usually break for coffee and cakes.

Table Manners

• Always wait to be seated by your host or hostess.

• If you're the guest of honor, sit at the side of the table, not at the head.

• Don't be surprised to see both knives and forks to the right of the plate. Spoons are always placed above the plate. Cloth napkins are used more often than paper.

• If you want to eat like your hosts, hold the fork in your left hand and the knife in your right, using the knife to push food onto the back of the fork.

• To indicate that you have not finished but are merely pausing during the meal, cross the knife and fork on your plate. When you have finished, place the knife and fork parallel on the plate.

• At informal dinners, expect

to receive a plate with the food already on it. At more formal dinners, food will be passed around on platters, and you can help yourself.

• If you serve yourself, or your hostess serves you, take only what you can eat. It's considered rude to leave food on your plate.

• When you are toasted, look at the drink, look in the eyes of the person offering the toast and then drink.

• When passing food or beverages to someone, always say *"Bitte"* which means, in this case, "You're welcome."

• Remember that it's better to leave too early than too late. Your host or hostess won't signal when it's time for guests to leave, but stay no later than 10:00 or 11:00 p.m.

Places to Eat

• Note the variety of eating places:

A *bar* serves only drinks, which are taxed heavily and are very expensive. Bars are separate establishments, not part of a restaurant.

A *cafe* serves coffee, cakes, *schnapps* and cognac.

"Exquisite," are restaurants reserved for the wealthy and for Westerners. If you want to entertain someone, they will enjoy eating at one of these restaurants.

A *gaststätte* is a more modest, less expensive restaurant, that is usually part of an inn.

A *konditorei* is usually a very attractive pastry shop. You can eat the pastry there with coffee or take it out.

A *restaurant* is a traditional restaurant.

• For a bargain meal, look for stands in the streets where you can buy sausages, fish or *schnitzel* (veal cutlet).

• Make reservations in advance, as restaurants are scarce.

• Don't expect to have a private table in a restaurant. People will join you, and you can feel free to join them. Parties of three or more will often split up if they can't get a table together.

• To call the waiter, say *"Herr Ober."* To call a waitress, say *"Fräulein."*

• Realize that service may be very slow, because most food is cooked to order.

Specialties

• Try these foods throughout East Germany: *bockwurst* (sausages); *kasseler rippenchen* (smoked pork chops); *kartoffelpuffer* (potato pancakes); *thüringer rostbrätel* (grilled sausages); *leber im grünen bett* (sauteed liver with herbs and wine);

plinsen (pancakes made of wheat, buckwheat and lemon); *spickgans* (smoked and pickled goose); *hoppel-poppel mit salat* (hash with lettuce and sour cream); and *falscher hase* (mock hare, meat loaf).

• For dessert, try *bienenstich* (pastry with honey and nuts) and *Berliner pfannkuchen* (jelly doughnuts).

• Depending on your feelings about slightly unusual food, you may want to try, or avoid, *eisbein* (pig's knuckle) and *schabelfleish* (raw hamburger meat.)

HOTELS

• To insure a room, make reservations when you apply for your visa. Otherwise, contact the official travel organization or use a room reservation service in the railroad station of a large city.

• Note that hotels for Westerners do accept major American credit cards.

• Realize that hotels may keep your passport during your entire stay. You will need a driver's license, even if you don't plan to rent a car, since another form of identification may be needed away from the hotel.

• To insure good service from the desk clerk, tip 10 marks when you arrive.

• Be sure to leave your key at the desk when you go out.

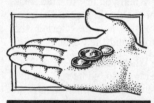

TIPPING

• Be discreet when tipping. Officially, tipping is not done in East Germany; in practice, people usually tip in hotels and restaurants.

• Restaurants: Round off the bill to the nearest mark.

• Taxis: Round off the fare to the nearest mark or give one mark.

• Porters: Tip one mark.

• Washroom attendants: Sometimes there is a posted fee; if not, leave one mark.

• Cloakroom attendants: Give a one-mark tip.

PRIVATE HOMES

• Always arrange a visit in advance, even though there is no customary hour for visiting. Never drop in on someone unannounced.

• To stay with friends or relatives in the German Democratic Republic, write at least three months in advance (four or five months would be better) to the *Reisebüro der DDR* in Berlin. You will have to fill out many forms and go through a great deal of red tape—without any guarantee that your request will be granted.

Gifts: Bring flowers when you're invited to a meal and present them unwrapped. Realize that roses have romantic implications.

If the family you're visiting has children, bring them a small toy or a game.

If you're a house guest, consider giving gifts from the U.S. such as whiskey or blue jeans. You could also take your hosts to an *Intershop*, a government-run store that sells merchandise unavailable elsewhere in the country and have them choose a gift. You must use Western currency to buy goods at these stores.

BUSINESS

Hours

Business hours: 8:00 a.m. to 4:00 p.m., Monday through Friday.

Bank hours: 8:00 a.m. to noon and 2:30 to 5:30 p.m., Monday through Friday, and from 8:00 a.m. to noon on Saturday.

Shop hours: These vary tremendously from town to town. Check the hours posted at shops in each town.

Business Practices

• Note that Tuesday is the best day to make an appointment. Don't suggest an appointment before 9:00 a.m. Businesses don't accept appointments on Wednesday.

• To attend the Leipzig Business Fair, held in March and September, obtain a special pass from an airline or travel agency. Present the pass at your point of entry and you will receive a free visa, valid only in Leipzig and vicinity.

• Before making travel plans,

wait for an official invitation from an authorized company; you will then be given a special permit for business travel.

• Cultivate patience in business dealings. Decisions are always made by committees, so prepare to wait months, or even years, and make several trips to East Germany before completing business arrangements.

• To please an East German business person, extend an invitation for a luncheon business meal. If you are invited out, you can offer to pay—but don't make your offer too insistently.

• Ask your business counterpart's spouse to come along if you wish. In this situation your spouse may come also.

Gifts: Give an unusual brand of scotch whiskey or bourbon.

HOLIDAYS AND SPECIAL OCCASIONS

Holidays: New Year's Day (January 1), Good Friday, Whit Monday (eight weeks after Easter), Labor Day (May 1), German Democratic Republic Day (October 7), Christmas (December 25) and December 26.

• On May 1, expect to see military parades and government-inspired rallies. Never photograph either of these functions. Realize there will be a great deal of drinking afterwards.

TRANSPORTATION

Public Transportation

• Pay at the ticket window for the subway in Berlin (the only city in East Germany with a subway).

• To ride buses and streetcars, put exact change into the paybox located on the vehicle. Pull the lever and tear off a ticket.

• Note that taxis are hard to get. It's better to call for a taxi than to wait at a taxi stand.

Driving

• It is helpful, but not required, to have an international driver's license.

• To travel through East Germany to another country, obtain a transit visa at the border. Your visa is stamped with the time and you are allowed a certain amount of time to get through East Germany. If you exceed the time allotted, you will be questioned. If you must spend the night en route due to a breakdown, stay only at an Interhotel. Don't get out of your car on the transit highway, and avoid chatting with people.

• Be especially careful to wear seat belts if you've rented a car in East Germany or are driving the car of a friend or relative. Although seat belts are not required by law, no East German insurance company will pay accident damages unless you were wearing a seat belt.

• Keep your eye on the speedometer, as speed limits are strictly enforced.

• If you're stopped by the police for a traffic violation, you will either pay a fine on the spot or you will be taken to a local magistrate, who will determine the fine.

• Don't drink and drive. Your blood alcohol level must be zero, which means that you can't even have one beer or glass of wine with a meal. If you're caught, there is a jail sentence.

LEGAL MATTERS AND SAFETY

• Carefully read the brochure you receive when you enter East Germany. This brochure contains the regulations you must abide by, including rules on driving, changing money, and forbidden areas.

• Register with the police if you plan to stay more than 24 hours. Ask for exact instructions at the border.

• Realize that anti-Communist newspapers, magazines or books will be confiscated at the border as you enter the country.

• Don't bring East German currency into the country, or take any out. On arrival, you'll have to fill out a currency declaration form, stating how much money you have in all currencies. Keep the form, as well as the receipts you'll get every time you change money. You'll be asked for these when you leave.

• Change money only in stores, official exchange offices and restaurants. Don't exchange money with anyone who approaches you on the street, or you could be sent to prison.

• If you want to visit East Berlin for one day, you must arrive at the border between 7:00 a.m. and 8:00 p.m, and leave by midnight. There are two points of entry: "Checkpoint Charlie" for pedestrians and cars, and *Bahnhof Friedrichstrasse* for pedestrians. At either point of entry, it's not uncommon for border guards to frisk travelers and search their luggage and cars thoroughly.

At the border obtain a day visa; it costs 5 marks and must be paid for in Western currency.

You must leave East Berlin from the same point you entered.

While in East Berlin, you must change at least 25 marks worth of Western currency. Get a stamped receipt for this and present it when you leave. You have to spend this much while you're in the country—if you have any left when you leave, it will be confiscated.

• To stay in any part of East Germany longer than your visa permits, apply to the *Reisebüro der DDR*. This will not automatically secure permission to extend your visit, however.

• If you are stopped by the police for any reason, be cooperative and very courteous; never show anger. You might mention the beauty of the country or offer them cigarettes.

• Be assured that in East Germany the crime rate is very low. Women are seldom harassed, although the authorities recommend taking a taxi after dark.

• Be aware that medical help is not available to visitors of East Germany.

KEY PHRASES

See Germany

CHAPTER SEVEN

Most travelers imagine that they'll find the English very stuffy and starched. And that is indeed one side of the coin: the gentleman going to work in "the City," wearing pinstripes and derby, and the oh-so-proper lady shopping in Harrods. But turn the coin, and you'll find punk-rockers with hair dyed purple and eccentrics of all types.

All English have at least one thing in common—a respect for privacy so strong that they sometimes seem aloof. Yet, if you ask people for help, they will give it cheerfully.

We've included Scotland and Wales in this chapter, because the customs in these countries are generally the same as those in England. We've indicated only where they differ. But be sure to note these differences, and whatever you do, don't call a Welshman or a Scotsman English!

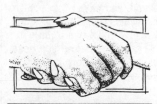

GREETINGS

• When greeting someone, shake hands and say "How do you do?" The person will respond with "How do you do?" as well. No one will expect an answer to the question.

• When introduced to a woman, wait for her to extend her hand. Men should remove their gloves when shaking hands with a woman. Women can keep their gloves on.

• Address a surgeon as "Mr.," not "Dr."

• Address a knight as "Sir" with his first name. (Sir Alec Guinness would be called "Sir Alec.") If you'll be meeting royalty, members of the nobility or the upper clergy, check for polite forms of address in *Whitaker's Almanac* or *Pear's Almanac*.

• If you want to avoid obvious Americanisms, say "Hello," not "Hi."

CONVERSATION

• Both in business and socially, you may use first names after a short acquaintance. (Take your cue on this from the English.)

• Good topics of conversation: the city you're visiting; history; architecture; gardening; and the positive aspects of the British role in world affairs, both past and present.

• Topics to avoid: politics (especially socialism), money and prices, England's decline as a world power, religion and Northern Ireland. Also avoid asking any questions about a person's profession.

• Don't be surprised to hear

the British end a sentence that is really a statement with a question. Example: "The sun rises in the morning, doesn't it?" No one expects you to answer the question.

• Expect to find the British somewhat more subtle and less straightforward in conversation than Americans. The British are reluctant to be very direct for fear of offending someone.

• Note that British humor tends to be satirical and sarcastic. Bathroom jokes are common on TV shows and in popular stage shows.

• If a conversation turns to an argument, keep cool and be ultra-polite. In arguments, the English will become cooler and cooler, rather than overtly angry.

SCOTLAND AND WALES

• Take care how you refer to a Scot or a Welshman. Remember that Great Britain includes three national groups, each one proud of its national identity. Also note that while a Scotsman may drink scotch, he does not want to be called a Scotchman. Scot or Scotsman are the correct terms.

• Also be aware that it is in poor taste to joke about what men wear (or don't wear) under their kilts, or about the heritage of kilts or bagpipes.

TELEPHONES AND CORRESPONDENCE

• Note that the English "ring up" instead of "call on the phone"; they "call" when they go to someone's home.

• Ask for a "call box" or a "telephone kiosk," not a telephone booth. Dial the number first, listen for a beeping sound, and put in 5 pence to be connected. That amount will give you a two-minute local call. Every time you hear beeps, put in more money. If you overpay, the money will not be refunded from the phone, but it will be sent to you if you call and give the operator your name and address.

• You cannot make a person-to-person call unless you are phoning outside the United Kingdom.

• Ask the operator to "reverse charges" when you want to make a collect call.

• Don't be surprised if people answer the phone by giving the last four digits of their phone number.

• Begin formal letters with "Dear Sir" or "Dear Madam" and end with "Yours faithfully." A less formal letter can begin "Dear Mr. (Mrs.) Jones" and close with "Very truly yours" or "Yours sincerely."

PUBLIC MANNERS

• Use "please" and "thank you" whenever appropriate to avoid appearing rude. The English use these words much more than Americans do.

• Avoid demonstrative gestures, such as slapping someone on the back or putting an arm around someone's shoulder. It's unusual to display affection to anyone but family members and very close friends.

• Never stare at people or bother them in public. (Many celebrities say they enjoy being in England because people leave them alone.)

• If you're a woman, don't feel insulted when porters, newspaper vendors, and bus or train conductors call you "Love," "Duck," "Dearie," or even "Darling." These are common expressions. Female vendors may also call a man "Love."

• Go to the end of the "queue" (line) and wait your turn for buses, taxis, trains, and in cinemas, theaters and shops. The English become outraged if you "jump the queue"—attempt to push ahead.

• Never shout in public.

• Expect to hear the national anthem—"God Save the Queen"—at the end of some movies and plays. Stand during the playing.

• At a cricket match, keep quiet and clap whenever someone makes a good play—regardless of what team they're on. You may want to go with someone who can explain the game to you, as the rules are complicated. Casual dress is appropriate.

• If you smoke, offer cigarettes to everyone in your group before lighting up.

• In markets, don't handle fruits and vegetables. Vendors become very displeased if you do.

DRESS

• In cities, you can wear shorts and jeans, as long as they are clean and neat.

• If you really want to fit in, wear tweedy clothes for casual occasions: slacks with sweaters and sporty jackets for both men and women.

• For business meetings, men should wear suits and ties, and women should wear dressy suits.

• You can wear almost anything, from clean jeans to dressy outfits, to theaters and concerts. Dress at these events has become increasingly informal.

• Get dressed up for dining in restaurants. Men should wear jackets, and some restaurants require men to wear ties, so it's a good idea to bring one along. Women should wear dresses or skirts and blouses.

• If the invitation says "Formal," it could mean a variety of costumes, from morning coat to tails. Take your invitation to one of the many formal wear rental shops. They will be able to tell you what you should wear and can outfit you if you don't have the required costume with you.

MEALS

Hours and Foods

Breakfast: 7:30 to 8:00 a.m. on weekdays; 8:30 to 9:00 a.m. on weekends. A light breakfast is cereal, toast, and coffee or tea. An "English" breakfast is a feast: juice and/or cereal; bacon and/or sausages; eggs; toast, sometimes fried in bacon fat; and, sometimes, kippers (smoked herring served hot); kidneys; fried mushrooms; and fried tomatoes.

Lunch: 12:00 to 2:00 p.m. The usual fare is sandwiches, salads, fruit or dessert, and coffee (served after, not with, dessert). Accompanying beverages may be beer, cola, lemonade or orange "squash" (concentrated orange syrup diluted with water). On Sunday, however, the main meal is at noontime and almost always features a roast, called "the Sunday joint."

Tea: 3:30 to 4:30 p.m. Tea can be a light snack or a

full meal ("high tea"). "Savories" (small sandwiches of cucumber, egg and watercress) come first, followed by sweets: "biscuits" (cookies), pastries, and "gateaux" (cakes). Tea accompanies the entire meal. "High tea" features at least one hot dish, such as meat pie, and is usually eaten a little later, in place of dinner.

Dinner: 7:00 p.m.; 8:00 p.m. for a dinner party. At a dinner party, the meal begins with cocktails (gin and tonic, whiskey or sherry) and small appetizers, such as nuts or "crisps" (potato chips). The "starter" (first course) is often soup or a prawn cocktail. Then there's meat or fish with potatoes and vegetables; salad accompanies the meal. Dinner ends with cheese and crackers, dessert, and coffee and liqueurs (port, cognac or Grand Marnier).

Breaks: At most businesses, workers take a coffee break at 10:30 a.m. and a tea break at 3:00 p.m.

SCOTLAND AND WALES

Breakfast: In Scotland, breakfast traditionally consists of porridge; toast with marmalade and butter, and tea with milk. Bacon and eggs are usually reserved for Sunday.

In Wales, the meal starts with porridge, followed by bacon and eggs and fried bread.

Lunch: Traditionally the main meal of the day in Scotland, lunch is becoming a lighter meal now that many women work outside the home. Nowadays, people typically eat "broth" (homemade soup) and a sandwich, followed by fruit or cheese and biscuits.

In Wales, the traditional meal is fish or meat with two vegetables. Dessert may be steamed pudding or canned fruit with cream. Beer or tea may accompany the meal.

Dinner: In Scotland, dinner will begin with soup, followed by a main course of meat with two vegetables. Bread or rolls and butter are always served, but salad is not common. Dessert ends the meal.

Those people who eat a main meal at noon have tea around 5:30 p.m. instead of dinner. Common dishes at this meal are boiled eggs and toast, Welsh rarebit, macaroni and cheese, or fish and salad. Bread and jam, scones, cakes or biscuits follow.

At 5:00 or 6:00 p.m., the Welsh eat a light evening meal (such as cold meat and pickles with bread and butter, or sausages and beans). Tea accompanies the meal.

Table Manners

• You may want to eat as the English do, with the fork in the left hand and the knife in the right. The fork is held with tines turned down, and the knife is used to push food onto the back of the fork.

• When you have finished eating, place your knife and fork on the plate side by side and vertically.

• To be polite, decline a second helping the first time it is offered.

• Don't smoke at a formal dinner until after the toast to the Queen at the end of the meal.

• Some people don't object to others smoking between courses, but be sure to ask permission before lighting up.

• Don't expect to be served tea after lunch or dinner—coffee is the usual beverage offered.

• If you are dining with someone of the upper class, expect the women to follow the traditional practice and withdraw after dinner, leaving the men alone for brandy and cigars.

• At a dinner party, plan on leaving between 11:30 p.m. and midnight. The meal itself will probably end about 11:00 p.m.

Places to Eat

• Expect to get smaller portions than you would in the U.S. at every meal except breakfast.

• In less expensive restaurants, you may be seated at a table with a stranger. It is not necessary to initiate conversation.

• A single woman can signal that she does not want to be picked up by bringing a book or magazine to read when eating in a restaurant.

• Two types of popular English eating places to try are fish-and-chips shops and pubs.

Look for genuine fish-and-chips shops primarily in English country towns. You'll get fried fish and chips (french fried potatoes) wrapped in a paper container. Try adding malt vinegar to the fish and french fries, as the English do.

For a taste of the local social life, go to the neighborhood pub. All pubs serve drinks and most serve lunches and light meals.

Pub hours: These change slightly from region to region, but are generally weekdays and Saturdays from 11:30 a.m. to 3:00 p.m. and from 5:30 to 11:00 p.m. Sunday hours are 12:00 to 2:00 p.m. and 7:00 to 10:30 p.m.

• Women who are alone might prefer the saloon bar section in a pub, rather than the public bar. Women can go into a pub alone, without indicating to men that they want to be picked up.

• Bear in mind that children

are not allowed in pubs, unless there is a garden where they can eat and play.

• Order beer by the pint or half-pint. Also specify the kind you want—"ale," "stout" (Guinness is the strongest), "lager" (the English equivalent of American-style beer) or "bitter." For example you would order "a half of bitter" or a "pint of stout."

• Women should be aware that ordering a pint is considered unladylike; a half-pint is better. A typical "woman's drink" is lager and lime.

• You may want to try gin and tonic, or sherry, both of which are popular drinks with the English.

• For an American-style martini, ask for gin and French or an American martini. If you simply order a martini, you'll get vermouth.

• You'll find that beer is served at room temperature, and other drinks are served without ice. (There may be an ice bucket on the counter in some pubs.)

• If you're in a pub with a group, it's customary to "buy rounds" so that each person takes his or her turn in paying for the group.

SCOTLAND AND WALES

• Note that pub hours in Scotland and Wales may vary slightly from those in England. In Scotland, Sunday pub hours vary from region to region; in Wales, pubs are closed on Sundays.

• In Scotland, try ordering whisky (spelled without an "e"), the national drink. Order a "malt whisky" rather than a cheaper blended variety and drink it neat or add water, never ice.

• Be aware that most restaurants outside of major cities in Scotland close around 8:30 p.m. In Wales, you should check to see if restaurants serve dinner, as many serve only a main meal at noon, then close.

Specialties

• Try these English specialties: cock-a-leekie soup (chicken and leek soup); crumpets (similar to English muffins, served at breakfast and teatime); Cornish pastries (turnovers filled with meat and potatoes); Scotch eggs (hard-boiled eggs covered with sausage meat and batter and deep-fried); bangers and mash (sausages and mashed potatoes); steak and kidney pie; and toad-in-the-hole (sausages baked in pastry).

For sweets, try clotted cream (a thick cream of butter-like consistency, served with scones and jam); gooseberry fool (pureed gooseberries mixed with custard); and trifle (sponge cake soaked in sherry or whiskey topped with custard, fruit and cream).

SCOTLAND AND WALES

• In Scotland, try cullen skink (fish soup); partan bree (crab with rice and cream); haggis (sheep's stomach stuffed with sheep's innards, spices, oatmeal and suet, eaten on New Year's Eve and Robert Burns' night, January 25); bannocks (flat cakes of oats, barley or rye, baked on a griddle in the oven); crowdie (a kind of cottage cheese with double cream and salt added, served with oatcakes and butter at teatime); Dundee cake (a rich fruit cake); black bun (fruit cake in a pastry crust, traditionally served on New Year's Eve); Aberdeen Angus beef; herring; salmon and trout.

• In Wales, try chicken and leek pie; sewin (sea trout); Glamorgan sausages (bread crumbs, grated cheddar cheese, and egg yolk, shaped like sausages and deep fried); and faggots (meatballs made of pig's liver, bread crumbs, oatmeal, onions and spices, baked and served hot or cold).

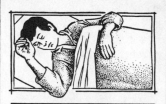

HOTELS

• If a clerk asks "Shall I knock you up in the morning?" he or she wants to know if you would like a wake-up call. The clerk may also ask if you would like "early morning tea." This is tea delivered to the door of your room as soon as you wake up.

• Note that breakfast is usually included in the price of a hotel or "Bed and Breakfast" room (a room in someone's house).

• At "Bed & Breakfasts" (B & Bs), don't expect to have breakfast late in the morning, as you would in a hotel. Breakfast will usually be offered during a one-hour period, most often between 7:30 and 8:30 a.m. Rarely, except on weekends, can you have breakfast after that hour. The menu for breakfast will be fixed and will usually offer some form of eggs with sausage and/or bacon. Don't ask for any variations—unless your hostess offers options.

• Don't be surprised to be charged for a bath in a B & B. Most operate on a very tight profit margin, and hot water is very expensive.

SCOTLAND AND WALES

• In Scotland, remember that hotel rooms can be very cold, even in summer. Ask when you book if there is central heating or a room heater.

• Breakfast in a hotel or B & B may differ from the traditional Scottish breakfast of porridge. Bacon and eggs are often offered in a hotel or B & B, especially in the winter.

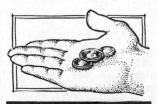

TIPPING

• Restaurants: Leave 12-15% if the service charge isn't included in the check.

• Taxis: Give 12-15%.

• Porters: Tip a minimum of 20 pence per bag.

• Washroom attendants: Leave a 10-pence coin.

• Maids: If you're lucky enough to spend a weekend with a family that has a maid, leave her 5 pounds at the end of your stay.

PRIVATE HOMES

• Always phone ahead before visiting.

• If you're visiting for an evening, don't expect your host to show you around the house. Don't wander through the house or garden on your own.

• If you are staying with a family, be sure to make your bed and tidy your room every day. You could also offer to clear the table after meals and help with the dishes. Unlike hosts in some other countries, the English are not reluctant to accept help from guests.

• If you make a long-distance call from the phone in a private home, call the operator beforehand to find out how much it will cost. Don't plan to settle when the phone bill arrives, since calls are not itemized.

• Also offer to pay for local calls as bills are computed on a per-call basis.

• Ask your hostess when it would be convenient for you to take a bath, since the water sometimes has to be heated first. The English are very frugal with hot water.

Gifts: If you're invited to dinner, bring flowers or—even better—send flowers in advance. Other good gifts are wine, champagne or a box of chocolates.

BUSINESS

Hours

Business hours: 9:00 a.m. to 5:00 p.m., Monday through Friday. A few businesses are open from 9:00 a.m. until noon on Saturday.

Bank hours: 9:30 a.m. to 3:30 p.m., Monday through Friday. Some are open Saturday mornings. In some small towns, banks are open only two or three days a week.

Shop hours: 9:00 a.m. to 5:30 p.m., Monday through Saturday. Some stay open until 7:30 p.m. on Wednesday or Thursday, and some close on Saturday afternoon. In small towns, shops observe "early closing" one day during the week and shut at 1:00 p.m.

Business Practices

• Be sure to make business appointments in advance.

• Avoid June, July or August for business trips, as the English usually take their vacations then. Many business people also take off the week between Christmas and New Year's.

• If you're asked to speak to a group of English business people, plan to remain to answer questions.

• Bear in mind that business dinners are more popular in England than business lunches. Spouses are often included in business dinners. Also expect to be entertained at a restaurant rather than at home.

• A businesswoman entertaining a male English colleague can avoid awkwardness with the check by making arrangements in advance with the maitre d' of the restaurant. If her colleague still protests, she can insist that she is not personally paying—her company is.

Gifts: Note that gift-giving is not a normal part of business, perhaps because of the clear distinction between business and personal dealings. It is best not to offer a gift before one is given to you.

SCOTLAND

Business Hours

• Hours are generally the

same except that banks are open from 9:30 a.m. to 12:30 p.m., and from 1:30 to 3:30 p.m., Monday through Thursday. On Thursday, banks also reopen from 4:30 to 6:00 p.m. On Friday, banks are open from 9:30 to 3:30 p.m. They are closed Saturdays and Sundays.

Business Practices

• Assume that a dinner invitation is likely to be in a business person's home, as home entertaining for business is more popular in Scotland than in England. You may want to reciprocate by inviting your host and hostess for dinner in a restaurant.

HOLIDAYS AND SPECIAL OCCASIONS

Holidays: New Year's Day (January 1), Good Friday, Easter Monday, May Day (the first Monday in May), Spring Bank Holiday (the last Monday in May), Summer Bank Holiday (the last Monday in August), Christmas Day (December 25), Boxing Day (December 26).

• Note that almost all shops close on public holidays, and public services, such as buses, are cut down. This is especially true for the three days around Christmas.

• Guy Fawkes Day (November 5) commemorates the capture of Guy Fawkes, who plotted to destroy the Houses of Parliament in 1605. The English celebrate with chestnut roasts, bonfires and burning effigies of Guy Fawkes. (This is not a public holiday however.)

• Boxing Day is traditionally the servants' holiday, to compensate for work on Christmas. On that day the employer would give them Christmas boxes—often leftover food—hence the name.

SCOTLAND AND WALES

• All public holidays are the same as those in England, except that Scotland adds January 2 and has its Summer Bank Holiday on the first Monday in August, instead of the last. Wales adds St. David's Day (March 1), the anniversary of the death of the patron saint of Wales.

• In Scotland on *Hogmanay* (December 31), many people have parties lasting until 7:00 a.m. the next day. On the morning of a new year there is what is called "First Footing." To insure good luck in the coming year, the first person who enters a home should be a tall, dark male carrying a piece of coal, a black bun and a bottle of whisky, from which he gives the host a drink.

In the afternoon, friends, neighbors and relatives gather at one house to wish each other "Happy New Year." Each guest brings a small gift to be used by everyone in the house, such as a calendar. Everyone partakes of a buffet, usually with ham, bread, black buns and shortbread.

TRANSPORTATION

Public Transportation

• If someone tells you to take the "tube" or "Underground," realize that he or she means take the subway.

• On the Underground, pay at the entrance. Fares are based on distance traveled. Keep your ticket because you must give it up as you leave the Underground at your destination.

• On some buses, pay as you enter; on others, choose a seat and wait for the conductor to come and collect your fare (take your cue from the other people getting on the bus). Fares are based on the distance traveled.

• On the Underground, choose an appropriate car— smokers' or non-smokers'. They are clearly marked on the outside.

• Smokers should use the top deck of double-decker buses; the bottom deck is for non-smokers. On single-deck buses, smokers should go to the back.

• Taxis can be hailed on the street, and minicabs (a regular small car, not the usual large London taxicabs) can be ordered by telephone.

• At night, if you see an empty taxi without its "for hire" light on, try hailing it anyway.

Driving

• Be very cautious when driving on the left side of the road for the first time, especially when you come to a roundabout (rotary), which must be entered clockwise.

• You must wear seat belts.

• Note that a "Halt" sign is a Stop sign; a "Diversion" is a Detour; and a "Zebra crossing" is a Pedestrian Crossing.

• Be aware that there is a 70 mph speed limit on motorways, even if it isn't posted.

• If you want to drive slowly on a motorway, remember to stay in the left lane. Other drivers may get angry if you're driving too slowly.

• Don't turn left at a red light.

• Acknowledge the courtesy of another driver by raising your hand to thank her or him.

• In Scotland, be aware that many service garages are closed on Sundays. Garages are few and far between in northern Scotland.

LEGAL MATTERS AND SAFETY

• Ask the English police for help with directions or any other traveling problems. You'll find that they are very friendly and helpful and tend to be tolerant of minor mistakes made by travelers.

• Although England is very safe, even in urban areas, an unaccompanied woman in an unfamiliar area may be wise to take a taxi.

• Expect to find a value-added tax (V.A.T.) added to the price of all goods. If you ship something out of the country from a store or plan on taking something worth more than 50 pounds out of the country with you, you don't have to pay this. Bring your passport with you to the store.

ENGLISH KEY PHRASES

American	English
candy	sweets
dessert	pudding
chips	crisps
french fries	chips
doctor's office	surgery
drug store	chemist
apartment	flat
elevator	lift
flashlight	torch
gasoline	petrol
to phone	ring up
raincoat	mac
subway	tube
toilet	loo (informal)
trunk of car	boot
hood	bonnet
soccer	football

SCOTTISH KEY PHRASES

American	Scottish
oh! (an exclamation)	ach!
small river or stream	burn
serious	dour
valley	glen
a mess	guddle
know	ken
boy	lad
girl	lass
lake	loch
dust and dirt	stour
small	wee

CHAPTER EIGHT

FINLAND

The Finns, oddly enough, share an outlook on the world with the Irish. Both peoples have lived for centuries in the shadow of great powers (Finland was long an outpost of the Russian Empire). Both the Finns and the Irish have developed a kind of wry humor as well as a cheerful fatalism.

When it comes to conversation, however, the two peoples are vastly different: the Finns are as quiet as the Irish are talkative. It sometimes seems that the Finns express themselves mainly in the language of color and form, as seen in the bold designs of their fabrics and ceramics. Be sure to look for these when you visit Finland.

You'll also want to experience that venerable Finnish tradition, the sauna. And if you really want to earn the respect of your Finnish hosts, plunge through a hole in the ice afterwards!

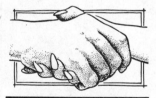

GREETINGS

• Shake hands when introduced, when greeting someone you know, and when leaving. Even children should shake hands.

• Don't be surprised if you see people offer friends both hands to shake simultaneously.

• Allow your host or hostess to introduce you to the others at a small party, which is the typical way for Finns to entertain. At a large party introduce yourself.

• Remember that business people prefer you to use their occupational title with the last name rather than "Mr." or "Mrs." If you aren't sure of someone's title, use *"Johtaja,"* which means "Director."

CONVERSATION

• Avoid using a Finnish person's first name until you are invited to do so.

• Good topics of conversation: sports, such as soccer, hockey, skiing and skating; and the history, sights and architecture of the city you're visiting.

• Topics to avoid: personal life, such as questions about someone's family or job, religion, socialism, or Finnish neutrality.

• Look in the eyes of the person to whom you're speaking.

TELEPHONES

• Look for public telephones in restaurants, cafes and phone booths. A local call costs 50 pennia.

PUBLIC MANNERS

• Remember that Finns don't show emotion in public, as Americans sometimes do. Finns kiss and hug only very close relatives, and friends they haven't seen for a long time.

• Be punctual for both business and social occasions.

• Wave when you see someone you know at a distance.

• Traditionally, men should remove their hats when greeting or talking to someone and when entering a house, church or elevator.

• Don't fold your arms. It's considered a sign of arrogance.

• Avoid crossing your legs so that one ankle rests on the other knee. It's considered too casual and rude.

• Note that smoking is forbidden in some official buildings and cafes.

• If you want to meet members of the opposite sex, go to one of many restaurants featuring dancing.

• Bear in mind that the sauna is central to Finnish life and is regulated by an unwritten code. The sauna itself is usually a small wooden house. There's a small dressing room for changing, and a main room where bathers sit or lie on wooden shelves. Heat comes from a small stove with hot rocks on top. From time to time water is splashed on the rocks to produce more steam. At the end everyone takes a shower or a swim in a lake or pool.

• Consider it a great compliment if you're invited to a sauna. You may even have a business discussion there. (However, this is unlikely if you're a businesswoman dealing with businessmen.)

• Be advised that the sexes usually have separate saunas, although close friends sometimes include both sexes in the same sauna. Traditionally, the women in the party have their sauna first, so that they'll be free to prepare the post-sauna refreshments.

• Expect the Finns to take their sauna naked. However, they won't be uncomfortable if you don't do the same. In hotels you'll be given a terry-cloth wrap which you can wear. You can also wrap a towel around you if you prefer. When people have saunas at summer homes on a lake, many of them wear bathing suits because they go for a swim after the sauna.

• Expect snacks after a sauna. Popular after-sauna snacks are sausages or salty fish with rye bread and butter. The salty fish is eaten to replace the salt lost by the body in the extreme heat. The beverage may be *Kalja*, which is similar to beer but non-alcoholic.

DRESS

• Expect people to dress rather formally and follow Paris fashions closely.

• Women wear dresses or suits for business, while men wear suits and ties. In the summer men can remove their jackets if their Finnish colleagues do.

• Anticipate that better restaurants will require men to wear jackets and ties.

• At dinner in someone's home, whether in the city or country, women should wear dresses, and men should wear suits and ties.

• Keep in mind that all men, even teenagers, wear ties and hats when they get dressed up.

• Wear formal dress for openings at theaters and concert halls. Short cocktail dresses for women and tuxedos for men are in order. Otherwise, women should wear dresses, and men suits and ties when they go to a play or concert.

MEALS

Hours and Foods

Breakfast *(aamiainen):* 7:30 to 9:00 a.m. People eat hot cereal, *pulla* (yeast bread), and either open-faced sandwiches of meat or cheese, or yogurt and fruit. The breakfast drink is coffee.

Lunch *(lounas):* 12:00 to 1:00 p.m. This is a light meal consisting of soup, sandwiches, salad and milk or buttermilk.

Dinner *(illallinen):* 5:00 or 6:00 p.m.; 7:00 p.m. for a dinner party. A family dinner will consist of meat, potatoes, vegetables or salad and pudding. Milk will accompany the meal.

At a dinner party, drinks usually precede the meal. Finns commonly drink beer or straight vodka or whiskey, although they sometimes have American martinis, or gin and tonics. The meal begins with soup, sometimes followed by a fish dish, such as smoked or salted salmon, or herring salad (herring mixed with sour cream, apples and onions).

The main course is meat, often a roast or stew, with potatoes and vegetables. Bread, usually a heavy, dark rye, and butter accompany the meal. Beer or sometimes wine is generally served with the meal, but you can request mineral water or fruit juice instead. Cheese and a sweet dessert end the meal. Coffee is served later in the evening, not immediately after dinner.

Breaks: Finns normally take coffee breaks at 10:00 a.m. and 2:00 p.m.

Table Manners

• Note that one of the Finns' favorite ways of entertaining is to invite people to a "coffee table" in the afternoon or evening. Cookies and cake—sometimes just one kind of each and sometimes an elaborate variety—and coffee are

served. Taste each of the pastries or your hostess will be insulted.

• At a dinner party, expect the host to sit at one end of the table, the hostess at the other. Guests then sit on the sides, often women on one side and men on the other. It is common for children to be included at meals with guests.

• Don't start eating before the host and don't leave the table before he does.

• At mealtime, refrain from drinking until the host has offered a toast. The host and hostess never receive toasts from others.

• Note that food is usually served buffet style at large parties. At a Finnish sandwich table, begin with smoked and salted fish, such as herring. Then take a fresh plate for the cold meats, which are roasted or smoked. Use another plate for the hot dishes. End the meal with fresh or stewed fruits, and cheeses. Coffee will be served later, sometimes with cookies.

• When the meal is not a buffet, wait to see if the hostess intends to serve the guests. Otherwise, help yourself from the plates and bowls of food that will be passed around.

• Remember that it's rude to leave food on your plate, so

take small portions at first.

• Be aware that people tend to press guests to eat more food and that this is their way of showing friendliness. However, if you simply can't eat seconds, say "No, thank you" politely.

• Keep in mind that the fork is held in the left hand and the knife in the right. You can leave silverware in any position on the plate when you have finished.

• Don't eat anything, including fruit, with your fingers. (For fruit, stick your fork into the fruit and peel it with your knife. Slice it and eat it with your fork.)

• When the meal ends, go to the hostess and thank her. Remember, however, this gesture does not signal the end of the evening.

• Stay about one and one-half to two hours after dinner.

Places to Eat

• Look for these types of eating places:

A *baari* is usually a milk bar—sometimes cafeteria style—where you can get soup, sandwiches, doughnuts and coffee.

A *kahvili* is a cafe or a shop that has pastries, coffee, tea or milk.

A *ravintola* is a restaurant.

• Be aware that Finns are more likely to entertain foreign visitors in restaurants than in their homes.

• Pick up the bill if you invite someone to join you for a meal in a restaurant. Bills in restaurants are never split.

• Only those restaurants and bars with licenses can serve liquor, and then not before noon.

• Try a Finnish favorite— berry liqueurs, which are often served ice cold—with your meals. Two popular choices are *mesimarja,* made of Arctic bramble, and *lakka,* made from cloud berries.

• Women should feel free to go into restaurants or bars alone.

• Avoid loud talking or noise in restaurants.

• In cafeterias and small lunch restaurants, expect to share a table with strangers, although this practice doesn't carry over to regular restaurants. In regular restaurants, wait to be seated.

Specialties

• Try these special foods: *vorsmack* (beef, mutton and salt herring); *merimiespihvi* (beef chunks baked with onions, potatoes and beer); *kalakukko* (fish and pork pie); *rapuja* (crayfish—it's considered a great delicacy and is eaten between July 21 and

October 31); *kiisseli* (a thick fruit pudding).

TIPPING

• Restaurants: Be aware that the tip is included in the bill, but you should leave a small additional amount on the table. Whenever the tip isn't included in the bill, leave 10-15%.

At a restaurant, tip the coat checker and the doorman each one Finnmark (at a fancy restaurant, give each 3 or 4 Finnmarks).

• Taxis: Don't tip, but round the fare up to the nearest mark.

• Porters: Tip 2 marks per bag.

• Cloakroom attendants: Give a 2-mark tip.

PRIVATE HOMES

• Don't be surprised if you're invited to take a sauna when you visit or come for dinner.

• When staying with a family, ask if you can help with the dishes. You will probably be refused, but it's polite to offer.

• Be sensitive to people who don't want smoking in their homes. If you want to smoke, ask if you should go outside.

Gifts: If you're invited to dinner, take or send cut flowers, which Finns prefer to potted plants. But don't take a large bouquet, as that would be considered ostentatious. You could also give a bottle of wine or a box of chocolates.

If you stay with a family, bring liquor, perfume, or historical dolls from the U.S.

BUSINESS

Hours

Bank hours: 9:30 a.m. to 4:00 p.m., Monday through Friday.

Business hours: 8:00 or 8:30 a.m. to 4:00 or 4:30 p.m., Monday through Friday.

Shop hours: 9:00 a.m. to 8:00 p.m. on Monday and

Friday; 9:00 a.m. to 5:00 p.m., Tuesday through Thursday; and 9:00 a.m. to 2:00 p.m. on Saturday.

Business Practices

• Most businesses close at 1:00 p.m. on the workday preceding a holiday.

• Don't plan a business trip for July or August, because many people take vacations then.

• Be sure to make appointments in advance. Try to make appointments with the managing directors of firms, because they are the decision makers.

• Remember that punctuality is extremely important.

• After a business deal is concluded, there's a long lunch, often followed by a sauna. At some point in a business visit, most foreigners are taken to a sauna.

• Include spouses in invitations to business dinners.

• Be prepared for the heavy drinking common at dinner. Space your drinks.

HOLIDAYS AND SPECIAL OCCASIONS

Holidays: New Year's Day (January 1), Good Friday, Easter Monday, Labor Day (May 1), Midsummer Day (celebrations start on the afternoon of the Friday closest to June 24 and continue through the Saturday), All Saints' Day (the Saturday nearest to the end of October or the beginning of November), Independence Day (December 6), Christmas (December 25), December 26.

• Note that May 1 is Labor Day, but since the 1920s many students and professors use the day to protest against communism. This celebration is called *Vappu*. On the evening of April 30, there are parties where people drink *sima* (fermented lemonade) and eat *tippaleita* (doughnuts). Students often parade in the streets. If you're invited to a *Vappu* party, bring champagne.

• December 6 is Independence Day. In the evening everyone turns out the lights and puts candles in the windows. People then take to the streets to walk about and admire the effect. These street gatherings are followed by parties.

TRANSPORTATION

Public Transportation

• Pay the conductor on the bus or trolley. In the subway, get a ticket at the booth. You pay one fare no matter how far you go.

• Note that there are many taxis. Look for taxi stands listed in the telephone book under *"autoasemat."*

Driving

• Be aware that the law requires the driver and any passengers in the front seat of a car to use seat belts.

• Know that traffic coming from the right has the right of way.

• Drive with headlights on both day and night.

• Blow the horn only in cases of danger.

• Keep in mind that you are subject to imprisonment or severe fines for driving under the influence of alcohol or drugs.

LEGAL MATTERS AND SAFETY

• To stay in Finland longer than three months, request permission from the passport police.

• Women should take a taxi after dark in any unfamiliar areas.

KEY PHRASES

English	Finnish	Pronunciation
Good morning	Hyvää huomenta	Whó-vahh whó-o-men-teh
Good evening	Hyvää iltaa	Whó-vahh íll-tah
Please	Ole hyvä	Óh-le whó-vah
Thank you	Kiitos	Kéy-eat-ohs
You're welcome	Ole hyvä	Óh-leh whó-vah
Yes	Kyllä	Cóol-lah
No	Ei	A
Sir, Mr.	Herra	Háir-rah
Mrs.	Rouva	Rów-vah
Miss	Neiti	Náy-tee
Excuse me	Anteeksi	Awn-ték-see
Good-bye	Näkemiin	Knáck-eh-me-een
I don't understand.	En ymmärrä.	En oeú-mer-reh
I don't speak Finnish.	En puhu suomea.	En póo-hoo swó-may
Does anyone here speak English?	Onko englantia puhuvea?	Ón-ko én-glahn-tya póo-hoo-vay

CHAPTER NINE

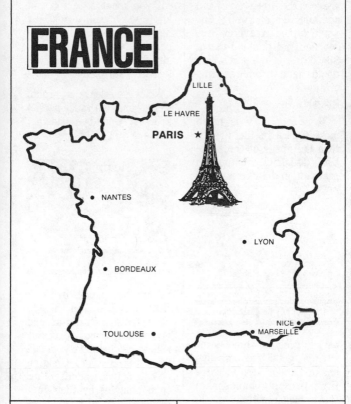

FRANCE

No people have a more undeserved reputation about their national character than the French. Many travelers decide not to visit France because they fear the alleged scorn and rudeness of the natives.

The French are **not** generally arrogant or rude. It's true that in Paris—as in any large tourist center—there are rude and unpleasant people. And if you're looking for

or expecting rudeness, you just may provoke it.

But generally the French are as kind as you could wish. In the French countryside especially, you will find warmth and acceptance. One traveler took a trip to Normandy and stopped in a shop in Bayeux, a town not far from the D-Day beaches, to buy a bottle of mineral water. When the shop lady determined that the traveler was American, she took the American's hand and said "Thank you." "For what?" the traveler responded, not thinking that a 30¢ bottle of mineral water could have produced this gratitude. "For saving us," the shop lady replied.

That shop lady is much more typical of the French than the image of the snobbish, disdainful creature so prevalent in the international press.

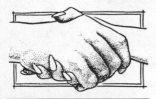

GREETINGS

• When greeting someone or saying good-bye, always shake hands. Don't use a firm, pumping handshake: shake hands with a quick, slight pressure. Children shake hands too.

• When you enter a room, greet everyone in it.

• In greeting a man, say "Good day, sir." Address a married woman or an older woman whose marital status you don't know with "Good day, madame." To a single young woman say "Good day, miss." Do not use the last name in greeting (i.e., "Good day, Mr. Dupont"), as this is considered too familiar.

• If you meet a person you know very well, use his or her first name and kiss both cheeks. Note that men usually don't kiss each other unless they're relatives.

• When you leave a group, shake hands with each person and say "Good-bye madame, (miss or sir)."

CONVERSATION

• Don't call people by their first names unless they're close friends. (Students and young people may relax this rule somewhat; take your cue from the French.) Children should not call adults other than relatives by their first names.

• Good topics of conversation: food, the area you come from, sports (especially soccer) and hobbies.

• Topics to avoid: the prices of things and where they were bought, what someone does for a living, income and age.

• Also avoid questions about personal and family life, as this is considered very private. Even a question such as "Do you have brothers and sisters?" is too personal.

• When you praise someone, don't be surprised if he or she makes a self-deprecating comment instead of saying "Thank you." The French are customarily modest about receiving compliments.

• Remember that dinnertime conversation is important to the French and that they will sit for hours at the table in lively discussion.

• Expect to find the French well-informed about the history, culture and politics of other countries. To gain their respect, be prepared to show some knowledge of the history and politics of France.

• When listening to someone, nod and respond with little comments throughout.

TELEPHONES

• Deposit 50 centimes for a local call. When you hear a tone, deposit more money if you want to continue. Some phones in cafes require *jetons* (tokens), instead of coins. Get these from the waiter.

• Answer the phone by saying *"Allô."*

PUBLIC MANNERS

• Avoid speaking or laughing loudly in public. Note that Americans tend to talk more loudly than the French, so drop your voice if you don't want to be conspicuous.

• Don't keep your hands in your pockets when speaking to someone.

• Don't chew gum in public.

• Don't select your own fruit and vegetables in markets or small stores; let the vendor serve you. If you pick up produce, the vendor is likely to tell you off in no uncertain terms.

• As you enter and leave a shop, say "Good day" to the sales clerk.

DRESS

• Note that dress in France, even casual dress, is more formal than in the U.S. Students and young people commonly wear jeans, but the middle class wear attractive, expensive clothing.

• For business meetings, men should wear conservative business suits with colored, striped or white shirts, and ties. Women should wear conservative suits or dresses.

• For the theater, men should wear dark suits, and women short dresses. Special openings call for tuxedos and long dresses.

• At the beach, you may change into your bathing suit right on the sands. Hold a towel around yourself and change under it.

• Don't be surprised if you see nude bathers or topless women at public beaches and swimming pools, especially along the Mediterranean.

MEALS

Hours and Foods

Breakfast *(petit déjeuner):* 7:00 to 8:00 a.m. A typical breakfast—in home, hotel or cafe—consists of *café au lait* (coffee with milk) or *chocolat chaud* (hot chocolate), bread, butter, jam and sometimes croissants. Breakfast is the only meal at which butter is served with bread.

Lunch *(déjeuner):* 12:00 to 2:30 p.m. Traditionally the main meal of the day, *déjeuner* consists of *hors d'oeuvres* (appetizers), a fish course (at a very formal meal), a meat course with vegetables, a salad, cheeses, fruit, pastries (on special occasions) and *demi-tasse* coffee (strong, black coffee in small cups). Wine accompanies the meal.

It is common for a business person to go home for a long lunch rather than visit a restaurant, though this is changing as more and more women work outside of the home.

Dinner *(dîner):* 7:00 to 9:30 p.m. Usually much simpler than the noon meal, *dîner* may be soup, a casserole and bread.

However, if it is a social occasion, it will be like *déjeuner.* On these occasions your host will likely offer you pernod, kir, vermouth or even champagne before the meal. Drinks are usually taken in the living room. Some hostesses serve an appetizer such as *pâté* or smoked fish. Others serve only nuts or small crackers so as not to spoil the appetite.

The usual after-dinner drinks are cognac, Grand Marnier, and Chartreuse. Many people make their own liqueurs from raspberries or blackberries and are very proud of them.

Table Manners

• If you are offered a drink before dinner, rise from your seat to accept it.

• Wait for the host and hostess to tell you where to sit at the table. The host and hostess usually sit at the center of the table opposite each other. Guests are seated in positions of descending importance to the right and left.

• Expect to have wine served with dinner and supper. The French consider it an aid to digestion and a stimulant to the appetite.

• Wait until the host has served wine to everyone and proposed a toast before you drink. Everyone will then say "To your health."

• Be aware that the host will continue to pour wine throughout the meal. If you do not care to drink much, take small sips, leaving your glass almost full.

• You may choose to drink mineral water, either sparkling or flat, in addition to or instead of wine.

• If you pour wine for someone, fill the glass only about three-quarters full.

• Note that tables are set with the forks and spoons turned downward. Use the spoon and fork placed above the dinner plate for dessert.

• You may choose to eat like the French, with the fork held in the left hand and the knife in the right. Do not switch the fork to the right hand after cutting. When only a fork is needed, keep it in the right hand. If you practice before leaving for Europe, you'll probably find this an efficient way of eating.

• Keep both hands on the table. It isn't polite to keep your hands in your lap, even when you're not eating.

• For salad, use a fork only. Don't cut it with a knife.

• Be sure to finish everything on your plate because leaving food is considered impolite and wasteful. You should also taste everything. (If you must follow a special diet, explain this briefly and quietly to your hostess.)

• Don't smoke between courses in either a home or restaurant.

• Put your portions of bread on the table next to the dinner plate (there won't be any bread-and-butter plates). Break the bread with your fingers. Never cut it.

• At family-style dinners, bread is often used to soak up gravy or to push food on the fork, but don't do this in more formal company or in restaurants.

• When you cut a piece of cheese from a wedge, don't cut off the point. Slice the wedge vertically, so that each person will have an equal share of the whole.

• If you have fruit for dessert, peel and slice it before eating it.

• To show that you have finished, place the knife and fork on your plate side by side, handles pointing to the right, fork tines up.

Places to Eat

• Look to see what an eating place is called to know what kind of food you'll get.

An *auberge* is an inn, often in the country, serving full meals and drinks.

A *bistro* is a bar, much like an English pub.

Brasseries are really restaurants, though they may be open for longer hours and may offer snacks as well as meals. Many *brasseries* specialize in Alsatian food and beer.

A *buffet exprès* is a cafeteria where customers eat standing up, but you won't find them as fast as American fast food restaurants.

Cafés usually limit their food menus to croissants and sandwiches. They are often open until 1:00 or 2:00 a.m., and some are open 24 hours.

A *relais de campagne* is a country inn, with menus ranging from snacks to several course meals.

Restaurants are, as the name suggests, regular restaurants. Hours are usually 12:00 to 2:30 p.m. and 7:00 to 9:30 p.m. (much later in Paris).

A *routier* is a roadside diner. Food there is simple but often good.

• Check the menus that are posted outside all restaurants so you know the prices before you enter.

• To call the waiter, say *"Garçon,"* (to call a waitress, say *"Mademoiselle")*. Never whistle or snap your fingers to attract the waiter's attention.

• In some restaurants you're expected to use the same fork and knife for the entire meal. If there is a knife rest on the table, place your utensils on it between courses.

• If you go with a group to a *café*, take your turn in buying a round of drinks, rather than splitting the bill each time.

Specialties

• A highlight of any trip to France is the opportunity to sample the special foods of the country's diverse regions. Try the pastries, bread, cheese (more than 400 varieties) and wine everywhere.

In Alsace and Lorraine try *choucroute garnie* (sauerkraut with sausage and pork), *pâté de foie gras* (goose liver paste) and *quiche Lorraine* (pastry filled with bacon, cheese, eggs and cream).

Bordeaux's specialties are *confit d'oie* (potted preserved duck), and *lamproie à la bordelaise* (eels cooked in red wine).

In Brittany, sample *crêpes* (especially those with jam or Grand Marnier and sugar poured over them), seafood, and *agneau pré-salé* (lamb reared on grass from salt marshes).

Burgundy is known for *boeuf bourguinonne* (the classic beef stew with wine, carrots, onion, and mushrooms), *escargots à la bourguignonne* (snails served in shells with garlic butter—usually six or twelve for a first course), *quenelles de brochet* (pike dumplings), and the cheeses of goat's or cow's milk.

In Normandy, sample *sole Normande* (poached sole served with a butter, egg, and cream sauce), *tripes à la mode de Caen* (a stew of tripe, cider, and vegetables), and *calvados* (the region's very strong apple brandy).

Provence offers *bouillabaisse* (a seafood soup made of saffron, herbs, garlic, tomatoes and olive oil), and *ratatouille* (a mixture of eggplant, tomatoes, onion, zucchini, and peppers, cooked in olive oil).

HOTELS

• In hotels and public buildings, note that *première étage* (first floor) refers to what Americans call the second floor. *Rez-de-chaussée* (*R.C.*) is what the French call the ground floor.

• If you're staying in a budget hotel, watch for one way they cut electricity costs. When you press the light switch in the stairway, the lights go on—but only for one minute. Press another switch on another floor to obtain more light.

• In French washrooms, be aware that "C" marks the hot water faucet, and "F" identifies the cold tap. Sometimes colors are used, with red signifying hot and blue cold.

• Don't expect to have a toilet and bath in your room unless you specifically ask for them (and pay more for the room).

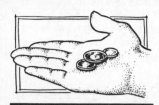

TIPPING

• Restaurants: Expect to find a 10-15% service charge added to checks (indicated by the words *service compris*—service included—on the menu). If the tip is not included, leave 10-15%. Even if the tip is included, leave some change on the table.

• Taxis: Tip 1 or 2 francs, more if the trip was a long distance.

• Ushers: Give 1 franc.

• Attendants in bathrooms: Give 50 centimes or a franc.

• Gas station attendant: Tip 2 francs if he provided extra services, such as washing the windshield.

PRIVATE HOMES

• Never drop in on someone in France, no matter how well you know them.

• When you are invited to visit a French home, don't expect a house tour. Guests are usually received in the living room, with doors to other rooms closed. Don't wander around, either outside or inside the house.

• When staying with a family, avoid making loud noises and don't bathe late at night, as the French are very concerned about what neighbors think of their behavior (though they rarely know them).

• Always ask before using the TV, phone or stereo.

• If you stay with a family for several days, keep the same cloth napkin for each meal. Each person will have his or her own individual napkin ring to keep it in between meals.

• If you stay for a week or more, offer to help with the dishes or even prepare a meal.

• In most French homes, the toilet is in a room separate from the bathroom. When leaving either room, close the door.

• Bear in mind that the electricity used to heat the water in most French homes is very expensive, and many French people do not take daily baths or showers. Try to do as the family does, and when you do take a shower, make it a short one.

• Remember to inform your hostess well in advance that you would like to take a bath or shower because the water often needs to be heated for an hour or two beforehand.

Gifts: If you're invited to a French home for dinner, bring a box of candy or cookies or an odd number of flowers (other than chrysanthemums—they're only for funerals). Only bring wine to good friends (and it should be an excellent, expensive wine or a bottle of champagne).

If you're staying for a few days, bring a gift from the U.S.: towels (which are much thicker and fluffier than the European variety), drip-dry sheets (flat if you don't know the bed size), books with photographs of your town or area, a typical product of your region (e.g., maple syrup, special textiles), good California wines. Give teenagers cassettes or records of popular music, or T-shirts with American sayings on them.

BUSINESS
Hours

Business hours: Generally 8:00 or 9:00 a.m. to noon, and 2:00 to 5:00 or 6:00 p.m., Monday to Friday. Many businesses open Monday at 2:00 p.m. and are open Saturday from 9:00 a.m. to 12:00 or 1:00 p.m.

Bank hours: 9:00 a.m. to 4:00 p.m., Monday through Friday.

Shop hours: 9:00 a.m. to noon, and 2:00 to 6:30 or 7:00 p.m., Tuesday through Saturday. Both shops and department stores are usually closed on Sunday and Monday. Note that stores are closed at lunchtime, so buy food beforehand if you are planning a picnic lunch.

Business Practices

• Expect to find many stores, restaurants, theaters and businesses closed during August, the most popular time for the French to take vacations.

• Avoid business trips to France the two weeks before and after Christmas and Easter.

• Best times to schedule business appointments: 11:00 a.m. or 3:30 p.m.

• Be sure to arrive on time for appointments.

• When you arrive, give your business card to the receptionist or secretary.

• If you don't speak French extremely well, hire an interpreter or speak English.

• Note that most business entertainment takes place in restaurants, rarely at home. Spouses are seldom invited to business lunches or dinners.

• If you are a guest at a business dinner, take your cue on ordering from your host. You may want to ask your host to recommend a choice, especially if he or she is the only one with a menu showing prices.

• If you wish to entertain French business people, invite them to *dîner* (dinner) rather than *déjeuner* (lunch).

• As either host or guest, never be flashy or loud. Don't make an issue of what food and wine you order and don't draw attention to yourself.

HOLIDAYS AND SPECIAL OCCASIONS

Holidays: New Year's Day (January 1), Easter Monday, Labor Day (May 1), Victory Day (May 8, end of World War II), Ascension Day (five weeks after Easter), Whit Monday (eight weeks after Easter), Bastille Day (the national holiday, July 14), The Assumption (August 15), All Saints' Day (November 1), Armistice Day (November 11) and Christmas Day (December 25).

• New Year's Eve is a very festive occasion. Families have a large meal, featuring raw oysters as a first course, often followed by turkey. On New Year's Day relatives give children money. If you visit friends, bring a small gift.

• On Mardi Gras (the Tuesday before Ash Wednesday), the French celebrate with costume parties and street processions. *Crêpes* are generally eaten on this day (traditionally to use up butter before Lent!).

• On Labor Day (May 1), people visit friends and neighbors and give each of them a sprig of lily of the valley for good luck and happiness. You may also see union demonstrations in the cities.

• Many of the French treat August as a month-long holiday. You'll find the seashore packed with vacationers, and many businesses, restaurants and museums are closed.

TRANSPORTATION

Public Transportation

• Give up your seat to senior citizens on buses and subways. They expect it and may be loudly indignant if you don't.

• If you want to become acquainted with someone on a train, you usually have to make the first move. The French tend to be reserved and discreet.

• If, however, someone is bothering you, don't hesitate to tell them to stop. If the person is persistent, speak to the conductor. Be assertive, but try not to make a scene.

• Bring bottled water on trains, even on a short trip, because there's no drinking water in the cars or lavatories. You may also want to bring along food on long-distance trains because the dining car may be removed with no advance notice.

• If the doors do not open automatically when the train stops, lower the window in the door and open the door from the outside. (It's easiest to get behind some natives and let them open the door.)

Driving

• Watch out for very fast drivers who pass constantly, even on narrow roads.

• Remember that the law requires everyone to wear seat belts.

• Seat children in the back seat, as this is required by law.

• Don't blow your horn in cities, as it is illegal.

• At an intersection, give the vehicle on the right the right of way.

• Don't turn right on a red light.

• You may find that women who are stopped for a traffic violation have an easier time than men. If you're a woman, try apologizing politely and you may avoid paying a fine.

LEGAL MATTERS AND SAFETY

• In large cities, take precautions against theft, particularly in the Paris Métro.

• Women should avoid using the Métro after 10:00 p.m.,

the long, dark corridors are not safe.

• Note that the drinking age is 18. There are no restrictions on drinking hours—you can drink 24 hours a day if you can find a bar open.

• Ask if a shop refunds the value-added tax to foreigners on items that cost more than 600 francs. If it does, get the store to fill out the appropriate forms (they will need your passport to do so). Take these forms to the airport when you leave and go to the office marked *La Détaxe.* Bring your passport and the items with you. They will check the forms, then notify the store by mail. The store will then mail your refund to your home address.

KEY PHRASES

Good day	Bonjour	bawn-zhoór
Good evening	Bonsoir	bawn-sswáhr
Please	S'il vous plaît	seel-voo-pleh
Thank you	Merci	mehr-see
You're welcome	De rien	de ree-en
Yes	Oui	wee
No	Non	nawn
Mr.	Monsieur	meh-syeur
Mrs.	Madame	mah-dahm
Miss	Mademoiselle	mahd-mwah-zehl
Excuse me	Excusez-moi	ex-qyou-zay mwah
Good-bye	Au revoir	o reh-vwahr
I don't understand.	Je ne comprends pas.	zhe ne kawn-prahn pah
I don't speak French.	Je ne parle pas français.	zhe ne pahrl pah frawn-say
Do you speak English?	Parlez-vous anglais?	pahr-lay voo ahn-gleh

CHAPTER TEN

If you think that Germans are always hard, cold, and ruthlessly efficient, visit during Carnival time in February, when you'll see continuous revelry in the streets, parades, parties, wild costumes and a general disregard for "upright behavior." One traveler went to Germany and rented a room in the home of a middle-aged German lady. The landlady laid down the rules: no men in the room ever—except

Carnival time!

At other times, Germans are more subdued in their entertainment, although they still enjoy getting together with neighbors for an evening of drinking and singing.

On the whole though, Germans do take life quite seriously. You will see this reflected in German newspapers, magazines, television and films, and you will experience it firsthand when you talk to Germans.

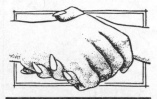

GREETINGS

• You should generally shake hands at meetings and departures, although customs on this vary from region to region. When you're unsure of the handshaking custom in a certain area, watch what the people around you are doing.

• Don't keep one hand in your pocket when shaking hands.

• Upon arriving at a small party, shake hands with everyone present.

• Realize that while it's acceptable to introduce yourself to people at a party or business meeting, it's better to be introduced by a third party.

• When you are introducing two people in a formal situation, such as a business meeting, a reception or a formal dinner party, give the name of the younger or lower-ranking person first.

• Men should rise when a woman enters the room. Men traditionally stand when speaking to a woman who is standing; however, if the man is much older or of a higher social standing, he may sit down. Women need not rise when someone enters the room.

• Although, traditionally, you would address an unmarried woman as *Fräulein* (for example, *Fräulein Schmidt)*, you should now only address women under 20 in this way. All other women, married or otherwise, are addressed as *Frau (Frau Schmidt)*.

• Be sure to use professional titles in southern Germany, and in small towns; however, they may not be commonly used elsewhere in Germany. When appropriate, address doctors, professors, lawyers and clergymen by "Mr." or "Ms." and the title (for example, *Frau Doktor,* Ms. Doctor).

• Address the spouse of a professional simply by "Mr." or "Mrs." and the person's last name.

CONVERSATION

• Use last names until you are invited to use first names. It is customary for two people who have become good friends to share a sort of ritual drink. If such a suggestion is made by a German friend, you should intertwine right arms, drinks in hand, and say "To brotherhood." Following this ritual, use first names and the informal form of you *(du)* in German conversation.

• Good topics of conversation: the German countryside, travel abroad, hobbies and sports, such as soccer. (Be aware that Germans take the sport of soccer very seriously. Never say anything negative about the sport or the local soccer team.) Don't expect Germans to know anything about American baseball or football.

• Topics to avoid: World War II, especially questions such as "What were you doing during the war?" and personal life. Avoid asking questions such as "Are you married?" or "Do you have children?"

• Expect Germans to have strong opinions on political issues, both domestic and international. They will also want to know your opinion on international events, in particular any German-American issues.

• Realize that if Germans seem cool and reserved at first, it is because they believe it's inappropriate to be casual and overly friendly with strangers. If you're going to be in Germany for a long time, you may feel isolated at first, since it takes a long time for friendships to develop.

• Don't expect to receive compliments even when you've done something very well—and don't offer compliments too freely. Compliments embarrass, rather than please, most Germans.

• Don't be surprised to find Germans outspoken. For example, where Americans would think it tactless to tell a friend that her outfit was unbecoming, Germans think it is merely being honest.

• Keep in mind that Germans consider it a sign of disrespect to speak while keeping your hands in your pockets.

TELEPHONES

• Observe that there are two kinds of public phones. The first is for local and regional calls only and has slots for 10-pfennig coins. A local call costs two 10-pfennig coins. The second, for local and long-distance calls, has slots for 10-pfennig, 50-pfennig and 1-mark coins.

• For a local call, deposit two

10-pfennig coins before dialing. When a sign lights up, deposit more coins, because this means your speaking time is over.

• Make long-distance calls from a post office rather than from a hotel room or a coin-operated phone, as it's cheaper and easier.

• Answer the phone by giving your last name instead of saying "Hello."

PUBLIC MANNERS

• Upon encountering someone you know at a distance, wait until you are within close range before offering a greeting. Although you will probably see and hear young people yelling at one another across the street, never shout greetings yourself.

• When entering and leaving a shop, always say "Hello" and "Good-bye" to the sales clerk

• Be conscious of the importance Germans attach to privacy. If the door to a room is closed, never enter without first knocking, whether you're in a home or an office.

• To attract someone's attention, raise your hand with the index finger extended.

• Never put your feet on the furniture.

• Don't be surprised to see few smiling faces during your stay. While a smile is a simple expression of pleasure or good will to Americans, in Germany it is a way to express affection.

• Never whisper or cough during an opera, concert or play, or you may be told off by your German neighbors. You'll notice that Germans are not only extremely quiet during a performance, they're extremely still and don't shift seating position at all.

• Men should walk in front of women into a restaurant. However, men should allow older women or persons of a higher status to enter a room or a house first.

• When walking down the street with a woman, a man should walk on her left side (normally the curb side). A woman walking with two men walks between them, as should a man walking with two women. A young girl walking with an older woman should be on the left side.

• Never take photographs near military installations or near the border between East and West Germany. Don't take photographs inside a church while a service is in progress.

Those museums and galleries that forbid photography post signs to that effect. If you'd like to take a close-up, be sure to ask permission first.

DRESS

• Teenagers can feel comfortable wearing the same casual clothes they would in America, but anyone older may want to dress a little more carefully than usual. Smart pants, shirts and sweaters are German standards. Jeans are fine if they're not worn out or dirty. Note that, in the summer, most German men wear sandals for casual wear. Tennis shoes are not worn except for sports.

• In southern Germany, don't be surprised if you see people wearing traditional costumes, such as *lederhosen* (leather shorts), *dirndls* (full, gathered skirts), jackets, and alpine hats, even in large cities.

• Wear conservative clothes in dark colors for business. Both men and women wear suits and men should wear ties. In warm weather, it's okay to take off jackets if German colleagues do so first. In summer, women should wear suits or short-sleeved dresses, but nothing sleeveless.

• When invited to dinner, women will often find dresses or skirts and blouses more appropriate than pants.

• For plays, concerts and operas, men should wear dark suits and ties, and women should wear fancy short dresses. For an opening night, men should wear dark suits, and women long dresses, so ask if it's an opening when buying your tickets.

• If you are prone to be chilly, keep in mind that you must check your coat at theaters; you're not allowed to wear or carry them into the auditorium.

MEALS

Hours and Foods

Breakfast *(frühstück):* 7:00 to 8:30 a.m. The meal usually consists of rye bread, rolls, butter and jam, and coffee with milk.

Lunch (mittagessen):
1:00 p.m. The midday meal is usually a large one. It begins with soup, followed by meat, potatoes, vegetables and salad. Rye bread (but no butter) and beer often accompany the meal. Germans don't usually take dessert and coffee after the meal; they have a coffee and pastry break at 4:00 p.m. instead.

Supper (abendessen):
Served between 6:30 and 7:30 p.m. The evening meal is usually lighter than the midday meal, consisting of cold meat, eggs, salad, cheese or open-faced sandwiches.

• If you're invited to dinner, don't be surprised if you're entertained in a restaurant rather than in a home. If the dinner party is in a home, it will usually be for a special occasion, such as an engagement party.

For such a party, drinks, such as sherry, vermouth or wine, will be served before dinner in the living room. There usually are no appetizers with drinks. The meal will follow the same courses as a typical noontime meal. Wine will accompany the meal and after-dinner drinks will be served with coffee, often one of three strong brandies: *kirschwasser* (cherry brandy), *himbeergeist* (raspberry brandy), *pflaumenwasser* (prune brandy).

Table Manners

• When invited to dinner, be on time. Remember that the Germans do not generally have long cocktail hours.

• Expect the male guest of honor to sit to the left of the hostess and the female guest of honor to sit to the right of the host.

• At a dinner party, don't drink until the host has toasted everyone and taken the first drink.

• Clink glasses only when the toast is offered for a special occasion, such as someone's birthday. If a toast is offered to you, return the favor later in the meal if you like. It is traditional that a man toasts a woman, never vice versa.

• Help yourself from the platters of food passed around the table.

• To eat German-style, keep the fork in your left hand and the knife in your right. Use the knife to push food onto the fork.

• Even when you're not using your knife, hold on to it.

• When fish is served, you may also be given a special fish knife and fork to use. The fish knife looks like a butter knife and the fish fork like a salad fork. If you aren't given special utensils, cut your fish with the fork you have.

• Avoid using a knife to cut

potatoes, pancakes or dumplings. To do so suggests that the food is not tender enough.

• Never eat with your fingers. Use a knife and fork to eat sandwiches and usually even fruit. (In some homes people do eat fruit with their hands, so take your cue from your hosts.)

• When you've finished eating, lay the knife and fork vertically side-by-side on the plate.

• Smoke between courses only if you see others doing so. Smoking usually begins after coffee is served. Always ask permission before smoking.

• Plan to leave shortly after dinner. If you've come at 7:00 p.m., leave no later than 11:00 p.m. Guests are expected to make the first move to leave. If your host doesn't refill your glass, consider it a clue that it's time to go. When the hostess asks you to stay after you've started to leave, stay another 30 minutes.

Places to Eat

• Look for the following eating places:

A *bierkeller* offers beer and food, such as sausages, pork cutlets and spare ribs, all accompanied by sauerkraut.

A *cafe* serves drinks and snacks.

A *gasthof* or *wirtshaus* is a regular restaurant. Don't go here if you only want a drink.

A *konditorei* serves pastry with coffee or tea.

A *schnellimbiss* is a snack bar, where you can get quick food. You will probably eat standing at a counter.

A *weinstube* offers wine and a limited selection of snacks. Bread sticks and pretzels and sometimes *harzer,* a cheese that you mix with onions, caraway seeds and wine and spread on rye bread are available.

• Expect the opening and closing hours for places serving alcohol to differ by region, since the local communities control these times.

• Before entering a restaurant, check the front window, where a menu with prices will be placed.

• Seat yourself except in the best restaurants. If there's no vacant table, look for an empty seat at a table with other people. Ask permission before you sit down, but don't be surprised if the people at the table strike up a conversation with you.

• Address a waiter as *"Herr Ober"* and a waitress as *"Fräulein."* Be patient if service is slow, and realize that there has been a major shortage of labor in the hotel and catering business.

• Don't ask for coffee with a meal; it's only drunk after a meal.

Specialties

• Germany is famous for its beers, white wine, wiener-schnitzel and sausages.

Also try the following: *kalbsvögel* (rolled veal stuffed with spinach, egg and bacon); *sauerbraten* (beef marinated in vinegar, sugar, raisins and crumbled gingersnaps for several days and then prepared like a pot roast); *hasenpfeffer* (rabbit stew); *weisswurst* (a white sausage of veal and pork); *bratwurst* (pork sausage); *leberwurst* (liver sausage); *würstchen* (a sausage much like an American hot dog); *spätzle* (noodle dumplings); and *schwarzwalder kirschtorte* (Black Forest chocolate and cherry cake).

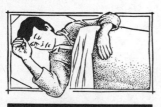

HOTELS

• Be prepared to fill out an intricate registration form when you check into a hotel.

• A service charge is included in the bill, so don't tip anyone

but the porter.

• If your room does not have a bath, get the key to the bathroom from the desk clerk. There may be an extra charge for this.

• Don't be surprised if you're charged extra for heat in your room.

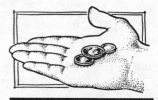

TIPPING

• Restaurants: Keep in mind that a 10-15% charge is usually added to the restaurant check as a tip (don't confuse this with the 13% value-added tax which is also added). It isn't necessary to leave an additional tip, but most people round the check out to the nearest mark. Let the waiter or waitress know that the change is theirs, rather than just leaving it on the table.

• Hotel porters: Tip 1 mark per bag.

• Taxis: Give a 10-15% tip.

• Gas station attendants: If they perform some extra-special service, tip 1 mark.

• Cloakroom attendants: Have 50 pfennigs on hand as a tip.

PRIVATE HOMES

• When staying with a German family, remember to turn off all lights if you're the last to leave a room. Even small children are expected to do this in order to conserve energy.

• Always close inside doors, such as bedroom, bathroom or living room, behind you.

• When staying with a family living in an apartment, be especially quiet from 10:00 p.m. to 7:00 a.m. and between 1:00 p.m. and 3:00 p.m., when people may be sleeping.

• If you need to make a call from a private home, ask permission first, since people are charged for each individual call. Offer to pay for the call.

Gifts: When invited to dinner, bring flowers and present them to your hostess unwrapped. Bring a small bouquet—large ones are considered ostentatious—and be sure that the bunch contains an uneven number of flowers (but never 13). Realize that red roses are reserved for expression of ro-mantic love, and calla lilies are traditionally funeral flowers.

Don't bring wine (unless it's a special California wine) as a dinner gift because your host might think that you consider his wine cellar inadequate.

If you stay with a family, bring American college sweatshirts for the children and teenagers. For your hosts, bring drip-dry table-cloths, bourbon whiskey, small pocket calculators and classical or rock records. Avoid giving perfume, soap or clothing, other than scarves, since such gifts are considered too personal.

BUSINESS

Hours

Business hours: 8:00 or 9:00 a.m. until 4:00 or 5:00 p.m., Monday through Friday.

Bank hours: 8:30 a.m. to 1:00 p.m. and 2:00 to 4:00 p.m., Monday through Friday, and Thursday until 5:30 p.m.

Shop hours: 8:00 or 8:30 a.m. to 6:00 or 6:30 p.m.,

Monday through Friday, and from 8:00 a.m. until 2:00 p.m. on Saturday.

Business Practices

• Address a business letter to the firm rather than to an individual executive (begin your letter, "Dear ladies and gentlemen:"). When a letter is addressed to a specific executive who happens to be away, there is a long delay in responding.

• Note that if two Germans sign a business letter, it means that both individuals make decisions.

• Avoid making business appointments in July, August or December.

• Plan business appointments between 11:00 a.m. and 1:00 p.m. and between 3:00 and 5:00 p.m. Avoid planning Friday afternoon appointments, as many offices close at 2:00 or 3:00 p.m.

• Never suggest a breakfast meeting. It is unheard of in Germany.

• Make appointments well in advance. If you're in Germany, you can request an appointment for a short, informational meeting only a few days in advance. For a lengthier meeting, plan one to two weeks ahead.

If you're arranging a meeting by mail from the U.S., try to allow at least a month, as airmail letters take about a

week to travel each way.

• Keep in mind that Germans may ask to schedule appointments at times earlier or later than is usual in a U.S. business day.

• Be punctual. Germans consider punctuality very important.

• Expect to have a general conversation before getting down to business. A German will probably inquire about your flight, your accommodations, where you are from in the U.S., and similar general questions.

• Realize that German business people operate more slowly than Americans. They believe that a good job requires time, and they proceed in a very deliberate fashion. In fact, Germans generally don't trust the quality of businesses that specialize in fast service.

• Keep in mind that the atmosphere at a business meeting is serious; don't joke or tell humorous stories.

• Bring plenty of business cards with you.

• Although most business people prefer to use German, be assured that many will deal with you in English.

• If you go out to lunch with German colleagues, plan to discuss business before, but not during, the meal.

• When an occasion is to be

strictly social, spouses may be included; otherwise they are not.

HOLIDAYS AND SPECIAL OCCASIONS

Holidays: New Year's Day (January 1), Good Friday, Easter Monday, Labor Day (May 1), Ascension Day (five weeks after Easter), Whit Monday (eight weeks after Easter), Day of Unity (June 17), Prayer and Repentance Day (mid-November), Christmas Day (December 25) and December 26.

• Carnival is a three-day celebration that ends on Shrove Tuesday (the day before Ash Wednesday). There are parades, costumes, parties and revelry not seen at any other time of year. Normal business stops, and "anything goes."

TRANSPORTATION

Public Transportation

• Buy tickets for buses, streetcars and subways at newsstands or ticket machines.

• Stamp your ticket in a machine at the bus stop or subway entrance and keep it in case an inspector comes to check.

• When you enter a train compartment, greet everyone in it and ask if the seat is occupied. There is no drinking water on trains.

Driving

• Note that seat belts are mandatory.

• Be aware that children under 12 must sit in the back seat.

- Be alert, since driving in Germany is a challenge. Drivers in Germany tend to be impatient, and often tailgate.

Be watchful also for the many bicycles, motorcycles and scooters on the streets and highways.

- Be aware that there is no speed limit on highways.

- Look for emergency telephones along the highways. Many of the operators speak English; but if you find one who doesn't, ask to be connected to someone who does.

- Never drink and drive. Your license will most likely be revoked if you are in an accident after you've been drinking.

- If you're stopped for a traffic violation, pay the fine, which is usually small. If you wish to press the matter further, don't argue; go to a police station.

LEGAL MATTERS AND SAFETY

- Note that drinking hours differ from community to community. Bars and restaurants generally stop serving liquor at 1:00 a.m. on weekdays and 2:00 a.m. on Saturdays. Some nightclubs can serve liquor later than that. In Berlin, there are no fixed closing times.

- Realize that prostitution is legal in Germany and is tightly supervised by the government. Many cities have one street where the prostitutes sit in shop windows. Other women are not allowed on these streets.

- Women can feel safe going almost anywhere in Germany, without worrying about verbal or physical harassment.

- Be warned that women are safer taking taxis after dark in larger cities. In small towns, it's safe to walk alone if the streets are well-lit. Avoid train stations at night.

- If you buy goods in Germany and bring them out of the country, you can get the value-added tax that is included in the price of the goods refunded. Get a form from the shop and present it to the customs officials to get stamped as you leave the country. Your refund will be mailed to you when you get home.

KEY PHRASES

English	German	Pronunciation
Good day	Guten Tag	Góo-tun ták
Good morning	Guten Morgen	Góo-tun máwr-gun
Good evening	Guten Abend	Góo-tun áh-bent
Please	Bitte	Bít-uh
Thank you	Danke	Dúnk-uh
You're welcome	Bitte	Bít-uh
Yes	Ja	Ya
No	Nein	Nine
Sir	Herr	Hair
Mrs., Madame	Frau	Frow (rhymes with how)
Miss	Fraülein	Froy-line
Excuse me	Verzeihung	Fare-tśy-oong
Good-bye	Auf Wiedersehen	Oẃf vée-der-zeyn
I don't speak German.	Ich spreche nicht Deutsch.	Eech Spŕeh-cheh neécht dóytsh
Does anyone here speak English?	Spricht hier jemand Englisch?	Spréecht here yáy-mahnd ehń-gleesh

CHAPTER ELEVEN

GREECE

Almost everyone is familiar with Zorba the Greek, whose free spirit and love of life typify much of the Greek personality. To Zorba, dancing was life. And so too, to the Greeks. Sitting in a taverna, you'll often see both men and women spontaneously leap to their feet and dance. Dancing is as central to Greek life as television is to the American.

The Greek personality is warm and demonstrative. One Greek who came to the U.S. to study, had an affectionate personality that was almost embarrassingly effusive. She went home to Greece for a visit and reported that her relatives had said, "How cold you've become!" Travelers will find this warmth and acceptance a real boon when they travel in Greece.

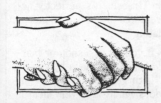

GREETINGS

• When introduced to someone, shake hands firmly. Also shake hands when greeting or leaving someone you already know.

• Expect close friends of the same sex to kiss and embrace one another when they meet. Men may only do this after a long absence.

• Unlike the practice in some European countries, you should not address people by professional titles when you greet them or converse with them.

CONVERSATION

• Wait for your Greek colleagues to use first names before you do.

• Good topics of conversation: international politics, music, sports such as soccer, your host's family or job, or the favorite conversation opener—the weather.

• Topics to avoid: Cyprus, American involvement in Greek affairs, or any pro-Turkish feelings you may have.

• Be prepared for Greeks to ask you rather personal questions, such as the amount you earn. Don't be offended, as this is their way of getting to know you. Try to be tactful if you prefer not to answer the inquiries.

• Remember that Greeks sometimes indicate a negative response by tipping their head back slightly and raising their eyebrows (or sometimes by just raising their eyebrows) without saying a word.

TELEPHONES

• Look for public telephones at newsstands and in booths on the street. Deposit 10 drachmas and dial. (To place long-distance calls, go to a telephone office.)

• When you answer the phone, say *"Embros"* ("Here I am").

PUBLIC MANNERS

• Expect to find the Greeks very demonstrative and physically affectionate. It's fine for you to be likewise.

• Don't wave American-style (showing your palm with fingers extended). It's an insult. Instead raise your index finger while keeping your palm closed.

• If you compliment a Greek, don't be surprised if he or she makes a puff of breath through pursed lips to ward off the jealousy of the evil eye.

• Note that many men finger worry beads constantly. This activity is thought to calm people and has no religious significance.

• Don't expect an orderly line at a bus stop or bank. People simply elbow ahead in such situations. Do as the Greeks do, or you'll be left waiting at the curb.

• Never joke about or show disrespect to the Greek flag or national emblem.

• Keep a flexible schedule, as punctuality is not important in Greece. It's perfectly acceptable to arrive 30 minutes late.

• If you go to a shop or market, try to bargain by asking "Is this the final price?" Vendors will make it very clear if they don't want to bargain. Start by offering half the asking price.

• Realize that Greeks smoke constantly, even while eating.

• Women shouldn't go behind the altar in a Greek Orthodox Church.

DRESS

• You can wear jeans in cities, but don't wear shorts anywhere.

• For business, women should wear shirtdresses or suits, and heels. Men should wear suits and ties in the winter. In the summer, Greek businessmen dress more casually, but it makes a better impression if you wear a suit and tie to begin with.

• If an invitation reads "Formal Dress," women wear long dresses, and men tuxedos.

• When invited to dinner at

someone's home, women should wear dresses or dressy pants; men should wear jackets and ties in the winter, but not in the summer.

• Be aware that women visiting churches or monasteries should have their arms covered and should wear skirts, never pants.

MEALS

Hours and Food

Breakfast *(to proeeno):* 7:00 a.m. Expect a roll or bread, with butter and jam or honey, and coffee, either Turkish or instant.

Lunch *(toh gevma):* 1:30 to 2:00 p.m. Some people have a light meal: a sandwich or salad, cheese and yogurt. Others have a main meal: appetizers, meat or fish with salad, fruit or yogurt with honey, and Turkish coffee. They drink beer or wine, and water with the meal.

Dinner *(toh theepno):* 8:30 to 9:30 p.m. A family dinner consists of the same courses as the main meal described at lunch except that a sweet follows the fruit course.

A dinner party will begin with appetizers such as meatballs, or cheese or spinach pies served with *ouzo,* an aniseed liquor usually served with water, or *retsina,* a wine with resin added. (Greece also produces good unresinated wines.)

The main course could be roast lamb or a dish such as *moussaka* (eggplant with meat sauce and cheese) with potatoes or rice pilaf and a salad. Wine will be served throughout the meal. The meal will end with fruit, Turkish coffee and, sometimes, brandy and scotch.

Table Manners

• If you're invited to dinner, arrive about 30 minutes late; people don't expect you to be on time.

• Realize that Greeks enjoy the company of friends most at meals; eating is incidental to that.

• Enjoy the relaxed atmosphere at meals. Close friends or relatives often share foods and eat from one another's plates.

• Use your fingers to help yourself to the appetizers that are usually served before lunch or dinner, often on one plate in the middle of the table.

• Don't be surprised if your hosts pressure you to drink, especially if you're a man.

Don't use the excuse that you have work to do; your hosts will simply tell you to take it easy for the day. If you really don't want to drink, take very small sips, so that your glass remains almost full.

• If you're the male guest of honor, sit to the right of the hostess. If you're the female guest of honor, sit to the right of the host.

• Note that, traditionally, women do all the serving while men stay with the guests.

• Expect that the oldest guest will be served first.

• Use the spoon above your plate for dessert. The fork will be on the left and the knife on the right.

• Note that some foods can be eaten with your fingers. Take your cue from your host.

• Keep your wrists on the table; don't put your hands in your lap. In informal company you may even put your elbows on the table.

• Bread accompanies every meal, but don't expect a bread-and-butter plate. Put your bread on the table.

• Plan to eat a great deal to avoid offending your host. If there's one dish you don't care for, say that you really loved one of the other dishes, and eat a bit more of that.

• To show that you're finished, cross your utensils, the knife under the fork with the fork tines down; or remove your napkin from your lap and put it next to your plate.

• Note that coffee is served Turkish-style, unless you ask for Nescafe. It is served in small cups and is very strong. You can ask for it bitter, medium or sweet.

• If you're invited to dinner, stay until about 11:00 p.m. If the conversation is lively and animated, feel free to stay longer and leave when the conversation is dying out.

Places to Eat

• For variety, try these types of eating places:

A *galaktoplia* is a milk shop. You can order yogurt, rice pudding, custard and sticky, sweet desserts.

A *kafenion* is a coffee-house or cafe. The emphasis here is on conversation. Both men and women frequent *kafenions* in the city, but in the country only men go.

A *zakharoplastio* is a pastry shop. They serve soup, homemade yogurt, puddings, coffee, alcohol and soft drinks. Women often go here rather than to cafes. Also, since nightclubs in Athens now have to close at 2:00 a.m., many people go to pastry shops late at night. If you're out late, stop in at one to watch the people.

• Look for stands on the

street and at beaches that serve snacks, such as: *souvlakia, giro, tyropitta* and *spanakopitta*. (See Specialties section for descriptions.)

• Seat yourself in most restaurants.

• Don't ask the price of a meal before ordering, as it's considered rude. As a rule of thumb, meat is usually inexpensive, and fish expensive.

• Except in the most deluxe restaurants, walk into the kitchen and choose the food you would like. (An especially useful custom in places where the menu is written only in Greek!)

• Remember that most frying is done in very heavy olive oil. You may want to stick to bland foods that aren't fried (if you don't relish a fried egg in olive oil, for example).

• To attract the waiter's attention, say "please." Some people bang on their glass with a spoon to summon the waiter, but that's not considered polite.

• Do be very assertive with waiters to attract their attention and to get what you want when you want it.

• If you are a woman traveling alone, choose one of the more elegant restaurants for your evening meal to avoid being harassed by men.

Specialties

• Be sure to sample some of these Greek specialties: *dolmades* (grape leaves stuffed with rice); *keftedes* (meatballs); *barbounia* (red mullet fish usually grilled); *kalamarakia* (squid); *souvlakia* (lamb and vegetables grilled on a skewer); *moussaka* (casserole of eggplant and ground lamb); *spanakopitta* (spinach pie); *tyropitta* (cheese pie); *giro* (pressed lamb and herbs cooked on a vertical spit, with slices carved off and served on pita bread with salad); *taramousalata* (a dip made of salted roe of grey mullet).

• For dessert, try *baklava* (a pastry with thin layers of flaky dough, nuts and cinnamon in a honey syrup).

• If you're not interested in exotic foods, avoid *miala* (brains) and *kokoretsi* (intestines stuffed with sweetbreads, livers and spices).

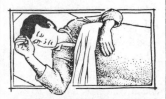

HOTELS

• When you check in, be aware that the hotel clerk will usually ask you to leave your passport overnight.

• Even in a luxury hotel, don't expect the same amenities you would find in luxury hotels in other European countries, such as TV, little packages of soap or refrigerators.

• In Athens, try to avoid taking a room facing the street; they tend to be very noisy.

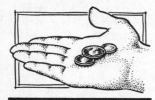

TIPPING

• Restaurants: Even though the tip is usually included in the bill, leave an extra 50 drachmas on the table (not on the plate with the check).

• Taxis: Give 10% only if the trip was long or the driver was very helpful. Generally the driver doesn't expect a tip.

• Porters: Give 10 drachmas per bag.

• Cloakroom attendants: Give 10 to 15 drachmas.

• Ushers in cinemas, theaters and at concerts: Tip 15 to 20 drachmas.

PRIVATE HOMES

• Visiting time usually begins about 5:30 p.m., but telephone ahead to ask if it's convenient for you to come. You'll be offered cold water and preserved fruits (take a spoonful of fruit and then drink some water), *ouzo*, pastries and Turkish coffee.

• If you arrive at 5:30, leave by about 7:30 (earlier if you hear preparations for dinner); otherwise, your hosts will feel obliged to invite you to dinner. If they do invite you, don't stay unless they really insist.

• Don't compliment your host or hostess on a specific object, such as a knicknack or a vase, or he or she will insist on giving it to you.

• If you stay with a family, expect that your hosts will want to be included in your plans for the day. Even if you would prefer to be alone, find a polite way of accommodating their wish to be included. For example, suggest meeting for lunch or in the late afternoon.

• If you spend several days with a family, help with small chores, such as setting the table. Offer to help with the dishes, though your offer probably will be refused.

• If you have been wearing sandals, wash your feet before going to bed.

• As a courtesy, ask before you take a bath. Hot water tanks in Greece are very small, so use only a small amount of water in case someone else wants a bath.

• Don't expect to find a shower curtain. The shower itself is like a telephone receiver and can be held in the hand. Be careful in using this type of shower because the metal hose connecting the shower to the pipes can twist unexpectedly and can send water all over the floor outside the tub.

Gifts: If you're invited to dinner, bring a flower arrangement or a potted plant. (Cut flowers are so inexpensive in Greece that they aren't a suitable gift.) Be sure that the plant or arrangement is wrapped when you present it to your host or hostess. If possible, send them in advance. Other good gifts are wine, brandy or pastries.

If you're staying with a family, bring whiskey, towels, sheets (buy queen-size because beds are usually large) or pocket calculators from the U.S.

If a family has children, they expect visitors to bring gifts to them, even for a casual visit. If you're invited to drinks or dinner, bring the children candy. If you're staying with a family, bring the children toys.

BUSINESS

Hours

Business hours: 8:00 a.m. to 1:30 p.m., and 4:30 to 7:30 p.m., Monday through Friday, and 8:00 a.m. to 1:30 p.m. on Saturdays. Many businesses are also closed on Wednesday afternoon.

Bank hours: 8:00 a.m. to 2:00 p.m., Monday through Saturday.

Store hours: 8:00 a.m. to 1:30 or 2:30 p.m., Monday through Saturday. Many are also open from 5:30 to 8:30

p.m. on Tuesday, Thursday and Friday.

Business Practices

• Avoid business trips during June, July and August and during the week before and after Christmas and Greek Orthodox Easter (see Holidays below).

• Realize that many businesses close on Wednesday afternoons, so you may find it difficult to make appointments then.

• Be sure to make prior appointments with people in business or government, but this is not necessary if your business is with a retailer.

• Be on time because punctuality is expected of foreigners, although it is not necessarily reciprocated.

• Bring business cards printed in English and give one to everyone you meet on business. This is to ensure that your name is spelled correctly.

• Expect your business colleagues to offer you Greek coffee and ice water. Other popular beverages for business discussions are *ouzo* and sometimes whiskey.

• Don't try to impose a deadline on a meeting (i.e., "We have to work this out by 6:00 p.m.") Greeks work out all the details of a business arrangement with those involved, and a meeting lasts as

long as is necessary to do that.

• Don't be surprised if your business contacts pick you up at the airport, even if it's very early in the morning, or take you out to every meal and are generally extremely hospitable. Personal contact is very important to Greeks, and they go out of their way to take care of business guests.

Gifts: Give your business contacts pens, pocket calculators, leather desk items.

HOLIDAYS AND SPECIAL OCCASIONS

Holidays: New Year's Day (January 1), Epiphany (January 6), Independence Day (March 25), Shrove Monday, Good Friday, Easter Monday, Labor Day (May 1), Pentecost, Feast of the Virgin Mary (August 15), National Day (October 28), Christmas (December 25), and December 26.

• Before you go, check to see when Greek Orthodox Easter is, as it changes every year. It is held on the first Sunday after the first full moon after the first day of spring after the Mosaic Passover.

• Don't invite Greeks to dinner or other entertainment on Good Friday. Religious people consider that a day of mourning.

• Visitors are welcome at Easter celebrations. Church services begin at midnight on Saturday, with people lighting one another's candles outside the church. After the church services there are parties. There's a meal of lamb that has been roasted outdoors, followed by dancing and games.

• In Greece, people celebrate their patron saint's day rather than their own birthday. (For example, everyone named George will have visits from friends and relatives on St. George's Day.) If you know someone celebrating a name day, take a small gift to her or his house. You'll then be offered light refreshments

TRANSPORTATION

Public Transportation

• Pay when you get on and make sure you have change. Bus fares depend on the distance traveled.

• Hail a taxi from the street or call one from a hotel. Sometimes when you are riding in a taxi, someone will shout to the driver to stop. If that person is going in the same direction that you are, the driver will allow her or him to get in. If the other person's destination involves a detour, don't pay for that part of the trip. This practice is illegal, but it's frequently done.

Driving

• If you plan to drive in Greece, get an international driver's license before you arrive and carry it with you at all times.

• Be very cautious when driving, as Greek drivers tend to ignore traffic laws, pedestrian signs and traffic lights. They also tend to weave in and out of traffic and pass on the right, as well as the left.

• Wear your seat belt, as this is required by law.

• Note that although vehicles approaching from the right have the legal right of way, in practice right of way depends on who gets to an intersection first.

• Do not use your horn in cities (this is illegal), but use it in the country, especially on mountain roads, as a signal that a car is coming around a curve.

• Be aware that the police can stop you for a traffic violation and demand payment of a fine immediately. They usually speak a few words of English or will find someone who does.

• Always park on the right side of the street.

LEGAL MATTERS AND SAFETY

• To find an English-speaking police officer, look for tourist police departments with headquarters marked in English.

• Women should take a taxi at night unless they know the area they're in well. Verbal harassment from men is common. They should also avoid the *Plaka* area after dark if they're alone.

• Feel free to go to gambling casinos, but be aware that any Greek accompanying you must bring his or her income tax return to prove that he or she can afford to gamble.

• If you have more than $500 in any currency when you leave Greece, you must declare it; however, you don't have to declare travelers' checks. To take any archeological items out of the country, you must get an export license.

KEY PHRASES

English	Greek	Pronunciation
Good morning	Kaliméra	Kah-lee-méh-rah
Good evening (afternoon)	Kalispéra	Kah-lee-spéh-rah
Good night	Kaliníkta	Kah-lee-ník-tah
Please	Parakaló	Pah-rah-kah-lów
Thank you	Efcharistó	Ef-kah-ree-stó
You're welcome	Típota	Tée-po-tah
Yes	Ne	Neh
No	Óchi	Ó-[ch]i (gutteral)
Sir, Mr.	Kírie	Kée-ree-yay
Madam, Mrs.	Kyria	Kée-ree-yah
Miss	Despinís	Theh-speen-ées
Excuse me	Me sinchorite	May seen-[ch]ó-ree-tay ([ch] is gutteral)
Good-bye	Chérete	[Ch]éh-reh-teh ([ch] is gutteral)
I don't understand.	Den katalaveno.	Then kah-tah-lah-véh-noo
I don't speak Greek.	Den meeló eleeneeká.	Then mee-ló ell-een-ee-ká
Does anyone here speak English?	Milá kanis angliká?	mee-láh káh-nees ahngleekáh

CHAPTER TWELVE

HUNGARY

Hungarians have a strong sense of both personal and national pride, a pride that until recently made Hungarian gentlemen scorn any job that could be regarded as money-making. The only three occupations suitable for a gentleman were public affairs, land ownership or the military.

The key to the Hungarian character is the ability to survive and adapt. The country's history has been a long series of invasions: Genghis Khan, the Turks, the Hapsburgs, the Nazis and the Russians. Through it all, they learned to adjust to what they could not change. And, perhaps because they are acutely conscious that one never knows what the future holds, they have developed a reputation for living beyond their means.

GREETINGS

• Shake hands when introduced, when greeting someone and when departing.
• Notice that when two good male friends meet after a long absence, they shake hands and embrace, making cheek-

to-cheek contact: first the left cheek, then the right. Close female friends embrace but don't shake hands.

• Address people by their professional titles followed by "Mr." or "Ms." Don't add their last name (for example, *Epitesz ur,* "Mr. Architect"; *Mernokno,* "Ms. Engineer").

• If someone doesn't have a title, or you don't know it, address that person by his or her last name, followed by "Mr." "Mrs." or "Miss" (there is no equivalent of "Ms." in this case); for example, *Bean ur,* (Mr. Bean); *Beanne* (Mrs. Bean) or *Bean kisasszony* (Miss Bean).

• Wait to be introduced at formal parties. At informal gatherings, introduce yourself.

CONVERSATION

• Use first names only after a Hungarian suggests it.

• Good topics of conversation: food, wine, what you like about Hungary. Since foreign travel is restricted, tell Hungarians what you have seen in other parts of the world. While they will love to hear about your ex-periences, avoid sounding like a "know-it-all."

• Topics to avoid: politics and religion.

• Don't be surprised by sudden, abrupt changes in subject. Hungarians often have an "official" opinion and also a private opinion. A subject change may mean one has said too much or has come too close to voicing an unacceptable political opinion.

• If you compliment Hungarians about anything, expect them to belittle their achievement, rather than simply saying "Thank you."

TELEPHONES

• To call from a public phone, deposit a 2-forint coin. (Wait for the dial tone; it may be slow in coming, or one may not be immediately available.) This will give you a six-minute local call. If you want more time, insert more money before the time is up or you will be cut off.

• When using a phone in a private home, offer to pay for each call (two forint for a local call). If your hostess won't accept payment, give her flowers at a later time.

• Make long-distance calls from the post office or from private phones.

• When answering the phone, say "Hello." Be aware that many Hungarians end phone conversations with close friends or relatives by saying the Hungarian word for "kisses," which sounds like "pussy" in English.

• Be conscious of the fact that phone calls may be monitored.

PUBLIC MANNERS

• A man should always walk to the left of a woman or an honored guest of either sex.

• If you try to buy opera or concert tickets and are told that they are sold out, tip the ticket seller 10 forint, and he or she may discover that more tickets are available. This is common practice, and you won't get into trouble for it.

• Never photograph soldiers or military installations.

DRESS

• Wear shorts only on country outings or at the beach. Jeans are acceptable for casual dress.

• For business, men wear suits, white shirts and ties. Women wear suits or dresses.

• For visits to concerts and theaters, men and women should wear business dress.

• For the opera, wear formal dress—dark suits for men and long dresses for women.

MEALS

Hours and Foods

Breakfast *(reggeli):* 8:00 to 9:00 a.m. The usual meal is bread, butter and jam. Eggs are seldom served; when they are, they are soft-boiled. Espresso is served with hot milk.

Lunch *(ebed):* 1:00 to 2:00 p.m. This is the main meal of the day. There's usually soup, often a thick meat soup or, in the summer, a cold fruit soup, followed by the main course, often a pork stew with paprika or wienerschnitzel and salad. Dessert follows, then espresso.

If people are entertaining, *schnapps* (brandy) or wine will be served before the meal, and wine will be served with it. Dessert will be elaborate, perhaps a *dobos torta* (a 12-layer cake with chocolate filling), or pancakes with a cream cheese filling and a wine sauce. Drinks served after the meal may include Tokay, a sweet dessert wine, or Pear William, a strong pear-flavored brandy.

Supper *(vacsora):* 7:00 to 8:00 p.m. This is a light meal consisting of open-faced sandwiches, or salad and cold cuts, and tea. Dessert is not served with the light evening meal. If it's a dinner party, it will be much like the noon meal described above.

Breaks: At 5:00 p.m. many people meet friends for cake and coffee.

Table Manners

• Observe that the host and hostess sit at opposite ends of the table, with the guest of honor at the hostess's right.

• As each course is served, wait for your hostess to begin before eating.

• If wine is served, the guest should propose a toast before drinking. Say "To your health."

• Before starting to eat, wish everyone a good appetite.

• Taste food before adding salt, pepper or paprika, or you will insult your hostess.

• Start with small portions of various dishes, as the food may be very rich, and you're expected to eat everything on your plate. If you can't finish something, apologize to your hostess.

• Try eating with the fork in your left hand and the knife in your right, as the Hungarians do. Push food onto the back of the fork with your knife.

• When eating fish, use only a fork or the hostess will think the fish is not tender enough.

• Don't ask for ice water, as it is not served in Hungary, and your hosts may not know what you mean.

• When complimenting the hostess on the meal, expect that she will make light of her efforts.

Places to Eat

• Note the variety of eating places:

A *bisztró* or an *étel-bar* is a snack bar.

Borozó serve nothing but alcoholic drinks and are mainly frequented by men.

Cukrászda are pastry/tea shops; specialties are *dobos torta* (many-layered cakes), marzipan balls dipped in chocolate, and glacéed chestnuts.

An *eszpresszó* is a coffee bar.

Étterém are large, elaborate restaurants.

Önkiszogáló éttérem are self-service restaurants.

Taverns serve snacks, which are eaten with draft beer or apricot or plum brandy.

Vendéglö or *maszek* are usually simple, family-run restaurants, following ethnic and country traditions.

• Restaurants are officially divided into four classes. Most hotel restaurants are "above class," which means that they are better than all the ranked restaurants. Of the ranked restaurants, the highest class is I, and the lowest is IV. Look for the classification on the menu, near the entrance to the restaurant.

• Expect prices in restaurants to be higher in the evening, because there is usually live music.

Specialties

• Hungarian food can be very rich and spicy. Try the following Hungarian specialties: *halászle* (a type of fish soup made from carp and potatoes or pasta); *pörkölt* (a paprika-flavored stew of pork served with sour cream and dumplings); *töltött paprika* (green peppers stuffed with ground meat in a tomato sauce); *töltött káposzta* (stuffed cabbage); *fátanyéros* (a mixed grill of veal, pork, beef and sausages, served on a wooden platter and accompanied by red cabbage, pickles and potato salad); *idei sült liba* (roast goose served with cucumber salad); and *rétes* (strudel).

Try also *palacsinta,* crepe-like pancakes used in almost every course. Two varieties are: *pörkölt palacsinta* (crepes filled with chicken, paprika and sour cream), and *palacsinta* (dessert crepes filled with cheese, raisins, jam or chocolate).

HOTELS

• Understand that hotels keep your passport overnight in order to register you with the police. If you're camping out, the manager of the campsite will do likewise.

• If hotels are booked up, ask a travel agent to find accommodations for you in private homes. This may even be preferable to a hotel, since you will have a chance to meet some Hungarian people.

• Consider another less expensive alternative to a hotel, renting a room or apartment through *IBUSZ* (the state travel agency). If you're renting sight-unseen, try to have a Hungarian associate check the accommodations out to be sure that there is hot water, a refrigerator and an elevator. Ask for your own house key, so that you won't have to depend on the superintendent or manager.

• Stick to large hotels and *IBUSZ*-organized tourist activities if you expect language to be a major problem.

• Don't expect air-conditioning in any but luxury-class Hungarian hotels.

• Bring your own soap and face cloths, as they are not always provided.

• In large hotels, ask the desk clerk to help you if you would like to get theater tickets or make restaurant reservations. Most of them speak English.

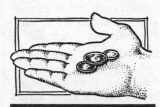

TIPPING

• Restaurants: Give 10% of the restaurant check to the headwaiter, who brings your bill. When an orchestra plays for your table, give the leader 10 to 20 forint.

• Porters: Give the head porter at a hotel 10 to 20 forint when you arrive. Otherwise give 10 forint per bag.

• Taxis: Tip drivers 10% of the fare.

• Cloakroom attendants: Tip 5 forint per person.

• Washroom attendants: Keep 2 to 5 forint handy for tips.

PRIVATE HOMES

• Families often live in apartments with very limited living space, so don't be offended if you're not invited to stay in the home of someone you know. When planning to visit friends or relatives, make arrangements to stay at a hotel if at all possible.

• Don't be surprised if friends or relatives don't invite you for dinner. Their home may be too small even to invite you for a meal. They may prefer to entertain you outside the home.

• If you are invited to stay with someone, don't try to help in the kitchen. Hungarians want guests to relax, not to work.

• Adapt yourself to the water supply available. Apartments have hot water only if there is central heating or an individual gas boiler in the flat. Feel free to take a daily bath or shower if there's hot water; otherwise, you'll have to settle for a cold shower.

• Don't expect to find American-style washers and dryers, as they don't exist in Hungary. People wash clothes in the bathtub and hang them outdoors to dry.

Gifts: As a dinner guest, bring Western liquor or wrapped flowers (other than chrysanthemums).

Provide a real treat for friends or relatives by taking them to a restaurant in one of the large hotels, such as the Hilton or Penta in Budapest. Realize, however, that the food and drink will be expensive.

If you're going to stay with

a family, consider bringing gifts from the U.S., such as cigarettes, liquor, perfume, clothing, dress fabric, permanent press sheets and tablecloths.

BUSINESS

Hours

Business hours: 8:30 a.m. to 5:00 p.m., Monday through Friday, and 8:30 a.m. to 1:30 p.m. on Saturday.

Government office hours: 8:00 a.m. to 4:00 p.m., Monday through Friday, and 8:00 a.m. to noon on alternate Saturdays.

Bank hours: 8:30 a.m. to 3:00 p.m., Monday through Friday.

Shop hours: 10:00 a.m. to 6:00 p.m., Monday through Friday, and 10:00 a.m. to 3:00 p.m. on Saturday. Some department stores are open longer on weekdays.

Business Practices

• Write business letters in English, unless you are fluent in Hungarian. Businesses expect to translate letters.

• Consider hiring an interpreter if you do not speak Hungarian or German well enough to conduct business. (German is widely spoken by educated Hungarians.)

If you're staying in one of the large international hotels, ask for an interpreter or contact *IBUSZ* or another major tourist agency.

If you are dealing with a business or factory in an outlying area, you will almost certainly need an interpreter.

• If you anticipate needing secretarial help during your business visit, stay at one of the large, international hotels; they will probably be able to help you find clerical assistance.

• Don't make business appointments in July and August or from mid-December to mid-January.

• Never make appointments on Saturdays, even if a business is open. No meetings are held on Saturdays.

• Take many business cards with you to give to everyone you meet.

• Since businesses are owned and run by the government, expect all business dealings to be conducted under government controls. If you need help with business protocol, contact the State Department in the U.S., or the Commercial Section of the U.S. Embassy in Hungary.

• If your business dealings are successful, consider hosting a cocktail party for your Hungarian colleagues. Greet all guests at the door and be prepared to give a short speech (in English).

• Suggest lunch if you want to have a meal with business associates.

• When you've developed a personal relationship with a business colleague, entertain at a dinner and include spouses.

Gifts: When you visit a large company to do business, have a package of cigarettes or a ballpoint pen for everyone or give nothing at all.

HOLIDAYS AND SPECIAL OCCASIONS

Holidays: New Year's Day (January 1), Liberation Day (April 4), Easter Monday, Labor Day (May 1), Constitution Day (August 20), Great October Socialist Revolution Day (November 7), Christmas (December 25), and December 26.

• On Easter Monday, Hungarian girls and boys participate in a celebration based on an old fertility ritual. Men and boys go from house to house visiting unmarried women and spraying them with perfume. The men then give the women a hand-painted egg and the women offer the men *schnapps.* In the countryside, they sometimes follow an older tradition; the women put on five or six dresses (they layer them) and go outside, where the men dump buckets of water on them.

• On May 1 there will be a military parade. Don't take any photographs. Expect restaurants to be crowded.

TRANSPORTATION

Public Transportation

• Be warned that the English pronunciation of "bus" means fornication in Hungarian! Pronounce the word "boos" or "ow-to-boos."

• Buy bus, streetcar and trolley tickets at kiosks or tobacco shops, called *traffik.* You pay one fare, no matter how far you travel.

• When boarding public transportation, put the ticket into a red machine to have it cancelled. If you travel with an uncancelled ticket, you can be fined.

• In the subway in Budapest, put a one-forint coin in the machine in the station and walk through. You won't get a ticket.

• Because some taxis don't have meters, be sure to have an agreement with the driver about the fare before you get in the cab.

• Buckle your seat belt as soon as you get in a taxi. The driver won't move until you have it fastened.

• Order a taxi by phone: go to a taxi stand located outside hotels, railway stations, theaters and at major intersections. Or try hailing a taxi on the street.

Driving

• Occupants of the front seat of a car must wear seat belts.

• Consider carefully whether you really need or want to drive in Hungary, as the penalties for an accident could be severe.

• Don't have even one drink if you're going to drive. There are constant spot checks by the police. If you've been drinking and are involved in an accident, you can be imprisoned for years. The minimum punishment for drunken driving is a very large fine.

• If you're involved in a minor accident that didn't involve drinking, you must immediately pay any fine the police may levy.

• If you're in an accident involving major damage, you should expect the police to confiscate your passport and forbid you to leave the country until matters are settled.

• If you're in an automobile accident where someone was injured, you'll have to attend a hearing. If you are convicted, there will be a fine or jail sentence.

• Realize that traffic police speak only Hungarian and so may not be able to help you if you need to get directions.

LEGAL MATTERS AND SAFETY

• Remember that you need a visa to enter Hungary. If you arrive by car or plane, you can get your visa on arrival. Bring three photographs with you. If you travel by train, bus or hydrofoil, you can't get a visa at the border. Get one in advance from a Hungarian consulate or embassy.

• Declare all money in any currency upon arrival. Don't try to bring in or take out more than nine dollars in Hungarian currency.

• Change money only at the border hotels, banks or travel agencies.

• Keep receipts each time you change money. You will probably be asked to show them when you leave the country.

• Never bring printed matter against the socialist system into the country. Don't bring a hunting weapon unless you have permission to do so (obtainable at Hungarian embassies or consulates).

• Be assured that Westerners have little difficulty leaving the country. Customs officers may check for Hungarian currency or works of art, neither of which may be taken out of the country.

• Be conscious of the "No Entry" signs posted near military and border areas and don't go too close.

• Never deal with anyone on the street offering to change money at an exceptionally favorable rate. You could lose your money or end up in jail.

• If approached by someone offering to buy an electronic gadget you have, don't agree. This is black market activity and not worth the risk of getting caught.

• To buy Western products, go to one of the "dollar stores," called *Intertourist,* found in shopping areas and in international hotels. Prices are comparable to those at duty-free shops. Show your passport and pay in Western currency.

• Note that there is no legal drinking age or hours—if you find a bar open, you can drink 24 hours a day.

• You can feel safe walking on the streets, even if you're traveling alone. Street crime is very rare, and travelers of both sexes are quite safe.

KEY PHRASES

English	Hungarian	Pronunciation
Good morning	Jó reggelt	Yoh rég-gelt
Good evening	Jó estét	Yoh ésh-teht
Good night	Jó ejszakát	Yoh eý-so-kaht
Please	Kérem	Kéh-rem
Thank you	Köszönöm	Kúr-sur-nurm
You're welcome	Nincs mit	Ninch mit
Yes	Igen	Í-gen
No	Nem	Nem
Sir, Mr.	last name ur	
Madam, Mrs.	last name ne	
Miss	kisasszony after name	Kiss-osson
Excuse me	Bocsánat	Bóh-chah-not
Good-bye	Viszontlátásra	Víss-ohnt-lah-tahsh-ro
I don't understand.	Nem értem.	Nem éhr-tem
I don't speak Hungarian.	Nem tudok magyarul.	Nem tóo-dok mó-jo-rool
Does anyone here speak English?	Beszel itt valaki angolul?	Béss-ehl eet váh-lah-kee óng-goh-lul

Yes, most of the clichés about Ireland are true. It is green with a capital "G," the people love to talk, and many of them love—almost as much—to have a drink.

The Irish will make you feel completely at home within minutes—within seconds if your ancestors were from Ireland. You can be completely yourself, and the Irish will enjoy—or at least cheerfully tolerate—your crotchets and eccentricities.

Don't worry about offending anyone in Ireland by using the wrong fork or forgetting to shake hands. The Irish have survived blows more severe than a lapse in protocol. In fact, the ways to offend the Irish are few: unkindness, defending the British behavior in Ireland over the centuries, and probably the worst lapse of taste—not buying your round in the pub.

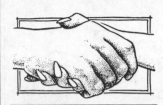

GREETINGS

• Shake hands when you're introduced, every time you meet and leave people you don't know well, and when you meet a good friend you haven't seen for a long time.

• Wait for a woman to extend her hand before you do.

• At a large party, introduce yourself. At a small party, allow your host or hostess to introduce you.

• Remember that the only occupational titles commonly used in addressing people are Dr. and Professor.

CONVERSATION

• Although it's common to use first names after a short acquaintance, use last names at first meetings and whenever the Irish address you in those terms.

• Enjoy the legendary Irish eloquence by engaging the people you meet in conversation.

• Good topics of conversation: the beauty of the Irish countryside, Gaelic culture, Irish handicrafts, sports, such as soccer and horse racing, and the weather (in Ireland you'll never run out of comments on the weather).

• Topics to avoid: Northern Ireland, Ireland's relationship with the United Kingdom, religion, feminism, and the contrasts between Ireland and America.

TELEPHONES

• To make a call from public phone booths, which are readily available in towns, lift the receiver and deposit 5 pence. Dial, and press button "A" to speak when someone answers. If there's no answer, press button "B" for a refund. In rural areas, lift the receiver and wait for the operator. Have change available because you'll have to keep putting more in to continue the call.

PUBLIC MANNERS

• Realize that the Irish are not very demonstrative and are not comfortable with people who are.

• When shopping, don't hand over the money to pay for your purchase until the clerk has wrapped your merchandise. If you start to hand the money over before this, the clerk may feel rushed.

• Be sure to take your proper place in "queues" (lines) for buses, theaters and in shops. Never push ahead.

• Don't expect to find bath houses at the beach. However, it's perfectly acceptable to change on the beach, while holding a towel around you.

DRESS

• Be sure to bring a raincoat, as this is a necessity year-round.

• If you want to fit in, wear tailored clothes for casual wear, especially tweeds and wools in dark colors.

• It's rarely warm enough in Ireland to wear shorts but when it is, wear them only at the beach—never in town.

• For business, men should wear suits and ties or tweedy sport jackets. Women may wear suits or wool blazers and wool skirts. Choose subdued colors.

• Unless it's a business meal, dress for a dinner party will be fairly casual. Men don't need to wear jackets and ties.

• Formal evening wear on an invitation means tuxedos for men and short cocktail dresses for women.

MEALS

Hours and Foods

Breakfast: 8:00 to 10:00 a.m. Expect a major meal. First course is juice (usually canned) and/or cereal. The second course is the "fry-up": eggs, grilled sausage, bacon, tomatoes, "black pudding" (blood pudding) cut up into small pieces and grilled, and brown bread and butter.

Eat the hot toast served with butter and marmalade afterwards because it's in bad taste to have marmalade with the "fry-up." For beverage choose tea or coffee.

Lunch: 1:00 to 2:00 p.m. Midday meals may be hot dishes, such as steak and kidney pudding, or boiled bacon and cabbage (the bacon is like roast pork which has been cured and boiled), or a cold meal, such as ham or cheese salad (ham or cheese slices with lettuce and tomato). Salads come with one type of dressing— "salad cream," a thinner, tarter version of mayonnaise.

Dinner: 5:00 to 8:00 p.m. The kind of dinner depends on how heavy the midday meal was. A light dinner (sometimes called "tea") may consist of cold cuts and salads or a "fry-up" (see breakfast).

A heavier dinner, which is served at a dinner party, might start with drinks. Vermouth, sherry, wine, whiskey and brandy are commonly offered. The meal begins with a fish course or soup, followed by meat, usually a roast with two kinds of potatoes, such as mashed and roasted, and vegetables. Then comes cheese and crackers, dessert and coffee or tea and port or spirits. Wine is often served with the meal.

Table Manners

• Bear in mind that refusing a drink is a major insult. If you really don't care to drink, explain that you don't drink for health reasons.

• If you are offered a drink, raise the glass before you take a sip and say "Cheers."

• When you eat in a private home, your plate may be brought to you with food already on it. Even though you have no choice in portion size or type of food, try to eat everything on your plate.

• Note that the small plate next to your dinner plate is not for bread but for the peelings removed from boiled potatoes. You're not supposed to eat the peelings. Bread is not usually served with dinner.

Places to Eat

• Try hotel restaurants in rural areas for a complete menu and good quality food.

• Go to a pub for a reasonably-priced lunch. Pub hours are 10:00 a.m. to 11:30 p.m., Monday through Saturday and 12:30 to 2:00 p.m. and 4:00 to 10:00 pm. on Sundays. Some pubs in major cities are closed between 2:00 and 3:30 p.m.

• Be prepared to receive huge portions in restaurants, even in gourmet restaurants.

• Note that pubs have two

sections: the bar and the lounge. Women traditionally frequent the lounge, though drinks are more expensive there.

• Don't expect drinks to be served with ice. You'll get ice if you ask for it, but only one or two cubes.

• If you want to try the Irish "national" drink, order Guinness stout, which is served cool. If you've sampled Guinness in the U.S. and haven't liked it, give it another try in Ireland. Many Irish won't drink the Guinness served in the U.S. Order lager served cold, and you will get the equivalent of American beer. Normally, Irish beer is served at room temperature.

• Be aware that women are expected to order half-pints (10 ounces) of beer or stout. Some pubs won't serve pints to women. On the other hand, a man who orders a half-pint will have his virility questioned.

• Try these other pub drinks: whiskey (Irish whiskey) and scotch (Scotch whisky), both usually drunk neat, shandy (beer and lemonade), gin and tonic.

• If you're with a group, buy a round of drinks. Women are not allowed to buy, however.

Specialties

• Foods to try in Ireland are "colcannon" (a mix of potato and cabbage); fish and chips; Galway oysters; grouse; "mixed coddle" (boiled bacon and sausages); pheasant; smoked salmon and fresh salmon; steak and kidney pie; and trout.

• If you're not interested in exotic foods, avoid "black pudding" (blood pudding), which is often served at breakfast, and "rognons" (kidneys).

HOTELS

• If you want fairly cheap accommodations, stay at a Bed and Breakfast (or "B & B"). These are usually rooms in someone's house. A large breakfast is included in the price of the accommodation and some B & Bs offer an optional "high tea" around 6:00 p.m. This may consist of a dish such as chicken and chips followed by cakes and tea.

In a B & B, ask when it is convenient to take a bath. Since you might be sharing a bathroom with the family, try to avoid using it when people are rushing to get off to work. You usually pay extra for baths.

• Note that "Guest Houses" in Ireland are more like hotels than Bed and Breakfasts, but the people are usually very friendly and will want to socialize with you. Most Guest Houses serve an optional dinner at 8:00 p.m.

• At a small hotel, if you have the chance, buy the manager a drink and have a chat. Don't be pushy about it, but take advantage of an opportunity if it arises. Managers can be very helpful in making your stay a pleasant one.

• Inquire at your hotel to see if they provide a "baby-listening" service through a connection between the main desk and your room. You won't need a babysitter if you go to the hotel restaurant; someone will come for you if your baby begins to cry.

• Anticipate that, in some hotels, hot water is shut off during the day and is not available until evening.

• Expect hotel rooms to be cooler than American rooms and plan your clothing accordingly.

TIPPING

• Restaurants: A 10-15% service charge is usually added to the check, and no extra tip is expected. In some restaurants children work as waiters and waitresses. You may want to give them some extra change as you leave.

• Never tip in pubs or in theaters.

• Taxis: Tip 10 pence for a short to moderate distance, 20 pence for a long ride.

• Porters: Tip 10 to 20 pence per bag.

• Cloakroom attendants: Tip 20 pence.

PRIVATE HOMES

• Assume that children will be involved in family functions.

• Don't be surprised to meet members of the clergy at family functions. They are accorded great respect by the Irish and should be deferred to.

• If you are a Catholic and staying with a family, plan to attend Sunday Mass with them.

• Dress modestly when staying in a private home. Always dress for breakfast and never walk around the house in a nightgown or pajamas.

• The Irish will not be surprised if you wish to bathe daily, but be sure to ask your hostess if it's convenient for you to have a bath. Note that many homes in Ireland do not have showers.

• Wash cloths are rarely used. If you aren't given one, don't ask for one.

• If you make phone calls, insist on paying for every one. Place calls through the operator, so that you will know the cost. Rates for tele-phones are very high, so the Irish don't use them for long chats.

Gifts: Good gifts if you're invited to dinner are a bottle of wine, flowers (especially if you know that your host will have chosen the wine for the meal), a box of chocolates or a selection of continental cheeses.

If you're a house guest, select a token gift, such as linen towels. Giving gifts, especially expensive gifts, isn't nearly so common in Ireland as in America. Avoid giving expensive or ostentatious gifts.

If someone gives you a gift, open it immediately.

BUSINESS

Hours

Business and government office hours: 9:30 a.m. to 5:30 p.m., Monday through Friday.

Bank hours: 10:00 a.m. to 12:30 p.m., and 1:30 to 3:00 p.m., Monday through Friday, and until 5:00 p.m. on Thursday.

Shop hours: 9:00 a.m. to 5:30 p.m., Monday through

Saturday.

Business Practices

• Although Gaelic is the official language of Ireland, don't make special arrangements for translations. It's spoken only in a section of western Ireland and is never used in business discussions.

• Avoid business trips to Ireland during the first week in May (when most business people are busy with trade fairs), during July and August, and the Christmas and New Year period.

• Make business appointments in advance, either by letter or telephone.

• Keep in mind that the Irish are not very time conscious and may not be punctual for an appointment. Someone who offers to meet you in five minutes will more likely turn up in half an hour.

• Business cards aren't commonly used, but bring them along so that you can leave them with a secretary if the person you want to see is unavailable.

• There are no general rules about including spouses in business dinners. If you intend to include the spouse of an Irish businessperson in a dinner party, mention this specifically.

Gifts: Giving gifts is not commonly a part of business dealings.

HOLIDAYS AND SPECIAL OCCASIONS

Holidays: New Year's Day (January 1), St. Patrick's Day (March 17), Good Friday, Easter Monday, June Bank Holiday (first Monday in June), August Bank Holiday (first Monday in August), Halloween, Christmas (December 25), St. Stephen's Day (December 26).

• On St. Patrick's Day, the Irish go to church sporting a sprig of shamrock in their lapels. There are parades in Dublin, but all in all, the celebrations are more low-key than those in the U.S.

TRANSPORTATION

Public Transportation

• Be aware that bus fare is based on the distance traveled. A conductor will come to your seat and collect the fare.

• Realize that the upper deck on "double decker" buses is for smokers.

• Look for taxis at taxi stands and on the streets, or telephone for one. Minimum charge is 50 pence.

• If you want to travel around the countryside, you'll find that bus routes cover most parts of Ireland.

Driving

• Wear a seat belt if you are the driver or front seat passenger in a car. Penalties are severe if you are caught not wearing it.

• Don't drive after drinking even two pints of beer. Failing a breathalyzer test can bring fines up to 500 pounds or six months in jail.

• If possible, avoid driving in cities during rush hours, 8:00 to 9:30 a.m., and 5:00 to 6:30 p.m.

• Remember that the Irish drive on the left side of the road.

• Note that all road signs are in English and Gaelic.

• Irish drivers tend to ignore the lines separating lanes, and in the country they often drive down the center of the road.

• In the country, be prepared to stop suddenly for farm animals.

LEGAL MATTERS AND SAFETY

• Don't bring any pornographic materials or books on the government's censorship list (most fiction will be allowed) into Ireland.

• Don't take more currency out of Ireland than you brought in.

• "The Irish guards" is the common name for the Irish police. They may stop you for an identity check, as they are very conscious of the problems in Northern Ireland.

• Hitchhiking is very common in Ireland and is safe, even for women. Never use the phrase "get a ride"; it's obscene. A driver will offer you "a seat" or "a lift."

• Don't be afraid to travel alone in Ireland. There are rough sections in the large cities, but you can find out about them at your hotel. If you want to meet people, go to the lounge section of a pub.

• Note that the drinking age is 18.

• If you get sick, remember

that every small town has a district nurse and doctors on call and that medical service is excellent and relatively inexpensive.

KEY PHRASES

American	Irish
country lane	boreen
insulted	cut
fried bread	dip
slow	dither
excellent	fairly
a meal	a feed
impertinence	guff
a couple of drinks	jar
raining gently	mizzlin
a loud-voiced person	thundergub
child	wain

CHAPTER FOURTEEN

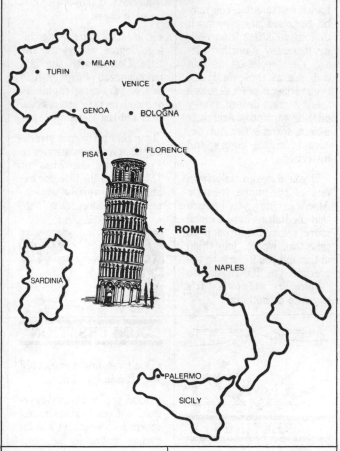

Visiting Italy is often a trip from legend to legend: the Forum in Rome, the Uffizi in Florence, the Piazza San Marco in Venice. Between legends, of course, there should be many stops for a nourishing bowl of pasta, a mellowing glass of wine, or a reviving cup of espresso.

The American image of Italy is composed partly of TV

commercials in which large maternal figures urge their children to eat ever more pasta, and partly of gaudy Italian restaurants. You may be surprised at how much that image differs from reality, especially in northern Italy. The people are as thin and chic as those in Paris; even residents of small towns spend a great deal of money on their wardrobes. And their houses feature tasteful decors in subtle colors and materials.

If you arrive in Italy from one of the more frenetic American cities, you'll notice that the Italians have a much more relaxed approach to time than we do. Join them in this and you'll come to appreciate the Italian phrase *"Dolce far niente"*—"It's sweet to do nothing."

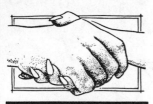

GREETINGS

• Shake hands when saying "Hello" and "Good-bye," no matter how brief the encounter.

• If there are no formal introductions, especially at parties, introduce yourself by stating your name and shaking hands.

• Expect a great deal of physical contact in greetings. Give someone you know well a kiss on each cheek.

• In greeting a man with a college degree, always use the title *Dottor* with the last name instead of *Signor*. Also address lawyers, engineers and architects by professional title and last name.

• In greeting a woman professional, or a woman married to a professional, use "Miss" or "Mrs." with the title, for example, *Signorina Avocatessa* (Miss Lawyer).

CONVERSATION

• Don't use first names until your Italian friend does.

• Good topics of conversation: food, restaurants, sports such as soccer and bicycling, and family life.

• Topics to avoid: American football (Italians don't understand it, nor are they interested in it), and Italian politics (unless an Italian brings it up).

• Never say anything negative about regional or national sports teams.

• Don't ask people whom you've just met what they do for a living.

TELEPHONES

• Buy *gettoni* (tokens) in a cafe or a tobacconist's shop for use in public telephones. (You can also use regular currency in some public phones now—check the phone first.) Usually one *gettone* gives you three to five minutes for a local call, though in some places, time for a local call is unlimited.

When you don't have unlimited time, the call is cut off automatically when your time is up. (Adding more *gettoni* won't help.) Call again or have the other person call you back at the pay phone.

• When you answer the phone, say *"Pronto."*

PUBLIC MANNERS

• Always stand when an older person enters the room. Italians are very respectful to elders.

• Participate in the ritual of the *Passeggiata*. Every evening, between 6:00 and 8:00 p.m., people dress up in good clothes and stroll through town. It's a good time to arrange to meet someone for coffee or an aperitif in a cafe.

Don't be shocked to see women walking arm-in-arm with other women and men walking with men in the same way. When you meet someone you know, stop, shake hands, chat a little and shake hands in parting. (Someone who knows many people may take two hours to go from one end of the street to the other.)

• Try bargaining in every store and market. Ask "May I have a discount?" Shopkeepers will say no if they don't want to bargain, but they won't be insulted.

• If you wish to photograph people, ask them first. They will usually be pleased.

• Don't photograph military installations, factories or in museums where signs are posted forbidding photography. Look around for signs showing a camera with an "x" across it.

DRESS

• Don't wear shorts in cities.

• For casual dress, men can wear pants and casual shirts, and women can wear pants or skirts. Jeans are fine if they're not worn or dirty. You'll notice that even casual wear in Italy is very elegant. You may feel uncomfortable if your clothes are in the least bit scruffy.

• Men and women should always wear suits for business meetings. Men should also wear ties.

• For the theater or opera, men should wear dark suits and ties, and women should wear dresses and heels. When it's an opening performance, dress formally in tuxedos and long dresses. (The formal event of the year is the opening of the La Scala Opera season in Milan in December.)

• Remember that women traditionally cover their heads and arms when visiting churches. Shorts are not allowed in churches.

MEALS

Hours and Foods

Breakfast *(la prima colazione):* 8:00 a.m. In the morning, eat a light meal of bread and butter and *cappuccino* (half strong coffee and half hot, foamy milk) or *cioccolato caldo* (hot chocolate).

Lunch *(la colazione):* 1:00 p.m. This is the main meal of the day. The meal usually begins with a pasta dish. The main course is meat (often veal), with potatoes or vegetables. Bread is served throughout the meal and salad follows. Wine and water usually accompany the meal.

The meal ends with cheese and fruit, followed by espresso (strong, black coffee served in small cups), which is drunk rapidly—not lingered over.

On Sundays or when there's company, aperitifs such as vermouth, Campari or Cynar (made from artichokes) are served before the meal. An *antipasto* (appetizer), such as *prosciutto* (thin slices of salty ham) and melon, or chopped liver on bread triangles, is also served before the pasta dish. Cheese follows the main course. Pastries, then fruit (to cleanse the palate after a sweet) end the meal. Espresso and a digestive (a bitter, after-dinner liqueur, such as Fernet Branca) follow.

Dinner *(la cena):* 8:00 p.m. Expect a light meal of soup, cold cuts, salad and fruit. If it's a dinner party, it will have the same courses described in the company meal above.

Table Manners

• Expect the host and hostess to sit opposite one another at the middle of the table, with the most important male guest to the left of the hostess, and the second most important male guest to her right. Female guests are seated next to the host in the same way.

• Allow the host or another man to pour the wine. Keep in mind that Italians would think it unladylike for a woman to pour wine.

• If you don't want your host to keep refilling your wine glass, simply keep your glass almost full by taking tiny sips.

• However much you enjoy Italian wines, don't get drunk. The Italians will think you extremely offensive. They view wine almost as a food, not as a vehicle for escape or relaxation.

• Wait to see if you should pass food around the table on serving platters, or if the hostess will serve everyone, beginning with the most important female guest.

• Don't begin eating until the hostess does.

• Before the meal, people often wish everyone a good appetite and an enjoyable meal.

• Don't be surprised if you find three plates at your place: the large one on the bottom is for the main course; the deep dish on top of that is for pasta; and the small plate on top of the others is for the antipasto.

• Expect forks to be to the left of the plate, and knives and soup spoon to be to the right. Be aware that the knife and fork above the plate are to be used for fruit. (Don't eat any fruit except grapes and cherries with your hands.) Above the fruit knife and fork is the coffee or ice cream spoon.

• If you'd like to fit in, eat with the fork in your left hand and the knife in your right, using the knife to push food onto the fork.

• Don't cut spaghetti or other types of pasta and don't twirl it around your fork with the aid of a spoon. Take two or three strands at a time and twirl them around your fork using the deep sides of the pasta plate, as you would a spoon.

• Use your knife (not your fingers) to pick up a piece of cheese and put it on bread or a cracker.

• Don't expect to find a plate for bread. Italians place a few slices of bread or a roll on the table at each place setting.

• At a family meal in a home, feel free to sop up gravy with bread if you see others doing it, but don't do it in a restaurant or at a dinner party.

• To be polite, decline seconds when they are first offered. Your hostess will insist, at which time it is just as polite to accept. If you want to refuse graciously when your hostess insists, tell her you really can't eat any more.

In the unlikely event that no one offers you seconds and you would like more, ask politely. The hostess will feel very complimented.

• When you finish, put the knife and fork parallel on the plate, with the fork tines facing down.

• Don't smoke between courses. It's considered impolite because it spoils the taste of the food that has been prepared for you.

Places to Eat

• Try eating in a variety of places.

A *bar* is a cafe where families go. You can get pastries, croissants, doughnuts, coffee, soft drinks, aperitifs or wine. If you are looking for an American-style bar, try large hotels.

An *espresso bar* serves small cups of very strong coffee. As the name suggests, espresso is not sipped but gulped. Stand at the bar, drink your coffee quickly and leave.

A *gelateria* is an ice cream parlour.

A *pizzeria* is a pizza parlour.

A *ristorante* is a more elegant and expensive restaurant.

A *rosticceria* offers prepared food to take out. They have chicken, duck, quail, pigeon and other small birds, which are coated with olive oil and fresh herbs and cooked on a spit over an open fire, and a variety of salads. Put together an excellent and inexpensive picnic to enjoy in a parkmor in your hotel room.

A *tavola calda* (literally "farm table") is a lunch bar, where you eat standing, sitting on stools at a counter or at a table.

A *trattoria* is a medium-priced restaurant that serves simple meals.

• Note that wine is the most popular drink. Try these widely available wines: Chianti, Barolo, Barbera (reds) and Verdicchio, Soave and Frascati (whites). The most popular brandy is *grappa*, made from grape skins.

• To attract the waiter or waitress's attention in a restaurant, raise your hand slightly and say *"Camariere,"* or *"Signorina."*

• If you suggest to someone that you have a meal together, pay the whole bill. If someone invites you, he or she will pay. Try to return the lunch or dinner invitation within the next few days, if possible.

If you invite people to dinner (or to a nightclub or movie), don't feel you must invite couples or must "fix up" a single man or woman. Italian women feel very comfortable attending group functions alone. If you should be invited to dinner, don't feel that you need a date.

• If you are a single woman, don't be afraid to eat alone in northern Italy. Avoid looking around a great deal, or you will find men staring and smiling at you. However, they will seldom come to your table to bother you.

By contrast, men will invariably come to your table and try to pick you up in southern Italy. If they persist, try moving to another table or enlisting the waiter's help. A last resort is to finish your meal quickly and leave.

• Ask for the check in a restaurant; it will not be brought to you until you do.

• If you see the words *"pane e coperto"* on the menu, anticipate a bread and cover charge.

• Keep the receipt from the check with you as you leave the restaurant. It's possible, though unlikely, that you might be stopped outside by the tax police, who will ask to see your receipt. Don't panic. They are not checking on you but on the restaurant's tax compliance.

Specialties

• Plan to experience different styles of cooking and different specialties in various regions of Italy.

• In Bologna, try *mortadella* (similar to bologna with peppercorns); *prosciutto* (dried, salted ham, served in paper-thin slices); and *tortellini* (small doughnut-shaped pastas filled with meat). Note the many pork dishes.

• In Florence and Tuscany, sample *bistecca alla Fiorentina* (steak from Chianiana cattle, charcoal-broiled with olive oil, salt and pepper); and *fagioli all'ucceletto* (white beans with garlic, olive oil, sage and tomato paste).

• In Genoa, order *gnocchi* (potato-flour dumpling) and *pesto* (a sauce made from crushed basil leaves, garlic, olive oil, Parmesan cheese and pine nuts, served with pasta).

• In Milan and Lombardy, look for *osso buco* (veal shank in tomato sauce with onions, wine and stock), and *polenta* (corn meal of a consistency like porridge).

• In Naples, taste *mozzarella in carrozza* (deep-fried cheese sandwich) and pizza

• In Rome, sample *abbacchio al forno* (roast suckling lamb), and *cannelloni* (tube-shaped pasta filled with meat or ricotta cheese and covered with a tomato sauce).

• In Sicily, try *caponata* (eggplant, tomatoes, green pepper and olives, cooked in olive oil) and *cassata alla Siciliana* (layers of sponge cake alternating with cream, ricotta cheese, candied fruit, chocolate and liqueur).

• In Venice and the Veneto, taste *fegato alla Veneziana* (thin slices of calves' liver sauteed with onions) and *risi e bisi* (rice and peas).

HOTELS

• When you check in, leave your passport at the desk for a few hours so that the clerk can fill out forms for the police.

• Be aware that the water taps read "C" for hot and "F" for cold.

• Leave your key at the desk when you go out. The management will be very upset if you don't.

• Women traveling alone should stay in first class hotels. If you go to the bar in a hotel, anticipate that someone will try to pick you up. If you simply want a drink, and a man approaches you, don't respond to him.

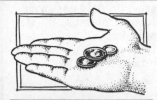

TIPPING

• Restaurants: Although a 10% service charge is included in restaurant checks, leave 10% more if the service was very good. Don't leave a tip when you have a drink or a cup of coffee standing at a bar.

• Taxis: Give an extra 10% to taxi drivers but keep in mind that a tip is included in the fare.

• Washroom attendants: Tip 100 lire.

• Church attendants who show you around: Tip 500 to 1,000 lire.

• Museum guides: Give 300 lire.

• Movie ushers: Tip 300 lire.

• Cloakroom attendants: Give 200 to 300 lire.

PRIVATE HOMES

• Remember that children usually eat with the family,

even when there are guests. Pay attention to them and include them in your conversation.

• If you spend several days with a family, expect to be given a napkin ring with a cloth napkin. At the end of each meal, fold the napkin and replace it in the ring. You'll be given the same napkin at each meal. (Ring designs are different, so your hostess can identify the individual napkins.) Napkins are usually changed every five days.

• Keep in mind that electricity is very expensive. Turn off lights when you leave a room.

• Always ask your host or hostess before you take a bath and use as little water as you can.

Gifts: When invited to a meal, bring individual pastries, a box of chocolates, flowers or wine. If you bring flowers, be sure to buy an odd number. Don't bring chrysanthemums; they're associated with funerals. Bring two or three bottles of wine, rather than just one. If you don't have time to buy a gift beforehand, send one the next day.

When staying with a family for several days, bring a dinner gift with you and send another gift after you leave. Good choices are whiskey and cognac; California wines; cigars; or something typical of your region in the U.S., such as crafts or quilts.

Never give a brooch, a handkerchief or a set of knives; they are all associated with sadness.

BUSINESS

Hours

Business hours: In northern Italy, hours are 8:30 a.m. to 12:45 p.m. and 3:00 to 5:30 p.m., Monday through Friday, and 8:30 a.m. to 12:45 p.m. on Saturday.

In central and southern Italy, business hours are 8:30 a.m. to 12:45 p.m. and 4:30 or 5:00 to 8:00 p.m., Monday through Friday, and 8:30 a.m. to 12:45 p.m. on Saturday.

Government office hours: 8:30 a.m. to 1:45 p.m., Monday through Friday. Senior staff members sometimes return to the office from 5:30 to 8:00 p.m.

Bank hours: 8:30 a.m. to 1:30 p.m., Monday through Friday.

Shop hours: About the same as business hours, though shops usually stay open until 7:30 or 8:00 p.m. In some towns, shops are closed one weekday.

Business Practices

• Don't try to make business appointments in August, as most firms are closed for vacation.

• Make business appointments between 10:00 and 11:00 a.m. and after 3:00 p.m.

• Correspond in Italian if you want immediate attention to your letter.

If you can't have your letter translated into Italian, send it in English, and the recipient will have it translated. If you write to large firms in English, you can expect them to respond in English.

• If you need an interpreter, hire one through your hotel or a travel agency.

• Bring business cards, although Italians don't use them very much.

• To make a good impression, be punctual. Italian business people are on time for meetings and will expect you to be.

• Don't discuss business immediately. Italians enjoy small talk first. Expect to answer questions about your family.

• To discuss business plans,

arrange to meet for lunch. If you have several dealings with the same person, invite the person to dinner and possibly a nightclub. This should be a strictly social occasion, and you should include spouses.

Gifts: Give a small gift to any staff members who were helpful to you. If the gift is for a woman, give flowers. If it's for a man, give a pen, silver key chain or an executive-style diary.

HOLIDAYS AND SPECIAL OCCASIONS

Holidays: New Year's Day (January 1), Easter Monday, Liberation Day (April 25), Labor Day (May 1), Assumption of the Virgin (August 15), All Saints' Day (November 1), Immaculate Conception (December 8), Christmas (December 25) and St. Stephen's Day (December 26).

• Expect people to celebrate the arrival of spring on *Pasquetta* (the Monday after Easter) with the first picnic of the year.

• Be aware that *Ferragosto* (August 15) is also celebrated with picnics in the countryside or at seaside resorts. *Ferragosto* originated as a pagan fair in the days of the Emperor Augustus, probably as a thanksgiving for the harvest.

TRANSPORTATION

Public Transportation

• You pay one fixed rate on city buses, no matter how far you travel. (This flat rate may vary from city to city, however.) Buy tickets at the newsstand or tobacconist closest to the bus stop. When you board the bus, put your ticket into the validation machine. Be sure to keep your ticket. Inspectors sometimes check for tickets, and there are fines if you don't have one.

• Use subways in Rome and Milan. The fare is a flat rate as well. In the subway stations, there are coin-operated ticket machines. Keep the ticket until you get off the subway, in case there is an inspection.

• To find a cab, go to a taxi stand. When you call a taxi,

you must pay the distance the driver has to come to pick you up. Be aware that there is an extra charge of 500 to 1,000 lire at night.

• Note that there are first class and second class intercity trains. You can reserve a seat in first class at the train station or at some travel agencies. In large cities buy your ticket before boarding the train. In smaller cities you can pay on the train, but there will be a surcharge.

• If you wish to go with someone onto the platform in a large city, purchase a platform ticket for a very small fee.

• Don't throw away your ticket before you get off the train.

• If you have reserved a train seat in advance and find someone sitting in it, call the train master to find you another seat.

• If you are a woman traveling alone by train, don't go into a compartment where there is only one man.

Driving

• Note that round signs mean that an activity is forbidden, square signs mean that it is allowed. Triangular signs warn drivers to be cautious.

• Be aware that there is no speed limit on highways and that Italians tend to drive extremely fast.

• On major highways, use S.O.S. telephones for emergencies. Push one button to call for a tow truck and another to call an ambulance. A light will come on when your message has been received.

• Watch out for three-wheeled vehicles, scooters, bikes and motorcycles.

• If you're stopped for a violation, pay the fine immediately or ask for an injunction, which allows you to pay at the police station. You can contest the ticket, but it's usually cheaper and easier to pay immediately. Bear in mind that fines can be very severe, ranging from $10 to $500, depending on the offense.

LEGAL MATTERS AND SAFETY

• Note that there is no legal drinking age and that bars and restaurants are allowed to serve liquor 24 hours a day.

• If you need a police officer in a large city, seek out one who speaks English. In small towns, police usually don't speak English, but they will try to find someone who can interpret.

• Should you need a lawyer, discuss the fee in advance. The Italian Bar Association does not accept cases on a contingent fee basis. To find a lawyer, ask at the Chamber of Commerce in Italy or at the American Consulate.

• Note that there is a 14% value-added tax, called the *I.V.A.*, included in the price of all goods. Stores are supposed to refund this to you if you plan to take the goods out of the country, but most stores in Italy won't make a refund unless you spend over $1,000 (although it won't hurt to ask). If they do agree to a refund, they'll give the money to you right away, and you must send proof later that you shipped the goods out of the country.

• Be aware that there are police officers on every long-distance train. If you have any trouble, ask for them.

• Avoid taking walks alone late at night. The Milan and Rome subways are usually safe for areas near the center of the cities, but if you have to travel a long distance after 11:00 p.m., take a taxi.

• In large cities such as Rome, Naples, Milan and Turin, be alert to avoid robberies. If you notice someone staring at your purse, necklace or bracelet, try to melt into a crowd of people. Carry your purse on the arm away from the street, as the thieves sometimes approach on bicycles or motorcycles.

KEY PHRASES

English	Italian	Pronunciation
Good day	Buon giorno	Bwon jór-no
Good evening	Buona sera	Bwonah sáy-rah
Please	Per favore	Payr fah-vó-ray
Thank you	Grazie	Grát-see-ay
You're welcome	Prego	Praý-go
Yes	Si	See
No	No	No
Sir, Mr.	Signor	See-nýor
Madame, Mrs.	Signora	See-nyór-ah
Miss	Signorina	See-nyor-ée-nah
Excuse me	Scusi	Scóo-zee
Good-bye	Arrivederci	Ar-ree-vay-déhr-chee
I don't understand.	Non capisco.	Non ka-pée-sko
I don't speak Italian.	Non parlo italiano.	Non páhr-lo ee-tahl-yá-no
Is there anyone who speaks English?	C'è qualcuno che parla inglese?	Chay kwal-kóo-no kay páhr-lah een-gláy say

CHAPTER FIFTEEN

NETHERLANDS

In the flat, canal-crossed country of the Netherlands, you'll find windmills and tulips, just as you expected. You'll also find some of the world's great art, some of the best Indonesian cuisine in the world (a benefit of Dutch colonialism), and some of the most eccentric young people.

You'll also find that the Dutch speak superb English, which makes it extremely easy for travelers to explore all the things The Netherlands has to offer and to get to know the Dutch people.

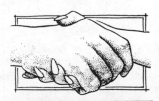

GREETINGS

• Always shake hands when greeting and leaving someone. Shake hands with young children too.

• When you're introduced to someone, repeat your name as you shake hands.

• If you're not formally introduced at a business or social gathering, introduce yourself to each person individually and shake hands. Just give your last name; don't say "Hello" or "How do you do?"

• Keep in mind that if you don't introduce yourself, the Dutch will consider you too casual and may even be offended.

• Note that close friends sometimes kiss when they meet. The ritual is to kiss on one cheek, then the other, and then back to the first.

CONVERSATION

• Avoid using first names until the Dutch suggest it.

• Good topics of conversation: Dutch politics; travel; vacations; and sports, such as soccer, cycling, ice-skating.

• The Dutch are very politically oriented, so be sure to read up before arriving in the Netherlands.

• Topics to avoid: American politics, unless you're prepared to hear some very strong views from the Dutch; money and prices, since the Dutch think that Americans always discuss money.

• Don't make jokes about the Royal Family. The Dutch are very fond of their royalty and would resent such remarks. Many homes have pictures of the Queen; people will appreciate your acknowledging them.

• You can ask about someone's profession or family but don't probe. Although the Dutch aren't as formal as the French or the Belgians, they still value their privacy.

• Avoid offering personal compliments until you know someone well.

TELEPHONES

• To call from a public phone, deposit one guilder and dial. When you hear a beep, put in more money. You'll find it easier to make calls from a post office, even if you're only calling locally.

• When answering the phone, state your name instead of saying "Hello."

PUBLIC MANNERS

• Don't touch or be physically demonstrative with anyone except relatives or good friends. If you are good friends with a Dutchman, you may occasionally touch his shoulder when shaking hands.

• Don't chew gum or keep your hands in your pockets while talking to people.

• Greet a friend you see at a distance by waving. Never shout.

• When entering a shop or a train compartment, always say "Good morning" or "Good afternoon" to everyone present. Each person will probably reply.

• Realize that a shop clerk waits on only one person at a time and even escorts the customer to the door. Never interrupt, no matter how great your hurry.

• When accompanying a woman, men should walk on the part of the sidewalk nearest the street.

• Men should stand when a woman enters the room.

• Feel free to strike up a conversation with another person in a cafe, even if you're a single woman.

DRESS

• Don't go sightseeing in halter tops or shorts. Blue jeans are acceptable, however.

• Men should wear suits for business meetings, and women should wear suits or dresses.

• When dining in a Dutch home, men should wear suits and ties, and women should wear dresses or skirts and blouses.

• For theaters and concerts, you can dress formally or informally, as you prefer. The exception is an opening night, when men usually wear tuxedos, and women cocktail dresses.

MEALS

Hours and Foods

Breakfast *(het ont bijt):* 7:30 a.m. Expect several kinds of breads and rolls, sliced meats and cheeses, hard-boiled eggs sometimes, and tea.

Lunch *(de lunch):* Noon in the countryside and 1:00 p.m. in cities. In the country, the midday meal will be the main meal of the day (see dinner). City dwellers lunch on open-faced sandwiches.

Dinner *(het diner):* 6:00 p.m., slightly later for a dinner party. Dinner often starts with tomato or a clear vegetable soup. The main course consists of meat (often braised beef) or broiled fish, boiled potatoes or rice, vegetables and salad. Note that there is not a separate salad plate. Dinner ends with fruit, ice cream or pudding—caramel, rice and fruit puddings are popular—and coffee.

At dinner parties, people sometimes start with sherry, but the most popular drink is *jenever* (gin, flavored with juniper berries), served chilled and straight. The meal will be much the same as that described above, and wine will usually be served.

Breaks: At 10:00 a.m., many people break for coffee and cookies or small pastries and at 4:00 p.m., they take tea and cookies.

Table Manners

• Keep in mind that in many homes the family offers a prayer before meals.

• Don't be surprised if the hostess serves herself first in some parts of the country. It was once customary for the hostess to taste the food first to prove it wasn't poisoned. Remember not to start eating before the hostess.

• Keep in mind the usual beverages with a meal are wine and water. Most Dutch drink beer only with Indonesian or Chinese food.

• Taste a small portion of every dish served, even if you know you don't like it.

• Strive to eat everything on your plate.

• Expect the hostess to offer second helpings after everyone has finished.

• Eat European-style with the Dutch, holding the knife in your right hand and the fork in your left. Items such as salad require only a fork kept in the right hand.

• Look for the dessert spoon above the dinner plate.

• Realize that all types of food are eaten with knife and fork, including sandwiches, fruit and sometimes even pieces of bread.

• Keep both wrists on the table. Don't rest your free hand in your lap.

• Don't expect bread to be served at dinner.

• If the hostess leaves the table and goes to the kitchen, the men should rise upon her return.

• Don't get up during a meal, even to go to the bathroom, as this is considered very rude.

• Feel free to smoke between dinner courses but be courteous enough to ask first.

• Normally you should stay about an hour and a half after dinner has ended. If everyone is having an especially good time, the party may last until 3:00 a.m. Usually the hostess will produce wine, beer and cheeses about midnight.

Places to Eat

• The following eating places are alternatives to restaurants, which are very expensive:

Bar/Cafes serve all kinds of alcohol. Some also serve small snacks. A common snack is an open-faced roast beef sandwich with an egg on top.

Broodjeswinkels, the deli-like sandwich shops, offer open-faced sandwiches, eaten with milk or buttermilk.

Snack bars all over the country serve soup, sandwiches, cakes, pastries, coffee and soft drinks. Those *snack bars* with an "A" license also have beer and wine.

• Try herring, salted and served on toast, a favorite Dutch snack. Look for street stalls where herring is sold. If you buy a herring filet at one of these stalls, hold it by its tail and take several large bites.

• Also experience a meal in an Indonesian restaurant for a special treat. Though the restaurants are inexpensive and informal, they offer an elaborate meal—the *rijsttafel* (rice table). Plain steamed rice serves as a foundation for 15 to 50 different dishes. Put some rice on your plate and add a spoonful of each dish around it. Eat the meal with a fork and spoon.

• Seat yourself at all restaurants except at the very elegant ones.

• When invited to a restaurant as someone's guest, be polite and order Dutch food from the menu. Someone entertaining several people at a restaurant usually chooses and orders for the whole party.

• When eating with a group in

a restaurant, pay your share unless you've been specifically invited as a guest. If someone does treat you to a meal, reciprocate as soon as possible.

• Expect excellent coffee in Dutch restaurants. Each year, one of the newspapers in the country rates the coffee in every restaurant and awards a major prize to the restaurant offering the best.

Specialties

• Try these Dutch specialties: *erwtensoep* (a thick pea soup, often served with bread and smoked sausage or pig's knuckle); *croquetje* (chicken and veal croquettes) and *uitsmijter* (a ham or roast beef sandwich with two fried eggs on top); *hutspot* (a stew of beef, mashed vegetables and herbs); *lamstongen met rozijnensaus* (lamb's tongue in a raisin and white wine sauce); and *flensjes* (small crepes, served for dessert).

Also try these Indonesian specialties, typically served at a *rijsttafel*: *saté* (pork cooked on wooden skewers and served with peanut sauce); *kroepoik* (shrimp crackers); *bebottok* (meat steamed in coconut milk); *babi pangang* (pieces of roast suckling pig in a spicy sauce); *seroendeng* (fried coconuts and peanuts); and *sambals* (different kinds of very hot red and green pastes).

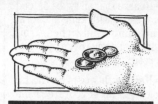

TIPPING

• Restaurants: Leave a little change on the table if the service was very good, although the tip is usually included in the restaurant check. In cases where the tip isn't included, leave 15%.

• Taxis: Ask if the tip is included in taxi fare. If not, give the driver 15% and add a guilder if he helps with luggage.

• Cloakroom and washroom attendants: Tip 25 Dutch cents.

• Porters: Give 50 Dutch cents per bag.

• Hotel doormen: If one hails a taxi for you, offer 50 Dutch cents.

• Ushers in theaters: Tip one guilder.

PRIVATE HOMES

• Notice how the Dutch take pride in their home furnishings, and offer compliments on them.

• If you're staying with a family, realize that you will be expected for meals unless you indicate otherwise. It's also courteous to let your hosts know when you'll be out and at what time you'll return home.

• Make your bed, tidy your room and offer to help with the dishes in a Dutch home.

• Bathe daily if you wish, but realize your Dutch hosts will be surprised if you wash and blow dry your hair every day

• Always ask permission to use the phone. If you need to make several calls from the home, offer to pay. If your hostess refuses, give her a gift.

Gifts: When invited to dinner, bring flowers. Unwrap them before presenting them to your hostess. Should your host pick you up at your hotel, it is acceptable to ask to stop at a florist on the way home. It's also courteous to send flowers or a plant the next day.

If you know there are children in the family, bring them candy.

Bring wine only to the home of close friends; many people pride themselves on their wine cellars and would be insulted.

If you stay with a family,

bring the newest paperback books and magazines; attractive paper napkins; typical American crafts, such as Indian jewelry; T-shirts with sayings.

BUSINESS

Hours

Business and government office hours: 8:30 a.m. to 5:30 p.m., Monday through Friday.

Bank hours: 9:00 a.m. to 4:00 p.m., Monday through Friday. In addition to this— 5:00 to 7:00 p.m. on Thursday.

Shop hours: 8:30 or 9:00 a.m. to 5:30 or 6:00 p.m. on weekdays. Some shops are also open from 7:00 to 9:00 p.m. on Thursday or Friday nights. Some small shops close from 1:00 to 2:00 p.m. All shops must close for a half day each week; the day varies from place to place and shop to shop.

Business Practices

• Use the correct titles in business dealings, especially when writing business letters. Titles for professionals such as lawyers or engineers can be complex. Buy an executive-style calendar that contains listings of the proper forms of address to be sure you're using the right title.

• Don't plan business trips from June through August or around Christmas. These are both popular vacation periods.

• Always make appointments well in advance; business people travel a great deal.

• Plan all business matters well in advance, since the Dutch are very organized and don't like anything impromptu or spontaneous. Avoid making spur-of-the-moment suggestions, such as "Let's go out to dinner tonight."

• Don't be surprised to hear English widely spoken and often used in business.

• Upon arriving for an appointment, men may be greeted by an attendant in a reception room and offered a cigar. Tip the attendant when you leave.

• Remember that every small occasion, even the arrival of a new secretary in an office, is celebrated with cream cakes for everyone.

• Be aware that Dutch business people like to entertain and to be entertained.

• If a host's wife comes with him to a lunch or dinner, the foreign business guest will be seated next to her.

• Note that businesswomen will encounter little resistance from Dutch businessmen if they want to pay for a meal, especially if they use a credit card.

• Ask if your host doesn't specify whether spouses will be included in the party. American spouses are frequently invited to business functions.

HOLIDAYS AND SPECIAL OCCASIONS

Holidays: New Year's Day (January 1), Good Friday, Easter Monday, The Queen's Birthday (April 30), Ascension Day (five weeks after Easter), Whit Monday (eight weeks after Easter), Feast of St. Nicholas (December 5; most businesses are open until noon), Christmas (December 25), and December 26.

• On the evening before the Feast of Sinterklaas (Saint Nicholas), children leave their shoes by the fireplace, with sugar lumps and carrots for Sinterklaas's horse. The next morning they receive a large gift, as well as small treats in their shoes. Good friends leave gifts at the door and run away.

On this day family members also give each other gifts, each with a humorous poem attached. For instance a teenaged girl may get a poem teasing her about her boyfriend. Each person also receives her or his initial in chocolate. If you're included in a celebration, have a gift, with a funny poem, for each family member. Popular foods for this day are: marzipan (almond paste) in different shapes, fondant and *speculaas* (spiced ginger cookies), with hot chocolate or hot wine to drink.

TRANSPORTATION

Public Transportation

• Use the same tickets for buses and subways. Tickets come in strips. Tear off the appropriate number of strips, depending on how far you will be traveling, and insert them into a machine to be stamped. This is basically an honor system, although inspectors occasionally check to see if fares have been paid.

• Note that tickets are less expensive if you buy them at the central office in advance of travel.

• Be very careful of streetcars, which have absolute right of way.

• Note that all taxis use meters. You can get one at a taxi stand or call. Fares are higher between 1:00 and 6:00 a.m.

Driving

• Be aware that seat belts are mandatory for everyone in a car. Children must sit in the back seat.

• Know that a vehicle approaching from the right has the right of way.

• Be cautious of bicyclists; they can be very aggressive.

LEGAL MATTERS AND SAFETY

• If you stay longer than three months, you must register with the police. Failure to do so can mean immediate deportation.

• A value-added tax is included in the price of all goods. You can get this back if you buy something worth more than 600 guilders from a big department store. Get a form from the store and present it to the customs official at the airport to get it stamped. Your refund will be mailed to you when you get home.

• Realize that prostitution is legal in The Netherlands. Women should avoid Zeedyk Street in Amsterdam, where many prostitutes sit in shop windows. It is considered bad taste for women to go there and stare.

• Also note that sex shops are legal and common, even in small towns.

• Ask at your hotel which areas in Amsterdam are best avoided.

• Know that the drinking age is 16 and that you can order alcohol in a bar or restaurant 24 hours a day.

• Women can go alone into a restaurant or bar without problem, but it isn't wise for them to go out alone after 11:00 p.m. They should use taxis if they need to be out late and watch their purses very carefully, especially on buses and streetcars.

KEY PHRASES

English	Dutch	Pronunciation
Good morning	Goedmorgen	Hóo-dun mórghen
Good evening	Goedeavond	Hóo-dun áh-vawnt
Please	Alstublieft	Ahss-tew-bleeft
Thank you	Dank u	Dahnk you
You're welcome	Geen dank	Hain dunk
Yes	Ja	Ya
No	Neen	Nay
Sir, Mr.	Mijanheer	Muh-náyr
Madam, Mrs.	Mevrouw	Muhv-rów
Miss	Juffrouw	Yuf-rów
Excuse me	Pardon	Par-dáwn
Good-bye	Tot ziens	Tawt seenss
I don't speak Dutch.	Ik spreek geen Nederlands.	Ik spráyk hane Náy-der-lunts
Does anyone here speak English?	Spreekt er hier iemand ingels?	Spráykt ehr hére ieé-mahnd eén-gehls?

CHAPTER SIXTEEN

NORWAY

TRONDHEIM

BERGEN

OSLO ★

DRAMMEN

STAVANGER

KRISTIANSAND

Thanks to the discovery of North Sea oil, Norway has one of the highest standards of living in the world. It is also the northernmost country in Western Europe, with fully half the country located above the Arctic Circle.

The Norwegian takes pride in being a self-reliant person who can also put aside personal interests for the common good. Great efforts have been made to save the country's natural beauties for everyone to enjoy.

People work very hard for nine months of the year, because the weather offers an opportunity to do little else. But at the first whiff of good weather, they rush off to enjoy their summer places and three months of summer sports.

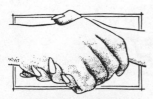

GREETINGS

• Shake hands when introduced, when greeting someone you know, or when taking leave.

• Wait for your host or hostess to introduce you at a small party. However, at a large party, it is best to introduce yourself.

• Rise when you're introduced.

• Use a person's occupational title before the last name if you're speaking to a professor, doctor, or engineer. Don't address a lawyer with an occupational title. Address a clergyman by his last name alone (for example, "Hello, Lyons").

• Don't be surprised if men are addressed simply by their last names. A greeting such as "Good morning, Jones" is very common and not considered rude.

CONVERSATION

• Use first names only with very close friends.

• Good topics of conversation: your hosts' interests or hobbies; politics; participatory sports, such as sailing, hiking or skiing; spectator sports, such as soccer; and what your hosts did on their last vacations.

• Topics to avoid: criticism of other peoples or customs and personal life (avoid questions such as "What do you do?" or "Are you married?").

• Realize that Norwegians are typically reserved about themselves and sometimes feel that Americans are too casual and glib about private issues. It will take time to get to know people personally.

TELEPHONES

• To make a local call from a public phone, deposit one

krone and dial the number. Have extra coins ready so that when you hear a beep signaling that time is up, you can deposit the additional coins quickly to avoid being cut off.

• Ask for an English-speaking operator if you need assistance.

• Remember that you can dial directly to over 40 countries from Norwegian phones. You can also make long-distance calls at a *telegrafkontor* (telephone office).

• Answer the phone by giving your last name or your phone number.

PUBLIC MANNERS

• Never speak in a loud voice.

• Avoid demonstrative gestures, such as slapping someone on the back or putting your arm around his or her shoulder.

• Feel free to take photographs in Norway, as there are few restrictions. At a village festival, where people wear traditional dress, first ask for permission to photograph individuals. They almost always will be very

pleased to pose for you.

• Look for slot machines in cafes and at the entrances to restaurants if you like to gamble. Most machines take one-krone coins and the proceeds go to charity.

• Wait for an attendant to clean the stall in a public bathroom before you use it. Pay a fee if one is posted; otherwise leave one krone.

DRESS

• Wear clean, pressed blue jeans and T-shirts for casual wear, but only if the fabric is not faded or torn.

• Wear shorts in the countryside only.

• Dress fairly casually for business. Men can wear sports jackets, but should always wear ties. Women should wear suits, dresses or dress pants.

• When you're invited to dinner in a home, men should wear suits, and women should wear dresses, skirts and blouses, or dress pants.

• Men must wear jackets and ties in better restaurants. This is not necessary in smaller or neighborhood restaurants, however.

• Dress fairly formally for the opening of an opera or ballet. Dark suits for men and cocktail dresses for women are appropriate.

• If you receive an invitation to a wedding or party that specifies formal wear, men should wear tuxedos or tails, and women should wear short or long dresses.

MEALS

Hours and Foods

Breakfast *(frokost):* 8:30 a.m. The usual meal offers cheeses, cold cuts, soft-boiled eggs, bread, and coffee or tea.

Lunch *(lunsj):* Around noon. This is a light meal of open-faced sandwiches (usually a thin piece of rye bread with artistically arranged meat, fish and cheese toppings) and fruit.

Dinner *(middag):* 5:00 to 6:00 p.m. for a family meal; 7:00 p.m. for a dinner party (6:00 p.m. in the winter). A dinner party begins with an appetizer (usually a small, special delicacy like smoked or cured salmon, fjord shrimp or a small meat salad) or soup, accompanied by white wine. At formal dinners, both appetizers and soup are served—soup first, then appetizer.

• The main course is usually some type of meat or fowl: roast beef, reindeer, goose or pheasant are common. Boiled potatoes and vegetables and sometimes a salad accompany the meat. Red wine is usually served with this course.

• Dessert follows—often ice cream with liqueur, or fruit (cloudberries, strawberries, or fruit salad) with whipped cream. Dessert drinks are usually either port or madeira. The meal ends with coffee and cognac or another liqueur.

Table Manners

• Be on time when invited to a meal. If there is a time for cocktails before the meal, it will be very brief. In some homes, people go immediately to the table for the meal.

• If there is a cocktail hour, expect your host to offer sherry, scotch or champagne but not mixed drinks. Sometimes smoked meats or cheeses accompany the drinks. Take small amounts of cheese, using the cheese slicer provided.

• Note that the host and hostess sit at opposite ends of the table, with the male guest of honor to the left of the hostess and the female guest of honor to the left of the host.

• Don't start eating until your host or hostess does.

• Keep in mind that food is passed around the table on platters except at formal dinners. Take small portions at first, since it's considered rude not to finish everything on your plate. However, if you don't care for something after tasting it, your hosts will understand that the food may be strange to you and won't be insulted if you leave it.

• Expect dinner to last several hours, as there are usually many courses and much conversation.

• Adopt the Norwegian eating style by keeping the fork in your left hand and the knife in your right. Use the knife to push food onto the back of the fork.

• Eat open-faced sandwiches with a knife and fork. Never pick them up with your hands.

• Indicate that you've finished eating by crossing your utensils in the middle of the plate.

• Try *aquavit*, a liquor made from potatoes, if it's served on special occasions. Toast someone by looking at her or him, sipping the *aquavit*,

looking at the person again, and then putting your glass down. A beer chaser follows the *aquavit*.

• You may drink water if you don't want to drink wine or beer. Bottled water, such as Perrier, is usually served.

• Wait to see what the others at the table do before you light a cigarette, although Norwegians commonly smoke between courses.

• Thank the hostess at the end of the meal. This doesn't signal the end of the evening, however.

• Don't be surprised if there's dancing in the home after a dinner party.

• Stay until 11:00 p.m. if you're invited to dinner in the summer. Since it stays light until midnight, your hosts may suggest taking a walk after dinner and then returning to their house for a liqueur. In winter people go to bed earlier, so plan to leave by 10:00 p.m.

Places to Eat

• Know what different kinds of food to expect in different eating places.

A *bistro* offers a wide selection of open-faced sandwiches, beer, wine and soft drinks.

A *kafe* offers open-faced sandwiches, coffee, tea, and sometimes beer and wine. In some communities *kafes* also serve hard liquor. (Note: some restaurants have the word *kafe* in their name, but they serve full meals and are not to be confused with real cafes.)

Kaffestovas are self-service cafeterias where you can get simple hot food such as meatballs, fishcakes and stews.

Konditori are pastry shops offering simple, open-faced sandwiches, pastries and coffee. No liquor is served.

• Also look for outdoor food stands where you can get snacks, such as sausages, waffles or hamburgers. It's okay to eat these snacks on the street.

• Ask to share a table if you go into a cafe and there are no free tables. This isn't done in a regular restaurant, however.

• Don't copy the young people you may see snapping their fingers to attract a waiter's attention. Instead, raise your hand and extend the index finger.

• Take only what you can eat at restaurant and hotel dining room *smorgasbords*. Norwegians are scandalized by waste of food. You can always return for second helpings.

• Expect to pay a separate charge for soda water when ordering a mixed drink like scotch and soda.

• Don't order wine and beer before 11:00 a.m. There are three types of beer: *Brigg,* which is low in alcohol; *Pils,* which is lager; and *Export,* which has the highest alcohol content.

• Don't order a drink with hard liquor except between 3:00 and 11:45 p.m. Hard liquor is not sold at all on Sundays or holidays.

• Women can safely go alone into a bar or restaurant.

Specialties

• You'll find fresh fish figuring more prominently on Norwegian menus. Sample these fish specialties: *gravlaks* (salmon cured with dill); *sild* (herring, prepared in many different ways); *kokt torsk* (poached cod); *reker* (fjord shrimp); *steke marinert makrell* (grilled, marinated mackrel); *fiskepudding* (fish pudding with bread crumbs and cream); and *torsk med eggesaus* (poached codfish steaks with egg sauce).

• Also try *fenalar* (cured and baked leg of mutton); *flatbrod* (crisp thin rye bread); *himmelsk lapskaus* (fruit salad with nuts, served with rum and egg sauce); and *rabarbragrot* (rhubarb compote).

• Take note of the following exotic foods that you may

want to try (or avoid): *hval biff* (whale meat; it tastes like liver, with the consistency of steak); *gjetost* (a cheese that tastes more like sweet fudge); *sylte* (head cheese, a fatty and gelatinous salami made of innards).

HOTELS

• Show your passport to the desk clerk when you check in. It isn't necessary to leave it, however.

• Take your room key with you when you go out.

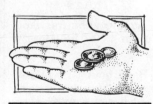

TIPPING

• Restaurants: Leave 3 to 5 extra kroner if the service was very good, although the tip is included in the bill.

• Taxis: Round the fare up to the nearest krone; the tip is included in the fare. When the driver performs some extra services for you, offer 10% of the fare.

• Washroom attendants: Look for signs posted in washrooms indicating the fee. If there is no sign, tip the attendant 1 or 1 1/2 kroner.

• Porters: Give 2 kroner per bag.

PRIVATE HOMES

• Arrive at 3:30 or 4:00 p.m. if you're going to visit someone in the countryside. People usually have their main meal at noon, followed by a nap. Late afternoon is reserved for visitors.

• Call in advance if you want to visit someone in the city.

• Be prepared to see Norwegian women removing long, brown woolen underwear from beneath skirts or dresses when entering a house in cold weather. Women visiting Norway during the winter months might also want to wear long underwear.

• Bring pastries or a box of chocolates when you're invited to come for a cup of coffee.

• If you visit people in the city, expect to be offered alcohol or coffee. If you visit people in the countryside, they are more likely to serve coffee and pastries.

• Feel free to go out by yourself if you stay with a Norwegian family. While your hosts will be pleased to show you around, they won't smother you by insisting on accompanying you everywhere.

• Offer to pay for any calls you make in a private home. Local calls from a home cost about 10 cents a minute, except after 5:00 p.m., when they're free.

• Offer to help set or clear the table when you stay with a family for several days. Your offer will probably be declined unless other guests are coming for the evening. In general, Norwegians enjoy playing host and prefer to have guests relax and enjoy themselves.

• Don't hesitate to bathe every day if you wish. Always ask if it's convenient, however, since the water may have to be heated.

Gifts: Bring a bottle of wine, chocolates, pastries or flowers when invited to a meal. Liquor is a welcome gift, since it's very expensive in Norway. If you bring flowers, remember that carnations and all white flowers such as lilies are reserved for funerals. Never give a wreath of any kind, even at Christ-

mas, as they too are reserved for funerals.

If you stay with a family, bring an example of an art or craft typical of your region. (Indian jewelry or a piece of scrimshaw are good examples.) You could also bring an American antique, a bottle of American liquor, or frozen steaks or roast beef. Meat is very expensive in Norway, so it's a much-appreciated gift.

BUSINESS

Hours

Business hours: 8:00 a.m. to 4:00 p.m., Monday through Friday.

Bank hours: Hours may vary in different communities, but most banks are open between 9:00 a.m. and 3:00 p.m., Monday through Friday. Many banks are open until 6:00 p.m. on Thursday. Banks close slightly earlier during June, July, and August.

Shop hours: 8:30 or 9:00 a.m. until 4:00 or 5:00 p.m., Monday through Friday; Saturday from 8:30 or 9:00 a.m. until 1:00 or 2:00 p.m.

Business Practices

• Avoid business trips to Norway in July and August, when many people take vacations. In early September, many people take a week off to go hunting. Other vacations fall during the two weeks before or the three weeks after Christmas, during the week before and after Easter, and the days before and after June 21, the midsummer festival.

• Schedule appointments between 10:00 a.m. and noon or between 2:00 and 4:00 p.m.

• Arrange appointments at least a week in advance if you're in Norway, or if you telephone or telex from the U.S. If you set up an appointment by mail, allow one week each way for international air mail.

• Be punctual. If you find you're going to be even a little late, telephone to explain.

• Don't be concerned about language or business customs. Many Norwegian business people are fluent in English and are well acquainted with U.S. business and trade practices.

• Remember to avoid bringing up personal matters and don't try to be too familiar. However, you may find Norwegian business people more relaxed than their Swedish counter-

parts. It is more common to have a casual conversation, or even make jokes, at a business meeting in Norway than in Sweden.

• Keep in mind that business people don't normally go to lunch, but rather eat sandwiches at their desks. If you invite someone to lunch, however, the offer will usually be accepted.

• Realize that it is common for a Norwegian business person to invite you home for a meal. However, don't expect spouses to be included at a business meal in a restaurant.

HOLIDAYS AND SPECIAL OCCASIONS

Holidays: New Year's Day (January 1), Maundy Thursday (Thursday before Easter), Good Friday, Easter Monday, Labor Day (May 1), Constitution Day (May 17), Ascension Day (five weeks after Easter), Whit Monday (eight weeks after Easter), Christmas (December 25), December 26.

• On Constitution Day, all the school children in the country parade in their hometown or city, waving Norwegian flags, while everyone else watches. The day is a celebration of spring, as well, and is the biggest celebration of the year.

TRANSPORTATION
Public Transportation

• Within city limits, you pay one flat rate on buses, trolleys and subways. There may be an extra charge if you go to a suburb.

• Pay the driver or conductor when you get on. Exact change is not required.

• Enter the trolley from the rear and then pay the driver or conductor.

• Put the exact change in the machine at the station entrance. A stamped ticket will come out.

• Keep your bus and trolley tickets if you plan to transfer. Tickets are stamped with the time and are good for an hour.

• Realize that taxis are in short supply during the rush hours (around 8:30 a.m. and 4:00 p.m.) Reserve a taxi in advance, or look for a taxi stand, indicated by a green box with a telephone in it.

Driving

• Allow extra time if you'll be driving outside Oslo, as the roads are narrow and bumpy. Also, allow time for crossing the many fjords by ferry.

• Never have even one drink if you plan to drive. There are frequent police roadblocks to check for drunken driving, and you can be fined, lose your license for a year, or spend three weeks in jail if you have even a little alcohol in your blood. No exceptions are made for foreigners.

• If you go to a party or restaurant where you will be drinking even a little, take a taxi home. Norwegians regard the taxi fare as part of the expense of an evening out.

• Keep in mind that speeding carries the same penalties as drunken driving.

• Park at meters in the city. Meters are free after 5:00 p.m.

LEGAL MATTERS AND SAFETY

• A value-added tax is included in the prices of goods.

Some shops and department stores will fill out a form that allows foreigners to get a refund on this tax when they leave the country.

• Note that liquor is sold by the bottle only in government-owned liquor stores, which are open from 10:00 a.m. to 5:00 p.m., Monday through Friday, and from 10:00 a.m. until noon or 1:00 p.m. on Saturday. Prepare to wait in a very long line. When traveling outside Oslo, be aware that not all towns have liquor stores.

• Only order wine and beer in a restaurant or bar after 11:00 a.m. Only order hard liquor between 3:00 and 11:45 p.m. Hard liquor is not sold at all on Sundays or holidays.

• Keep in mind that liquor is not served to individuals under 20.

• Request permission from the passport police if you plan to stay in Norway longer than three months.

• Women should know that it is safe to walk alone at night most of the time. However, as always, they should consider the neighborhood first and be cautious.

KEY PHRASES

English	Norwegian	Pronunciation
Good day	God dag	Goo dahg
Good evening	God kueld	Goo kuehld
Please	Vaer så snill	Váhr so sníl
Thank you	Takk	Tahk
You're welcome	Vaer så god	Vahr so goo
Yes	Ja	Yah
No	Nei	Nay
Sir, Mr.	Herr	Har
Madam, Mrs.	Fru	Froo
Miss	Frøken	Fróo-ken
Excuse me	Om forlatelse	Ohm fah-láht-el-seh
Good-bye	Adjø	Ahd-yér
I don't speak Norwegian.	Jeg snakker ikke norsk.	Yay snó-kehr ik-keh norsk
Is there anyone who speaks English?	Finnes der noen somkar engelsk?	Finz dehr nó-en sóhm-kchn én-gelsk

If you travel to Poland, you'll probably be surprised by how much the Poles know about the U.S. and by how interested they are in American life. Many Poles have relatives in the U.S. who keep in touch through letters and visits.

In Poland, you will be impressed by the post-World War II restoration of such old cities as Warsaw and Gdansk, and by the medieval beauty of Cracow. However, be very cautious in photographing the delights you find in these places. The government is extremely sensitive about anyone taking photographs of any person or place with any possible connection to the military or to Poland's labor movement. When in doubt, drink in the beauty but don't take the picture.

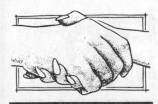

GREETINGS

• Shake hands when you're introduced, when you greet someone you know and when you leave. Men should wait for women to extend their hands first.

• A woman should not be surprised if a Polish man kisses her hand when he's introduced, when he greets her at subsequent meetings and when he leaves. American men need not kiss the hands of Polish women; they should simply shake hands.

• Know that when close friends or relatives meet, they embrace and kiss on one cheek, then on the other, then back to the first.

• Expect your host or hostess to introduce you, but if you find a large crowd when you arrive, introduce yourself.

• Realize that professional titles are commonly used. Address someone as "Mr." or "Mrs." plus their professional title (for example *Panie Doktorze,* "Mr. Doctor").

• When you're introduced to a married couple, don't be surprised if their last names sound slightly different. When a woman marries, she takes her husband's surname and changes the last letter to "a." (For example, Mr. Mayevski's wife would be Mrs. Mayevska).

CONVERSATION

• Don't use first names until a Polish person does. Using first names is a sign of true friendship and is considered so important that friends celebrate the occasion by having a drink together. The little ceremony is called *bruderschaft,* as it is in Germany.

• Good topics of conversation: daily life in the U.S., the state where you live, places you vacation, your family, Poland and its cultural history.

• You'll find Poles very curious about life in America. Many have relatives in the U.S. and will want to talk about them.

• Topics to avoid: religion, and Polish members of the Communist Party.

• Don't be surprised if Poles ask how much money you make per hour. This is another example of their curiosity about American life—they don't mean to be offensive.

• Observe that Polish men have rather traditional views of female behavior and are often most helpful to women who avoid being direct or abrupt in both business and social encounters.

TELEPHONES

• Look for public phones in hotels, restaurants, cafes, and in phone booths. They are widely used, since few people have private phones.

• Deposit 2 zloty to make a local call. You'll hear a tone when the money runs out. Deposit more money to continue the call.

• For long-distance calls, go to the post office.

• You'll find that only overseas operators speak English.

• Say *"Halo"* when you answer the phone.

PUBLIC MANNERS

• Try to talk quietly when you're in public, as Poles speak more softly than Americans.

• Never chew gum while you talk to someone.

• Never ever toss any garbage away. No one in Poland litters, and the Polish are shocked by anyone who does.

• Don't walk on the grass unless you see others doing so, or you could get a ticket.

• If you're lost, keep in mind that a puzzled look will inevitably bring an offer of help. People will be willing to find you a map or even take you home for a cup of tea and a rest.

• Bargain only in open markets, never in state-run stores.

• Realize that a woman who asks a man for directions may be seen as flirting. It is more appropriate to ask a Polish woman or a police officer for help.

• Be very discreet about taking pictures. Never photograph soldiers, military installations or industrial plants.

DRESS

• Men and women can wear jeans or other pants for casual dress. For dressier occasions, wear jeans with dressy shirts or blouses.

• When visiting a church, women should not wear short skirts or low-cut dresses, but they can wear pants.

• For business, men wear suits and ties, and women wear dresses.

• Men should wear jackets and ties, and women should wear dresses, skirts or dressy pants (designer jeans are fine) and blouses when dining in someone's home.

• Men wear suits, and women wear dresses to expensive restaurants.

• Remember that formal dress isn't necessary for the theater or the ballet. Men wear dark suits, and women wear dresses.

• When an invitation specifies formal wear for an occasion such as a New Year's Eve party, men wear tuxedos, and women wear long dresses.

MEALS

Hours and Foods

Breakfast *(sniadanie):* 7:00 to 8:00 a.m. Usually the meal consists of rolls, butter, jam and tea.

Lunch *(obiad):* 3:00 to 4:00 p.m. Poles do not take a lunch break at work, but eat the main meal of the day right after they get home. They begin with a beef, tomato or fruit soup, then have a meat course, with vegetables or salad. Beer or vodka accompany the meal. Next comes a stewed fruit or pastry and, finally, tea with lemon and sugar.

If you're invited to a meal, it will probably be on Sunday around 1:00 or 2:00 p.m., as most Polish women work Monday through Saturday. The meal will be much like the one described above, except that it will begin with appetizers like steak tartar (raw hamburger) or smoked eel, and vodka. The main course could be veal cutlet with seasonal vegetables or a dish such as stuffed cabbage rolls. Beer, vodka or wine accompany the meal.

Dinner *(kolacja):* 8:00 to 9:00 p.m. Usually a lighter meal, supper consists of a sandwich, pastry and tea.

Breaks: At 10:00 a.m., people stop work to eat a sandwich.

Table Manners

• Don't be surprised if the meal is served at a table in the living room, as most apartments are very small.

• Keep in mind that the guest of honor is seated at the head of the table.

• Note that toasting is a major feature of many meals. The host will probably toast you with vodka. Return the toast later in the meal by saying "To your health."

• When a Pole flicks his finger against his neck, realize that you're invited to join him for a drink of vodka.

• Don't try to match the Poles shot for shot when they drink vodka, unless you are a prodigious drinker. The vodka can be very strong, and they're used to drinking it neat and in one gulp. Either ask for a little in your glass or simply say that you've had enough.

• Wait until everyone has been served before you begin to eat.

• Notice that the table setting is like an American one, except for a small spoon for coffee that you may find above the dinner plate.

• Hold the fork in your left hand and the knife in your right; use the knife to push food on the back of the fork.

• Serve yourself from platters of food that are passed around the table, unless you receive a plate with food already on it.

• When beet soup is served, pick up the bowl and drink from it. You won't be given a spoon.

• Keep both hands out of your lap while you're at the table.

• When people insist that you take seconds, refuse politely twice and then accept on the third offer, if you care to. When you're full, leave a little food on your plate or your hostess will refill the plate immediately.

• Realize that coffee is in very, very short supply, so unless it is served, don't ask for it. It is usually only served after formal dinners.

• Don't leave early from a dinner party or your hosts will be insulted. Poles love to stay up and talk until the wee hours of the morning, even if they have to get up early the following day. Don't look for your hosts to offer clues such as yawning or telling you they have to get up early.

• Thank people for their kindness to you by taking them to dinner at a restaurant. Many Poles enjoy eating out, but don't often have the opportunity to do so.

Places to Eat

• Look for the following kinds of eating places:

A *bar mleczny* is a milk bar where you can get a fast meal; you eat standing or seated at a counter. You can choose ice cream, yogurt, drinks made with yogurt, fruit drinks with milk, and *pierogi* (vegetable-filled turnovers). Alcoholic drinks are not available.

Karczma are old, restored taverns and inns, with regional folk decorations.

A *kawiarnia* is a cafe, serving wine, soda, coffee, pastry and cheeses.

Restauracja are restaurants that are categorized from A to D, with A being the best. Look for the designation in the restaurant window before you go in. Also check the menu, which will be posted in a window.

• Realize that there's no such thing as an American-style bar. The closest approximations are found in cafes and hotels.

• Speak English in a restaurant and you'll be served more promptly and receive special attention.

• Realize that restaurants don't always have everything that's listed on the menu. It's a good idea to ask the waiter what is available before ordering.

• Be aware that each restaurant in Poland has one meatless day a week because of erratic meat supplies.

• Keep in mind that service is very slow in most restaurants. If you're in a hurry, go to a *mleczny* (milk bar).

• Since wines are imported and are extremely expensive, don't order until you know the price and quantity. Prices are usually given by the glass. When you order, specify carefully the quantity you want.

• Choose one of the more expensive restaurants if you are a woman traveling alone, or you may find men joining your table uninvited. If that should happen, move to another table or leave.

• Pay the waiter at the table.

• If food or service isn't satisfactory, look for the "complaint book," where you write down what displeased you. This won't ensure immediate action however.

Specialties

• Grains, potatoes, and cabbage are mainstays of the Polish diet. Some specialties are *barszcz* (beet soup with vegetables and sour cream); *golabki* (stuffed cabbage rolls); *karp po zydowsku* (steamed slices of carp on root vegetables, served hot or cold in its own aspic); *bigos* (a hunter's stew of pork, ham, sausages, beef or game, onions, mushrooms, and cabbage or sauerkraut); *kaczka* (wild duck with apples); *zajac* (hare in sour cream); *sarnina* (roast venison); *kielbasa* (sausage); *kolduny* (beef turnovers in *ulebiak* mushrooms and cabbage in pastry); *zrazy zawijane* (steak rolled up with mushrooms and served with rice); and *bryndza* (sheep's milk cheese with chives).

• Depending on your taste, you may want to try, or avoid, two appetizers: *tatar,* (raw hamburger accompanied by onions, pickles and anchovies), and *wegorz* (smoked eel—considered a delicacy).

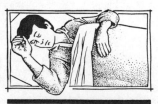

HOTELS

• Allow the hotel to keep your passport during your stay. Ask for it if you need it to change money or the like, and then bring it back.

• Leave your key at the desk each time you go out. Hotel room keys are enormous and would be awkward to carry.

• Ask the person stationed on each floor for extra towels or other supplies you might need for your room.

TIPPING

• Tip discreetly, because tipping is officially discouraged. However people still expect it, and you won't get into any trouble if you do.

• Restaurants: Restaurants usually include a 10% service charge in the check; if they don't, tip 10%.

• Taxis: Give drivers 5-10% of the fare as a tip.

• Porters: Tip 20 zloty per bag.

• Cloakroom attendants: Tip 5 zloty

• Washroom attendants: Look for signs that tell you how to pay the attendant who supplies toilet paper and towels. The usual charge is 2-5 zloty.

PRIVATE HOMES

• Plan to visit people on Sunday, the customary day for company.

• Call or write to find out if it's convenient to come before you visit. Never drop in unexpectedly, as your host will want to serve you something to eat and will be embarrassed if he doesn't have anything to offer.

• Eat only lightly before you go visiting to prepare yourself for the wine, tea and pastries that are offered. People are very insistent that guests eat.

• If you're visiting relatives during your stay, expect to receive many gifts, such as homemade preserves and hand-knit items.

• Don't be surprised if friends or relatives actually move out and stay with friends to give you the entire apartment while you visit.

• Offer to help clear the table and do the dishes when you are a guest for several days. In all likelihood your offer won't be accepted. Polish kitchens are extremely small,

and your hosts will tend to pamper you, but offering to help is a nice gesture.

• When vacationing, don't feel that your hosts must be included in every activity. They'll make suggestions on places to see and how to get there, but feel free to go off by yourself if you wish.

• Always ask if it's convenient before you take a bath. Unless the apartment is relatively new and has constant hot water, your host will need time to heat the water.

Gifts: When invited to a meal, bring flowers, candy, liquor or wine. Flowers are the first choice because they are expensive. Keep in mind that there should always be an odd number of flowers, and remember that chrysanthemums are reserved for funerals.

As a long-term guest, give a food gift, such as fruit. Poles appreciate gifts of food because it is necessary to wait in long lines when marketing.

Choose other gifts, such as chocolates, canned hams, cognac and perfume, from one of the government-run "dollar stores," where you can only buy goods with foreign money.

• When bringing gifts from the U.S., select coffee, cigarettes, American whiskey, records, a pocket calculator with batteries, an American canned ham, or ballpoint pens. For close friends, bring blue jeans, pantyhose, tights, and men's or women's corduroy pants.

BUSINESS

Hours

Business hours: 8:00 a.m. to 3:00 p.m., or from 9:00 a.m. to 2:00 p.m., Monday through Friday; 8:00 a.m. to 1:30 p.m. on Saturday.

Bank hours: 8:00 or 9:00 a.m. until noon or 2:00 p.m., Monday through Saturday.

Shop hours: 9:00 or 11:00 a.m. to 7:00 p.m., Monday through Saturday.

Business Practices

• Be aware that Polish people start the work day very early, with 8:00 a.m. appointments, and work through the traditional lunch hour. They also work all but one Saturday a month until 1:30 p.m. Schedule appointments for any time during the working day.

• To find the name of the right person to contact at a Polish firm, write to the commercial section of the American Embassy in Warsaw for help.

• You can write business letters in English, as most business people understand English or can easily have the letters translated. If you want to make the best possible impression, have your correspondence translated into Polish.

• Be patient when doing business with any state-operated organization and don't expect quick decisions. It may be necessary to negotiate arrangements over weeks or months, and you may possibly have to make more than one trip to Poland.

• Expect a Polish business person to suggest a 4:00 or 5:00 p.m. lunch date.

• Entertain Polish business people in the restaurant of an international hotel. Invite only department heads or those whose status is equal to your own. Don't include spouses in business invitations, unless you've been a guest in the family home.

• Don't empty your glass if you want to avoid drinking a lot at business meals. A glass is refilled as soon as it becomes empty.

Gifts: On your first visit to a company, consider bringing a bottle of whiskey or cognac as a gift.

HOLIDAYS AND SPECIAL OCCASIONS

Holidays: New Year's Day (January 1), Easter Monday, Labor Day (May 1), Victory Day (May 9), Corpus Christi (approximately eight weeks after Easter), Polish National Day (July 22), All Saints' Day (November 1), Christmas (December 25), and December 26.

• On May Day, there are rallies and parades. Don't take photographs. Be aware that there are no sales of alcohol for several days before and after May 1, nor are there sales on the day itself.

• If you're invited to a party on New Year's Eve, bring flowers, candy or wine.

TRANSPORTATION
Public Transportation

• Buy bus and streetcar tickets at newspaper stands and stamp your ticket in the machine as you board. Keep the ticket handy in case an inspector asks for it, or you'll have to pay a 500-zloty fine.

• Be aware that although taxis are inexpensive, the price doubles after 11:00 p.m. Line up at a taxi stand; the wait may be a long one. Let the elderly or sick go immediately to the head of the line.

• If you want to hitchhike, buy permit coupons at the border. Give coupons to the drivers when you are picked up. Drivers receive prizes at the end of the year for accumulating the largest number of coupons.

Driving

• Obtain an international driver's license if you plan to drive. Carry this and your passport at all times when you're driving.

• Wear a seat belt and be sure everyone else in the car does also, as this is required by law.

• Avoid driving at night, especially in the countryside. Unlit carts on the roads are a major hazard.

• Note that speeding and most other traffic violations result in a fine of 500 zloty (roughly $10.00), payable on the spot. If the police believe that you didn't understand the traffic signs, you may simply receive a warning.

• Drive only when totally sober. When Poles go out for an evening, the driver abstains from liquor completely. Your license may be revoked if you're caught drinking and driving, even if you've only had one beer all evening.

LEGAL MATTERS AND SAFETY

• You'll need a visa to enter Poland.

• For a stay of 48 hours or less (not including the day of arrival or departure) en route to another country, obtain a transit visa at the border.

• Realize that American magazines, newspapers, and books may be confiscated when you enter Poland.

• Don't attempt to bring Polish currency into the country or take it out.

• Don't sell your clothes if someone approaches you and asks to buy them; it's illegal.

• Register yourself with the local police if you're staying in a private home. Hotels do this for guests.

• Change money only at an official bank, or you could be arrested. Without proper receipts you can be detained for questioning or have the money confiscated.

• Be advised that women traveling alone should take taxis after dark.

KEY PHRASES

English	Polish	Pronunciation
Good morning; hello	Dzíen dobry	Dgen dó-bree
Good evening	Dobry wieczór	Do-bri vyé-choor
Good night	Dobranoc	Do-bra-nóts
Please	Proszę	Pró-she
Thank you	Dziękuje	Dgén-koo-jeh
You're welcome	Proszę bardzo	Pró-sheh bárd-zo
Yes	Tak	Tahk
No	Nie	Nyeh
Sir, Mr.	Pan	Pahn
Madam, Mrs.	Pani	Páh-nee
Miss	Panna	Páh-nah
Excuse me	Przepraszam	Pshe-prá-sham
Good-bye	Do widzeniz	Do-vee-dzhé-nya
I don't speak Polish.	Ja nie mówie po polsku.	Ya nyeh móov-yeh po pól-skoo
Does anyone here speak English?	Czy ktoś mówi po angielsku?	Chih któsh móo-vee po ahn-ghee-él-skoo

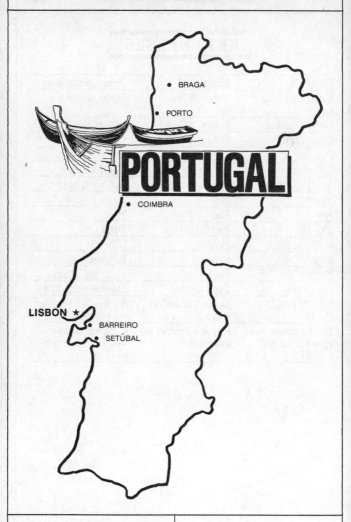

$\mathbf{A}$ visit to Portugal is usually a wonderful surprise, as most visitors don't have a "fixed" image of it beforehand. There's no equivalent of the Arc de Triomphe or the Tower of London planted in our minds before we go, and the beautiful countryside and the colorful fishing villages are quite unexpected.

The most amazing quality of the Portuguese, who are generally small and slender, is that they seem to eat 23 hours a day. And with every meal they consume large quantities of delicious bread.

Cultivate patience before you visit Portugal. Things don't get done overnight, or even over two nights. It once took Elizabeth Devine a week of daily visits to a travel agent to get a ticket from Oporto to Paris. On the other hand, she was never billed for the ticket!

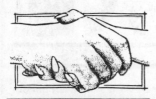

GREETINGS

• Men should rise when they are being introduced, but women need not.

• When you are introduced to someone, shake hands. If you are meeting a group of people, shake hands with each person.

• Don't shake hands when greeting close friends. Men embrace and slap one another on the back. Women kiss on both cheeks.

• Use a person's professional title before the last name if you're speaking to a doctor, lawyer, professor or engineer.

CONVERSATION

• Use first names only with close friends.

• Good topics of conversation: the beauty of Portugal, vacations, wines, hobbies, your and your host's families, and sports such as soccer.

• Topics to avoid: money issues, such as salaries and the cost of living, and personal questions about someone's job.

TELEPHONES

• When you make phone calls from cafes, pay the waiter at the end of the call. You can also use a phone booth. Deposit 5 escudos or more if you plan a long conversation. Should you deposit more money than necessary, it will be returned when you hang up.

• Go to the post office to make long-distance calls.

• When answering the phone, either give your name or say *"Está"* in a questioning voice.

PUBLIC MANNERS

• The Portuguese are very reserved with gestures, so don't be demonstrative.

• To wave to someone, extend your arm, palm up, and wave your fingers back and forth.

• You can bargain in markets where local crafts are sold, but don't bargain in shops or food markets.

• Both in public and private, defer to older people. Always wait until they have finished speaking before saying anything.

• Walk to the left of an older person, especially when you're going down the street.

• Don't eat anything but ice cream cones in the street.

• Be aware that going to the cinema is a social occasion in Portugal. People dress up and socialize in the foyer before the film and during the

two intermissions. Remember to buy tickets for movies in advance, just as you would for theaters in the U.S.

• Don't photograph military installations. In many places you'll see a camera with an "x" through it on a sign, which indicates that photography is forbidden. Often, the purpose is to promote the sale of slides, not to guard national security.

DRESS

• Dress more formally in Portugal than you would in America, even for casual occasions. The Portuguese tend to dress quite elegantly at all times.

• For business, men should wear suits and ties, even when it's very hot. However, if Portuguese businessmen remove their jackets, you may do the same. Women should wear dresses and heels.

• If you are invited to dinner, note that appropriate dress would be suits and ties for men, and dresses for women.

• For the cinema, men wear jackets and ties, and women

wear skirts and blouses, or dresses.

• An opera or theater opening calls for formal wear: tuxedos for men, dark dresses for women.

MEALS

Hours and Foods

Breakfast *(o pequeno almoço):* 7:30 to 8:00 a.m. The typical breakfast features bread, butter and jam, and coffee mixed with hot milk.

Lunch *(o almoço):* 12:00 to 2:00 p.m. Expect soup, then fish or meat with rice or potatoes and a vegetable. Salad accompanies the main course and may be served on the same plate. Wine and bread will be served with the meal (corn bread in the North and wheat bread in the South). The meal ends with fruit, dessert (a sweet or cheese and crackers) and coffee.

Dinner *(o jantar):* 7:30 to 8:00 p.m. This is a large meal with the same courses as lunch. At a dinner party, a fish course may be added before the main or meat course. Before-dinner drinks will

probably be dry, white port, or scotch for men and Cinzano for women. Wine is served with the meal, but in summer people sometimes drink beer. After dinner, *aguardente,* a very strong local brandy, may be served with the coffee.

Breaks: If you're invited to someone's home at 4:00 p.m., be prepared to sample a variety of appetizers, such as codfish cakes and Portuguese sausages baked in bread. Otherwise, people commonly have pastry and tea or espresso at 5:00 p.m.

Table Manners

• When dishes are passed around the table family-style, help yourself first, because you're the guest; then pass food to older people at the table.

• Don't start eating each course until everyone has been served.

• If there is a fish course, there will be separate utensils for it: a fish knife, which resembles a butter knife; and a fish fork, which looks like a salad fork.

• To eat as the Portuguese do, hold your fork in your left hand and your knife in your right. When you have finished, place the knife and fork, with the tines up, vertically on the plate.

• Never eat with your hands.

Even fruit should be eaten with a knife and fork.

• Don't put your hands in your lap when you're at the table. You can put your wrists on the table, but never your elbows.

• Keep your napkin in your lap. Don't tie it around your neck even when eating very messy foods, such as lobster.

• At a formal dinner, expect the host to say a few words to the guests before the meat course begins.

• Don't use bread to soak up gravy.

• You'll be pressed strongly to take second helpings. Take very small portions the first time, as you're expected to eat everything on your plate.

• Before leaving the table, fold your napkin.

• It's customary to smoke after a meal, but not between courses. Ask permission from your hostess.

• If you're invited to dinner, feel free to stay until 11:00 or even 11:30 p.m. Most people don't go to bed before 11:30 or 12:00 p.m.

Places to Eat

• Look for the following types of eating places:

A *cafe* offers coffee, drinks, small snacks, sandwiches and croissants with ham.

A *cervejaria* has a pub-like atmosphere and features beer, snacks (usually seafood such as clams and shrimps), or small steaks, which are cooked in heavy olive oil.

A *pastelaria* serves pastries, small snacks, coffee, tea, wine and local brandy.

A *restaurante* serves full meals. At the entrance, look for a sign telling whether the restaurant is first, second or third class. First-class restaurants usually don't have menus posted in the window.

• When you enter a first-class restaurant, wait for a maitre d' to seat you. In other restaurants, seat yourself.

• Don't hesitate to take children of any age into restaurants. Children eight years old or younger are charged half price. Very young children can share your food.

• Use a hand gesture to signal the waiter when you want to order and when you want the check.

Specialties

• A popular food in Portugal is *bacalhau* (salt-dried codfish). The Portuguese call it *"o fiel amigo"* ("the faithful friend") because there are over 300 ways to cook it. It is frequently prepared with tomatoes, olives, garlic and potatoes, and baked in the oven.

• Other Portuguese specialties are *bolinhos de bacalhau* (codfish cakes with parsley, coriander and mint); *caldo verde* (a popular soup made with mashed potatoes, kale and slices of sausage); *presunto* (air-cured mountain ham); *porco com amêijoas à alentejana* (pork in a marinade with clams, onions, pimentos, tomatoes, coriander and lemon juice); *lombo de porco com pimentos vermelhas doces* (marinated pork loin with sweet red peppers); *amêijoas na cataplana* (clams cooked in a special metal container and prepared with onions, hot pepper, garlic, paprika, sausage, tomatoes, parsley and ham); and *escabeche* (fish pickled with carrots, onions and bay leaves).

• For dessert, try *flan* (caramel custard) and *figos recheados* (dried figs stuffed with chocolate and almonds, and served with port).

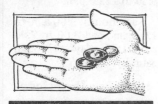

TIPPING

• Restaurants: If a service charge is included in your bill (and it usually is), leave an extra 50 escudos on the table. If it isn't, leave 10-15% of your bill as the tip.

• Taxis: No matter what the fare, give 25 to 50 escudos.

• Porters: Tip 20 escudos per bag.

• Cloakroom attendants: Tip 10 escudos.

• Washroom attendants: Tip 10 to 25 escudos.

• Gas station attendants: Tip 25 escudos.

• Ushers: Give 5 to 15 escudos.

PRIVATE HOMES

• Don't give yourself a house tour by wandering through rooms, and don't follow your hostess into the kitchen unless she specifically invites you there.

• If you're staying with a family for a few days, offer to help in the kitchen. Usually, but not always, your offer will be refused. To the Portuguese, hospitality means that they entertain, and that guests enjoy themselves.

• People who have entertained American house guests will understand if you want a daily bath, but others may not. Always ask your host or hostess if it is convenient for you to have a bath, because bath water may have to be heated in advance.

• If you must make a call from a private home, ask permission first and be sure to pay for your calls. Look up the prices for local calls in the telephone directory, but for long-distance calls, ask the operator to tell you how much the call will cost before you make it.

Gifts: Don't feel obligated to bring a gift if you are invited to dinner. Instead, reciprocate by taking your hosts to a restaurant.

If you feel more comfortable bringing a gift, select expensive chocolates as a first choice, and flowers as a second. Don't bring inexpensive flowers, and don't bring chrysanthemums. Never bring wine as a gift because it's relatively inexpensive, and most people have good wine cellars.

If you're staying with a family, consider bringing a gift from the U.S. People enjoy receiving American handicrafts, American Indian jewelry and books about the U.S. If you bring something electric, take into account the differences in electric current.

BUSINESS

Hours

Government and business office hours: 9:00 a.m. to 1:00 p.m., and 3:00 to 7:00 p.m., Monday through Saturday. Some government agencies are open at different times. As a precautionary measure, phone in advance to check on the time schedule.

Bank hours: 9:30 a.m. to noon, and 2:00 to 4:00 p.m., Monday through Friday, and from 9:30 to 11:30 a.m. on Saturday. Some banks in tourist areas have a currency exchange service open from 6:30 to 11:00 p.m.

Shop hours: 9:00 a.m. to 1:00 p.m., and 3:00 to 7:00 p.m., Monday through Saturday.

Business Practices

• Don't plan business trips during August, as people take their vacations then.

• Check your tentative itinerary with the Portuguese Tourist Office to be sure you don't plan a business visit during a town holiday, when businesses are closed.

• If you want to make business arrangements by letter before a trip to Portugal, have your letter translated into Portuguese.

• When doing business with a small company, be prepared to hire an interpreter, since you may not find anyone who speaks English working there.

• Keep a relaxed attitude about time. It's good manners to be punctual, but people will be very tolerant if you are late. Expect others to be from 15 to 30 minutes late.

• Ask for someone's business card only if he or she is a senior member of a company.

• When your business colleagues offer you a drink (usually coffee, a soft drink or an alcoholic drink), accept something.

• Plan to do business at lunch rather than at dinner. Dinner with business colleagues should be a social event, and spouses should be included.

Gifts: If you have established contact with business people in Portugal, ask them what gift they would like from the U.S. People often like to receive technical books, which are difficult to obtain, or computer programs.

HOLIDAYS AND SPECIAL OCCASIONS

Holidays: New Year's Day (January 1), Shrove Tuesday (the day before Ash Wednesday; in February), Good Friday, Liberty Day (April 25), Labor Day (May 1), National Day (June 10), Feast of St. Anthony (June 13; Lisbon only), Feast of St. John (June 24; Oporto only), Assumption Day (August 15), Proclamation of the Republic (October 5), All Saints' Day (November 1), Independence Day (December 1), Feast of the Immaculate Conception (December 8), Christmas Eve (December 24) and Christmas (December 25).

• When in Lisbon, join in the celebrations on the Feast of St. Anthony, patron saint of the city. On the evening of June 12, there are parades, and on June 13, businesses and stores are closed. There are folk dance competitions, and some areas of the city are closed off for dancing in the streets. If you are invited to someone's home, bring flowers.

TRANSPORTATION
Public Transportation

• On buses, the fare depends on how far you're going. Give the driver exact change when you get on.

• On streetcars in Lisbon, pay when you get on. Exact change isn't required.

• On subways in Lisbon, you pay a flat rate, regardless of the distance you travel. Buy a ticket as you enter the subway.

• Buy a ticket before boarding trains, or you will be fined.

• Hail taxis in the street. For a long ride outside of town you may have to pay the driver for the return trip as well. Taxis are very inexpensive.

Driving

• Be cautious when driving because roads are poor, and drivers tend to be very aggressive.

• Always wear seat belts.

• If a police officer stops you for a traffic violation, pay the ticket later. If you believe you did nothing wrong, explain your actions to the officer, and you may avoid the citation.

• Expect parking to be a chaotic free-for-all. Cars are parked almost everywhere, often on sidewalks. However, in areas close to the downtown section of cities, parking regulations are more strictly enforced. If you find that your car has been towed, go to the police station.

• As a pedestrian, be aware that drivers don't pay attention to crosswalks. Always watch for traffic when crossing streets.

LEGAL MATTERS AND SAFETY

• There are no restrictions on drinking hours, and there is no legal drinking age. Liquor and wine is sold in supermarkets and pastry shops.

• Be aware that women commonly attend nightclubs only when accompanied by one or more persons.

• Women may go into a cafe alone but should not go to a bar alone. It may bring unwelcome attention, since it is not a common practice by local women.

• To be on the safe side, women should take taxis after 8:00 or 9:00 p.m., when there aren't many people on the streets.

KEY PHRASES

English	Portuguese	Pronunciation
Good day	Bom dia	Bawng dée-a
Good evening	Boa noite	Bó-a nóy-tuh
Please	Por favor	Por fa-vór
Thank you (by man)	Obrigado	O-bree-gáh-doo
Thank you (by woman)	Obrigada	O-bree-gáh-da
You're welcome	De nada	Day náh-dah
Yes	Sim	Seeng
No	Não	Náh-oo
Sir, Mr.	Senhor	Sayn-yór
Madame, Mrs.	Senhora	Sayn-yór-a
Miss	Menina	Ma-née-nah
Excuse me	Con licença	Con lee-sénsa
Good-bye	Adeus	A-dáy-oosh
I don't speak Portuguese.	Eu não falo português.	Ay-oo náh-oo fáh-loo por-too-gáysh
Does anyone here speak English?	Há alguén que fale inglês?	Ah áhl-guyng kay fáhl een-gláysh

CHAPTER NINETEEN

ROMANIA

In the unlikely event that you fly from Paris directly to Bucharest, you may suffer a brief attack of "déja vu." With its wide boulevards and parks, Bucharest has often been described as the "Paris of Eastern Europe."

As a Western visitor to Romania, you will be the object of great curiosity. Travel abroad by Romanians is very restricted, and they are eager to know what life in America is like. They will probably be familiar with the less attractive aspects of life here, because those will have been stressed in the local press. But they will also be eager to know how you live: Do you have a car? What kind? How much do you earn? As a guest in the country, you'll have to walk a fine line between boasting of the numbers of luxuries Americans enjoy and defending our record on unemployment and rights for minorities and women.

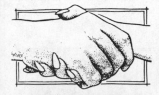

GREETINGS

• Always shake hands when being introduced. Also shake hands each time you meet and take leave of someone, no matter how many times you encounter that person in a day.

• Men should rise when being introduced, but women need not.

• When a Romanian man is introduced to a woman, don't be surprised if he kisses her hand lightly. An American man should simply shake hands with a Romanian woman.

• Expect great displays of affection among good friends. Members of the same sex greet one another by kissing on both cheeks, and male friends often kiss one another on the mouth.

• At a party, wait for your host or hostess to introduce you to each person there.

• Use a person's title before the last name if you're speaking to a male or female doctor, professor, lawyer or engineer.

CONVERSATION

• Be prepared for Romanians to treat you, a foreigner, in a formal manner. Follow their lead if they use your last name rather than your first.

• Good topics of conversation: sports; travel; and non-political international subjects, such as films, music, fashion and books.

• Topics to avoid: politics, the U.S.S.R. or Communism. Skirt controversial topics and never mention any negative aspects of Romania, such as the lines to buy food.

• When you first meet someone, don't ask questions about anything to do with the person's family, job or money.

• Be aware that every conversation with a foreigner is likely to be reported.

TELEPHONES

• Look for public phone booths on streets and in hotels, candy stores, cafes and restaurants. For a local call, deposit a 25-bani coin and dial. For long-distance calls from public phones, go to the post office, where you pay when the call is finished.

• When answering the phone, say *"Alo."*

PUBLIC MANNERS

• Do not photograph industrial plants or military installations. In fact, before taking any picture, check carefully for the sign showing a camera with an "x" through it (the international symbol for "No Photography Permitted"). Violating this ban is a serious offense in Romania.

• In public bathrooms, you must pay for toilet paper in addition to giving the attend-

ant a tip. Consider bringing toilet paper or tissues with you from abroad, as toilets outside the cities generally have only newspaper.

DRESS

• Note that jeans are worn everywhere in Romania by men and women.

• Everyone can wear shorts and thongs at the seaside, but don't wear them in cities.

• For business, men should wear dark suits, white shirts and ties. Younger men can wear lighter-colored suits and striped or colored shirts. Make sure that shoes are well-polished. In hot weather short-sleeved shirts without jackets are acceptable. Women should wear suits and heels.

• For dinner in a restaurant or in someone's home, dress up: suits for men and dresses for women. In better restaurants men must also wear ties.

• Don't bother to bring formal wear (tuxedos for men, long skirts for women), as it's not worn.

• When visiting a Greek Orthodox church, women should wear skirts and have their shoulders covered, though they need not cover their heads.

MEALS

Hours and Foods

Breakfast *(micul de-jun)*: 6:00 a.m. for those who work in factories; about an hour later for others. You can expect bread, butter, marmalade and a cup of tea or milk.

Lunch *(dejun)*: Noon. A family meal begins with soup, often vegetable or vegetable beef, or an appetizer such as eggplant salad. The main course could be fish, stew or stuffed cabbage. Some type of bread is usually served, and wine and water accompany the meal. Lunch ends with a dessert of fruit or preserves.

A more formal meal will begin with plum or pear brandy and appetizers, such as cubes of feta cheese, olives and small meatballs. The main course is often grilled pork or beef, served with salad. Dessert could be fruit, coffeecake, strudel or choc-olate cake. Turkish coffee and cognac are served after dessert.

Dinner *(masa de seara)*: 7:00 to 7:30 p.m. This is usually a fairly light meal consisting of leftovers, noodle or dumpling dishes, or cheese and rolls. Yogurt and tea follow. A dinner party will be the same as a formal noon meal.

Table Manners

• If you are a guest at dinner, you will sit at the end of the table opposite your host, so that everyone can hear the conversation.

• Expect several toasts at formal and informal meals. Touch glasses several times during the meal and say "Good luck" or "To your health."

• To eat Romanian-style, keep your fork in your left hand and your knife in your right hand.

• Don't put your napkin in your lap. Keep it on the table.

• When your plate is brought to you, be prepared to sample everything on it. Don't distress your host and hostess by suggesting in any way that you don't care for a particular food.

• When you are invited to dinner, plan to leave about 10:00 p.m. If you notice the host putting the cork back into the wine bottle, take this as a signal for guests to go.

Places to Eat

• Try the following alternatives to restaurants:

A *bar* sells alcoholic drinks, pastries, tea and coffee, as well as cigarettes.

A *braserie* serves coffee, alcoholic drinks, pastries and pretzels. Some also have grills.

In addition to standard restaurants, there are many outdoor restaurants serving complete meals.

• Ask the waiter what's available before ordering, as food shortages are common.

• As a usual rule, seat yourself.

Specialties

• Look for these special foods of Romania: *mititei* (grilled spiced, skinless sausages, served as appetizers); *sarmale* (cabbage leaves stuffed with pork balls); *mamiglia* (corn mush, served as a side dish with most meals); *ghiveci* (a variety of vegetables, cooked in olive oil and served cold); *pîrjoale* (highly spiced meat patties); *nisetru la gratar* (grilled Black Sea sturgeon); and *scrumbii la gratar* (grilled herring).

For dessert try *baclava* (layers of thin pastry filled with nuts and cinnamon and dredged in a honey syrup);

cataif cu frisca (a pastry soaked in syrup, served with whipped cream); and *placinta cu brinza* (sweet cheese pie).

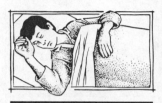

HOTELS

• To obtain a hotel room, it may be necessary to tip the registration clerk.

• When you check in, expect the hotel clerk to ask for your passport and keep it overnight, so that everything can be copied onto special forms for the police.

• Don't be shy about asking for advice on restaurants and tourist attractions. The hotel staff probably will be very helpful.

• Never leave valuables in your room. Leave them at the reception desk, where you'll be given a receipt.

• Should you break anything in your room, be sure to pay for it. Otherwise the chambermaid will have to pay.

• Don't take any of the hotel's towels or ashtrays as souvenirs. Before you pay your bill, someone will check to see if anything is missing, and you may be asked to open your suitcase in the hotel lobby.

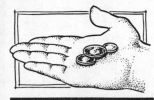

TIPPING

• Restaurants: If the service was excellent, leave an extra 5-10%, although 12% is automatically added to all checks. If the tip is not included, hand 10% to the waiter. Don't leave the tip on the table.

• Porters and taxi drivers: Tip 5 to 10 lei.

• For special services, people appreciate a package of cigarettes as a tip.

PRIVATE HOMES

• Don't plan a spontaneous visit to a private home, whether it's just for a drink or for a stay of several days. Your potential hosts must report to the local police that they would like to have you as a visitor. The police will then decide whether or not the visit will be permitted.

• Don't be surprised if your hosts offer to buy your clothes. You can sell them or give them as gifts. However, if you're approached on the street by someone wanting to buy your clothes, don't agree to sell them, as it could be an undercover agent.

• If you're staying in a private home, make a good impression by offering to help in the kitchen. The offer probably will be refused, but the family will be pleased that you want to share in household chores.

• If you really want to help, offer to shop and pay for some of the food. There are long lines to buy food, usually with a great deal of pushing and shoving. If both husband and wife work outside of the home, they probably have to wait in such lines after work to buy food for supper and would be especially grateful to you for undertaking this chore.

• Check with your hosts about taking baths. Sometimes water can be heated for daily baths, but in many apartments, hot water is available only twice a week.

• Should you call from a phone in a private home, offer to pay. If your host refuses to accept the money, buy him a gift before you leave the country.

Gifts: If you are invited to a meal, bring wrapped flowers (roses or carnations are good choices) or wine.

If you're staying with a family, good gifts to bring are jeans, perfume, cosmetics or coffee beans, which are in very short supply.

BUSINESS

Hours

Business and government office hours: 8:00 a.m. until 4:00 p.m., Monday through Friday, and 8:00 a.m. until 12:30 p.m. on Saturday.

Bank hours: 9:00 a.m. to noon and 1:00 to 3:00 p.m., Monday through Friday, and 8:00 a.m. until noon on Saturday.

Store and shop hours: 8:00 a.m. until noon (or from 9:00 a.m. until 1:00 p.m.) and 4:00 to 8:00 p.m., Monday through Saturday. Some also open from 8:00 a.m. until noon on Sunday.

Business Practices

• If you are writing a letter to a Romanian business, write in English. The recipient will then pay special attention to it.

• Find an interpreter through the National Tourist Office. If you are dealing with State Foreign Trade Enterprises, expect them to provide their own interpreter.

• To make a good impression, business people should stay at one of the country's prestigious hotels.

• Romanians are very punctual, so be sure to be on time.

• Bring a large supply of business cards, and make sure that your full title is printed on them.

• Although French is more widely spoken than English, you will usually find in business meetings that one or more of the people speak English. In some areas, Russian and Hungarian are also spoken.

• You must practice patience in your business dealings in Romania. People aren't operating from the profit motive—they will earn the same amount whether they make 50 or 500 sales in a year—so there is little reason for them to respond to pressure. You'll also find that the country's bureaucracy slows down decision making.

• Remember that once a successful relationship with a company is established, you can expect to do business with the company for a very long time.

• Make your own lunch or

dinner arrangements. Romanian business people attempt to keep office expenses to a minimum and do not entertain clients, as a general practice.

Gifts: To celebrate the signing of a contract or the Christmas holiday, give gifts such as lighters or pens with your company's name on them, but don't give expensive gifts.

HOLIDAYS AND SPECIAL OCCASIONS

Holidays: New Year's (January 1 and 2), Labor Days (May 1 and 2), Romanian National Days (August 23 and 24).

• Note that Christmas and Easter are not legal holidays and businesses and shops may be open. For those people who do observe these holidays, Christmas is celebrated on December 25 and Easter is celebrated according to the Greek Orthodox calendar (see Greece for an explanation).

TRANSPORTATION

Public Transportation

• Keep in mind that bus fare depends on the distance traveled. When you get on, tell the conductor where you want to go.

• Board streetcars at the rear door and pay the conductor, who will be on your right. Hold on to your ticket; inspectors sometimes get on to make sure everyone has a ticket. Exit via the streetcar's front door.

• Look for taxis on the street or at taxi stands. You'll find the stands near big restaurants and theaters or at railroad or bus stations. You can also phone for a taxi.

Driving

• You won't need an international driver's license to drive in Romania.

• Seatbelts aren't compulsory, but you must carry a red-reflector warning triangle in case of breakdown.

• Keep your passport handy in case you encounter a road-block where police stop people for security checks.

• If you are stopped for a traffic violation, expect an on-the-spot fine to be imposed.

LEGAL MATTERS AND SAFETY

• Never argue with the police.

• Don't bring any Romanian currency into or out of the country, as this is illegal.

• Be prepared for the customs officials to ask why you are visiting Romania. "Sightseeing" or "business" are the usual answers.

• When you leave Romania, you may bring out Romanian merchandise worth up to 1000 lei, tax-free. Anything in excess of this will be taxed.

• Don't tip anyone with foreign currency. It's illegal.

• Someone may approach you in a public place and suggest that you exchange money at a rate favorable to you. Don't do it. The practice is illegal, and the person could be an undercover police officer.

• Note that the legal drinking age is 18, but this is not strictly enforced. Recently the government has been trying to restrict the sale of liquor before noon, but this has not been very successful.

• Feel secure in walking alone after dark. Most people don't have cars, and the streets are crowded with pedestrians. Also, police patrol constantly.

KEY PHRASES

English	Romanian	Pronunciation
Hello; how do you do?	Bună ziua	Boó-na zee-wah
Good morning	Bună dimineața	Boó-na dee-mee-nay-áh-tah
Good evening	Bună seara	Boó-na say-áh-rah
Good night	Noapte bună	Nó-ahp-tay boó-na
Please	Vă rog	Vah-rog
Thank you	Mulțumesc	Muhl-tzoo-mésc
You're welcome	Cu plăcere	Koo plah-cháy-ray
Yes	Da	Dah
No	Nu	Noo
Sir, Mr.	Donnule	Dón-noo-lay
Madam, Mrs.	Doamna	Dó-ahm-nah
Miss	Domnisoara	Do-meen-ées-o-rah
Excuse me	Scuzați-mă	Scoo-zá-tee-mah
Good-bye	La revedere	Lah ray-vay-dáy-ray
I don't understand.	Nu înțeleg.	Noo int-zeh-lég
I don't speak Romanian.	Nu vorbesc românește.	Nóo vor-beéts ro-mahn-ésh-teh
Does anyone here speak English?	Vorbește cineva aici engleza?	Vor-bésh-teh shée-nay-vah aích en-gláy-zah

CHAPTER TWENTY

SPAIN

Spain—a synonym for romance: castles, the Man of La Mancha, the flamenco. Even bullfighting, which some visitors consider a barbarity, and which the Spanish regard as art, is romantic.

From this romance emerges the hero, a man unique, a man of pride and honor. To this day, the Spanish male's overriding concern is his honor.

When dealing with Spaniards, either socially or in business, never forget their pride in their individuality. And never offend a Spaniard's honor by causing embarrassment in any way. You would be affronting something that the people hold sacred.

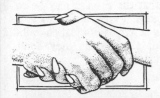

GREETINGS

• Both men and women should shake hands when first introduced to someone, as well as when meeting or leaving someone.

• Notice how frequently Spanish people show affection. Men who know each other well will embrace when meeting, and women will kiss each other on the cheek, as well as embrace. If you are meeting an old friend or a relative, do the same.

• Observe that a Spanish "last" name consists of the surname followed by the mother's maiden name. In correspondence, use both names (for example, Mr. Garcia-Lopez), but use only the surname (Mr. Garcia), in conversation.

• Keep in mind that even though a person who's older or of higher rank may call you by your first name, you should still address that person as Mr. or Mrs., with the last name.

CONVERSATION

• Use family names and titles in addressing people until you become well acquainted.

• Good topics of conversation: politics (but don't make political comparisons between Spain and the U.S.); U.S. lifestyles, and sports, especially soccer.

• Topics to avoid: religion; and an individual's family, job, interests or hobbies—until you are well acquainted.

• Never make negative comments regarding bullfighting.

TELEPHONES

• Look for public telephones in cafes, restaurants, phone booths and special public telephone buildings. For a local call, deposit 5 pesetas before dialing.

• Only make calls to places outside of Europe from phones at a telephone company office. Pay the cashier after you complete the call. If you're calling somewhere in Europe, you can make the call from a phone booth.

• If you make a call from a home, offer to pay, as people pay a charge for each call made.

PUBLIC MANNERS

• Realize that the American "okay" sign, with thumb and index finger forming a circle, is a vulgar gesture in Spain.

• Keep in mind that the Spanish have a casual attitude about arriving on time for social occasions, as well as business appointments. It is not only common, but acceptable, to be 15 to 30 minutes late.

• Don't be offended if people interrupt you frequently in conversation. In Spain it's not considered rude—just animated.

• If you ask directions, realize that the Spanish may be so eager to help that they give you wrong information, rather than admit they don't know.

• If several people start madly scrambling for a phone booth or taxi, smile and step aside. When they realize you're a tourist, they'll usually let you go first.

• Don't be surprised to see that men and women use the same public bathrooms, especially in small towns.

• If you enjoy gambling, look for booths on the street where you can buy lottery tickets, slot machines in bars, and casinos.

• Women should be aware that eye contact carries an important cue to men. When a woman returns a man's gaze, he interprets it as an expression of interest.

• Realize that Spanish men often call out expressions of admiration as women pass on the street. If you don't react or acknowledge them, the callers won't bother you.

• Check before you photograph. Don't take pictures of military areas and policemen in uniform and be aware that many museums will ask that you leave your camera at the door. If you wish to take a close-up of a person, ask the individual for permission first.

DRESS

• Don't wear bathing suits and beach attire anywhere but at the beach or in resort areas.

• Note that Spaniards dress elegantly, even for casual occasions. Don't wear scruffy or worn clothing if you want to fit in.

• For business, women should wear dresses or blouses and skirts, but never pantsuits. Men should wear jackets and ties, even in warm weather. It is customary to keep jackets buttoned, except when sitting.

• When invited to dinner, women should wear dresses, or skirts and blouses. Men wear jackets with ties and black shoes.

• Dress formally only for charity balls or official dinners. When an invitation specifies formal wear, women should wear long dresses, and men should wear tuxedos.

• Women may wear pants when visiting churches, but they should avoid sundresses and other clothing exposing the shoulders. No one should wear shorts in a place of worship. Women needn't wear hats or other head covering.

MEALS

Hours and Foods

Breakfast (el desayuno): 7:00 to 8:00 a.m. The meal consists of rolls, butter, marmalade, and coffee with hot milk, or cocoa. If you have breakfast in a restaurant, the waiter will pour half a cup of coffee, adding hot milk until you tell him to stop.

Lunch (el almuerzo): 2:00 to 3:00 p.m. This is the main meal of the day. It generally starts with soup, followed by a salad and the main course of fish or meat with vegetables. Wine and water are usually served with the meal. Fruit, followed by pastries and finally coffee, usually served in a small cup, end the meal.

Dinner (la cena): 9:00 to 10:00 p.m. If it's a family meal, dinner will be light. A typical meal could be a potato omelet or cold cuts, cheese and bread.

If it's a social occasion, dinner is often preceded by a stop at a *tapas* bar (see

Places to Eat). Before-dinner drinks include sherry, whiskey, and gin and tonic. Notice that the Spanish mix many kinds of liquor with cola; scotch and cola is a familiar combination. A dinner party usually includes soup or an appetizer, followed by meat or fish, vegetables and salad. Bread and wine will be served throughout the meal. Fruit is a common dessert, but if it's a social occasion, ice cream or cakes are often served. Coffee and cognac or other liqueurs end the meal.

Table Manners

• Notice that the guest of honor is seated to the host's right, while the hostess sits at the end of the table, opposite the host.

• Look for two plates at each place setting, one on top of the other. The top one is for the first course.

• The fruit knife and fork, or other dessert utensils, will be located above the plate. There is one glass for wine and another for water.

• Eat with the fork in the left hand and the knife in the right, using the knife to push food onto the back of the fork. Never use your fingers to push food onto the fork.

• Ask for juice or a soft drink if you do not care for wine. There is no pressure to drink socially. Plain or bottled water is usually served with meals.

• Be aware that there won't be a bread-and-butter plate. Bread is put on a coaster next to your plate, or simply placed on the table. Butter is only served with bread at breakfast.

• Keep your wrists on the table and your hands out of your lap.

• Observe the variety of ways that food is served. Food may be passed around the table on platters. Sometimes the hostess serves or offers the serving honor to a guest. When a family has a maid, she usually serves.

• Be honest if you aren't hungry, and you won't be pressed to eat. Spaniards don't like to see food wasted, so it is better to decline food than to leave it on your plate.

• Lay the fork and knife side by side on the plate to indicate you have finished. Leaving them on opposite sides of the plate suggests that you either weren't satisfied or that you haven't finished.

• Stay until about midnight, unless conversation is lively, and everyone is obviously having a good time. Spaniards tend to stay up late.

Places to Eat

• A unique feature of Spanish dining is the *tapas* bar, which offers a wide variety of appetizers and drinks. If you're going out to dinner in a restaurant, it's customary to begin the evening at about 7:00 p.m. by visiting a few *tapas* bars. Some people prefer to start about 8:00 p.m. and make their meal of the *tapas*. Some popular *tapas:* shrimp, octopus, marinated mushrooms, potato omelets, snails in hot sauce, small squid, and red peppers with oil. The least expensive *tapas* are olives and potato chips. Customary drinks with *tapas* are sherry, beer and wine.

Most *tapas* bars have some tables, but people usually eat standing at the bar. Each portion is usually enough for two and usually comes with two forks Bread is often served with *tapas*.

• Note the wide variety of places to eat in Spain.

An *asador* is a restaurant featuring steaks, roast suckling pig, roast lamb and fish.

A *bar* serves *tapas,* alcoholic drinks, soft drinks, coffee or tea.

Cafes serve *tapas,* sandwiches, some hot meals such as fried eggs or hamburgers, alcoholic drinks and coffee.

Marisquerias are restaurants that serve only seafood.

A *mesón* serves many varieties of *tapas* and wine. The decor is usually more pleasing than in a bar.

Pastelerías offer pastries, sandwiches, tea, coffee and soft drinks.

Tabernas are the oldest type of restaurants. They are usually family businesses and offer home-style cooking, with a standard menu and a few specials every day.

• Women are not advised to eat alone in a *bar* or a *mesón*.

• Summon a waiter by holding up an index finger and making eye contact. Never call out or shout.

• Be emphatically insistent when ordering meat cooked rare. Most restaurants overcook steak by American standards.

• You'll find that the food in restaurants is rarely hot or even warm. If you want a hot meal, mention it to the waiter specifically.

• Note that the waiter will not bring you the check until you ask. If you're in a rush, ask for the check when your food is served.

• Although some restaurants give the ceramic jugs in which wine is served to patrons, never assume that you may take one. You can also find similar jugs for sale in ceramic shops.

Specialties

• Try these Spanish treats: *churros* (deep-fried crullers served for breakfast); *gazpacho* (a cold soup of tomatoes, cucumbers, peppers, onions, garlic, olive oil and vinegar); *sopa de ajo* (garlic soup, with garlic cloves, olive oil, egg and bread); *cocido madrileño* (a meal of soup, followed by garbanzo beans and meat—ham, chicken, beef and salt pork—with three kinds of sauces, and carrots, leeks and cabbage); *paella* (rice with saffron, clams, mussels, squid, chorizo sausage, chicken, pork, ham and olive oil); *empanadas* (meat-filled turnovers); *tortilla de patata* (potato and onion omelet); and *zarzuela de mariscos* (Catalonian shellfish stew flavored with herbs and saffron).

• For dessert try *flan* (caramel custard) and *turrón* (candy made of almonds, egg white, and honey).

• Note that *anguilas* (eels sauteed in olive oil and garlic) are served squirming on the plate with the eyes sticking out. Don't be surprised, however, if a Spaniard recommends them, as they are considered an expensive delicacy.

• Also keep in mind that *morcilla* is fried blood sausage, and *calamares en su tinta* is squid prepared in its own ink.

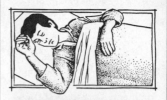

HOTELS

• Be ready to show your passport when registering. The desk clerk may need it to fill out forms, but you'll have it back within a few hours.

• Note that "C" on the water faucet or tap stands for "hot" and "F" stands for "cold."

• Leave your key at the reception desk when you go out.

• Make any complaint directly to the manager. For example, if your bed wasn't made properly, talk to the manager rather than the maid. Hotels and restaurants have official complaint forms that government inspectors check once a month. Ask to fill one out if you're not satisfied, and you may get a refund later.

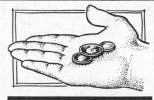

TIPPING

• Restaurants: Leave 15% if the tip isn't included in the bill. For exceptional service, leave another 5% on the table. Also consider complimenting the waiter personally, as such compliments are appreciated.

• Taxis: Give drivers 10% of the fare.

• Porters: Give 75 pesetas per bag.

• Cloakroom attendants: Tip 25 to 50 pesetas.

• Gas station attendants: Offer 10 to 25 pesetas.

• Washroom attendants: Tip 10 pesetas.

• House servants: Give 500 pesetas or a small gift to each house servant when you are a guest in a home for several days.

PRIVATE HOMES

• Call ahead before visiting, to make sure it's a convenient time. Visiting times are usually 4:00 to 6:00 p.m.

• Keep in mind that many people have a *siesta* or nap after the noon meal, so don't call or plan to visit at that time.

• Stay at least two hours when you visit a Spanish home, or you will be considered rude. If you're invited to a meal, you should also stay for a few hours afterwards.

• Realize that the Spanish are very formal about invitations, and won't extend a "spur of the moment" invitation.

• Consider it a great compliment to be invited to someone's home. Spaniards don't invite foreigners into their homes until they know them very well. They are more likely to entertain you in a restaurant.

• Keep in mind that children are regarded as very special members of the family. Whether you're paying a call or staying for some days with a family, be sure to pay special attention to the children.

• Note that in very traditional Spanish homes, the children do not eat with the adults. In most families, however, children and adults eat together.

• Bear in mind that your Spanish hosts will expect to spend the entire day with you while you are a guest in their home. Be diplomatic if you'd like some time by yourself. Offer to meet the family for dinner if possible.

• Please your hosts when you've been out for the day by bringing the children candy or a small toy.

• Avoid snacking in the home. Spaniards eat meals at set times and don't snack as Americans do. Never go to the refrigerator and help yourself.

• Realize that water is heated by electricity, which is expensive. Ask if it's convenient for you to have a bath or shower and don't use a lot of water.

• In homes employing servants, allow the maid to handle chores such as clearing the table. However, do offer to clear the table and do the dishes if there is no hired help. You probably won't be allowed to help if you're only there a few days.

Gifts: Choose pastries, cakes and chocolates as gifts, but no other types of food. Send or bring flowers when you're invited to dinner. Don't bring dahlias and chrysanthemums, as they are associated with funerals.

If you're a house guest, consider bringing gifts from the U.S., such as blue jeans, electric calculators, small electric appliances that are convertible or have 220 volt current, or American crafts,

such as quilts. Whistling tea kettles are a favorite, and American towels are much thicker than those usually available in Spain.

• When offered a gift, open it immediately.

BUSINESS

Hours

Business and government hours: 9:00 a.m. to 1:30 p.m., and 4:00 to 7:00 p.m., Monday through Friday, and 9:00 a.m. to 1:30 p.m. on Saturday. Some businesses are closed all day on Saturday.

Bank hours: 9:00 a.m. to 2:00 or 3:00 p.m., Monday through Friday, and 9:00 a.m. to 1:00 p.m. on Saturday. During the summer, banks close at 1:30 p.m., Monday through Friday, and at 12:30 p.m. on Saturday.

Shop hours: 9:00 or 10:00 a.m. to 1:00 or 2:00 p.m. In the winter, shops open in the afternoon from 4:00 to 7:00 p.m., in the summer, from 5:00 to 8:00 p.m.

Business Practices

• Allow ten days to two weeks when making an appointment from the U.S. by telex or telephone. If using international mail, allow three weeks to a month.

• Write in English when corresponding with Spanish business firms. An English letter translated into Spanish may not appear sufficiently formal and flowery and could offend the recipient.

• Don't make business trips to Spain from mid-July through the end of August, as most people vacation during that time.

• Good times of day for business appointments: between 10:00 a.m. and 12:30 p.m. Most business people take care of appointments in the morning and do paper work in the afternoon.

• Realize that everything, from businesses and government offices to schools, close from 1:00 to 4:00 p.m. for the *siesta*.

• Note that business people arrive at their offices around 9:00 to 10:00 a.m. At 2:00 p.m., they leave for a long lunch and return to work at 4:00 or 5:00 p.m., staying until 8:00 or 9:00 p.m. The usual time for a business lunch is 2:30 p.m.

• Use business cards in Spanish and English. A Spanish business card will have the two names used in all correspondence: the surname and the mother's maiden name.

• Be assured that most large firms conduct business in both English and Spanish.

• Use a Spanish contact to help you cultivate a relationship with business people or government officials. Spaniards value personal influence, and accomplishing anything on your own is very difficult.

• Never try to discuss business at the first meeting. You will be first judged as a person and asked questions about your background, education and interests. Then serious discussions can begin. Spaniards regard the impersonal efficiency often associated with Americans as very unpleasant, and so place great value on knowing business people as individuals.

• Never imply that someone hasn't properly prepared for a meeting. To do so would offend that person's honor, and to Spaniards, honor takes precedence over organization and efficiency. Also realize that imposing a decision in direct language is likely to be humiliating to your Spanish associates.

• Keep correspondence formal, even though you may have casual relationships in person with Spanish business people after the first meeting.

• Expect to be invited to business lunches and dinners. If

several people entertain you, reciprocate by inviting them all out to a meal together and include their spouses.

• Realize that it is very difficult for a woman to pay for a man's meal. Spanish men always expect to pay. When a businesswomen wants to entertain a Spanish businessman, she should speak to the maitre d' or waiter in advance and leave cash or a credit card. In the event that isn't possible, she should discreetly leave the table at the end of the meal to pay. When entertaining frequently, a women may be wise to use the same restaurant, so its staff will come to know her strategy.

HOLIDAYS AND SPECIAL OCCASIONS

Holidays: New Year's Day (January 1), Epiphany (January 6), St. Joseph's Day (March 19), Maundy Thursday, Good Friday, Labor Day (May 1), Corpus Christi (eight weeks after Easter), St. James Day (July 25), Assumption Day (August 15), Columbus Day (October 12), Immaculate Conception (December 8), Christmas (December 25).

• Realize that the Spanish exchange gifts (less elaborate than those in the U.S.) on January 6, rather than on Christmas. On the evening of the 5th, children put their shoes out on the balcony, and the next morning they find small gifts in them. If you are staying with a family at this time, buy a small gift for each child.

• Note that New Year's Eve is a time for family celebrations. At midnight, people drink champagne and eat one grape for each stroke of the clock.

• Be aware that each city celebrates its patron saint's day. The festivities can be very interesting, but if you're planning a business trip, check with the Spanish Tourist Office to make sure a holiday won't play havoc with your work schedule.

• Remember that when a holiday falls on a Tuesday or Thursday, it's customary to take a long weekend.

TRANSPORTATION

Public Transportation

• Buy your Madrid and Barcelona subway tickets at the subway entrance and keep them until the end of your trip. You pay one fare no matter how far you go. Realize that subways are always crowded and uncomfortably hot in the summer.

• Pay when you get on a bus and keep your ticket stub until you get off. You can save money by purchasing a book of bus tickets.

• Keep in mind that a *Tranvía* is a slow train, a *Talgo* is a fast, comfortable inter-city train and the *Rápido* is an express train with sleeping accommodations.

• Realize that refreshment service is usually not available on trains. It is best to bring your own food and drink.

Driving

• Be aware that an international driver's license is recommended but not required.

• Everyone in the front seat must wear seat belts outside city limits.

• Expect to hear car horns blowing loudly when a traffic light turns from red to green.

• Look for red and yellow striped poles, which indicate an emergency phone, when you need help on the highway. There are instructions in English. Press one button for an ambulance, another for a tow-truck. A light will go on when the message has been received.

• Be polite if you are stopped for a traffic violation; don't argue or become excited. Trying to bribe a policeman can lead to even more serious problems.

• Ask for a personal bail bond when you get your green card for insurance or when you rent a car. Without it, you could end up in prison for a long time if you have an accident.

• Note that the Spanish do not have strict laws about drinking and driving, as most European countries do, but if you drink and are involved in an accident, you will be heavily fined.

• Expect heavy fines and even imprisonment if you are involved in an accident in which Spanish people are injured, whether or not you have been drinking.

LEGAL MATTERS AND SAFETY

• If you want to get a tax refund on goods bought in Spain that you plan to take out of the country, ask when you buy the item. Some small stores will subtract the tax right away. (Bring your passport in case someone asks for proof that you are a foreigner.)

Other stores will give you a form to fill out. Take the form to a special counter at the airport (near the customs area). They will submit the form to the government and the government should then mail the refund to you. Seasoned travelers to Spain say that you should not count on receiving the refund.

• Realize that there is no legal drinking age in Spain and that there are no restrictions on when you can buy a drink in a bar or restaurant.

• Be advised that women going out alone after dark should take a taxi or a bus. The subways in Madrid and Barcelona have long, dark corridors that could be dangerous.

KEY PHRASES

English	Spanish	Pronunciation
Good day	Buenos días	Bwáy-nos dée-ahs
Good evening	Buenas noches	Bwáy-nahs nó-chase
Please	Por favor	Pór fah-vor
Thank you	Gracias	Grá-see-ahs
You're welcome	De nada	Day náh-dah
Yes	Sí	See
No	No	No
Sir, Mr.	Señor	Sen-yóhr
Madam, Mrs.	Señora	Sen-yóhr-ah
Miss	Señorita	Sen-yohr-ée-tah
Excuse me	Perdóneme	Pehr dó-nay-may
Good-bye	Adiós	Ah-dýos
I don't understand.	No entiendo.	No en-tyén-doe
I don't speak Spanish.	No hablo español.	No áhblo es-pahn-yól
Is there anyone who speaks English?	¿Hay alguien que hable inglés?	Ahy áhl-gyehn kay áh-blay een-gláys

CHAPTER TWENTY-ONE

SWEDEN

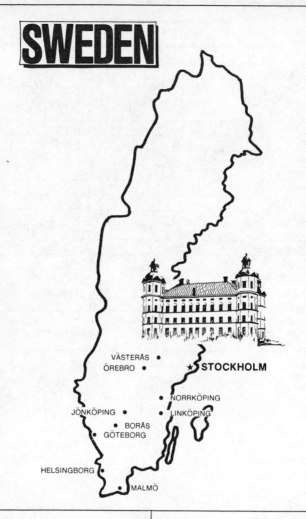

VÄSTERÅS •
ÖREBRO •
★ **STOCKHOLM**

• NORRKÖPING
JÖNKÖPING • • LINKÖPING

• BORÅS
GÖTEBORG •

HELSINGBORG •

• MALMÖ

Sweden may be best known for giving the world two Bergmans: beautiful Ingrid, and Ingmar, the brilliant director whose films have explored the darker side of humanity, a Swedish concern.

Swedes tend to be reserved but friendly. Oddly, you may find that they are more comfortable talking to foreigners than they are talking to other Swedes.

Swedes are at their very best—warmer and more open—during holiday celebrations. The Swedes are devoted to their deep and strong holiday traditions, some of which go back for centuries. They are also at their best when involved in sports. A friend who lived in Sweden for 14 years says, "When you see Swedes swimming or skiing, they have an almost pagan joy in nature. It's beautiful to watch."

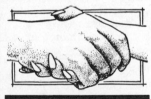

GREETINGS

• Shake hands when introduced. You don't have to shake hands with good friends, but always shake hands with older people when greeting them and when leaving.

• If there is no third party to introduce you when you enter a room filled with people, shake each person's hand and tell them your name.

• Use professional titles, such as "doctor," or "engineer," when addressing Swedes (e.g., "Hello, Engineer Ol-

son"). However, this may not be necessary with young people, who are not so formal.

• Note that, traditionally, the upper classes refer to each other in the third person and don't use the word "you" (they'd say "How is Mrs. Doctor Olson today?" rather than "How are you?"). This is changing, but if you want to be very correct when talking to an older person, do the same.

• When you meet someone after you've been to their house for dinner, say "Thanks for last time" right away.

CONVERSATION

• Use a person's last name preceded by "Mr.," "Mrs." or "Miss," unless you are friends.

• Look directly into the eyes of the person you are addressing.

• Good topics of conversation: Sweden's economy and high standard of living; sports, especially soccer and hockey; the city you're staying in; how Swedes spend their summers (or whatever time of year you are there); opera and ballet. You should know that Swedes are proud of their companies, architecture and history, and are pleased if foreigners know something about Swedish history and culture.

• Topics to avoid: prices (unless your hosts raise the issue first); casual sexual attitudes, suicide rates or alcoholism in Sweden; the country's neutrality during World War II; or anything that appears to be American criticism of Sweden.

• Be aware that compliments to people whom you've just met are regarded as insincere.

• Use the word "like" instead of "love," as the Swedes most often do.

TELEPHONES

• When making a phone call from a public phone, lift the receiver, deposit one krone and dial the number. If the call is long-distance, you'll hear beeps. Insert another krone.

• Note that Swedes answer the phone by giving their phone number or their last name.

• Most operators speak English, but if you reach one who does not, ask for the language assistance operator.

PUBLIC MANNERS

• Men should lift their hats when passing an acquaintance on the street. They should always remove their hats when talking to a woman.

• When you see someone you know at a distance, nod your head or raise your hand.

Don't embrace, touch or put your arm around anyone except a close friend.

• Wait patiently in lines for trains, buses and theaters.

• Women can talk to men in the bars of large hotels without danger or hassles. But men should know that Swedish women do not like to be "picked up." They enjoy being courted—often a lengthy process.

• Note that it is fairly common and accepted for couples in Sweden to live together without being married.

• Expect to see people changing into their bathing suits on the beach, either with or without a towel as a shield.

DRESS

• Take note that Swedes are very fashion-conscious and wear fashionable, high-quality clothes. Even casual clothing is elegant. The only time Swedes really dress informally is at summer homes in the country.

• When dressing for business, remember that men wear suits and ties, and women wear dresses or suits.

• Dress up for dinner unless you are invited to a picnic.

• When an invitation specifies formal wear, men should wear tuxedos, and women short cocktail dresses in a color other than black. The same attire is appropriate for the opera and ballet, although people are becoming somewhat less formal.

• Feel free to wear furs both during the day and in the evening.

• Don't expect to see the traditional Swedish costumes popular on travel posters and

postcards. These are only worn at festival times or in Lapland.

MEALS

Hours and Foods

Breakfast *(frukost):* 7:00 or 8:00 a.m., except in a summer house in the country. There breakfast is served when everyone is up, about 10:00 a.m. You will be served coffee, rolls, cheese, and sometimes, herring.

Lunch *(lunch):* Noon to 1:00 p.m. This meal can consist of either a hot dish or open-faced sandwiches (a thin piece of rye bread with artistically-presented toppings). Coffee follows dessert. Beer, mineral water or milk accompany the meal.

Dinner *(middag):* 5:00 p.m.; 7:00 p.m. for a formal dinner, which will have four courses. The first could be smoked salmon, caviar canapés, marinated herring or fruit soup. The second is meat (usually not beef, because it's so expensive), potatoes (usually boiled) and a vegetable. Salad follows, then a dessert such as ice cream and fruit, or crepes and fruit.

Wine will accompany a formal dinner, while beer may be served at a less formal meal. Coffee may be served after dessert with brandy or cognac. It will never be served with the meal.

Table Manners

• Be aware that Swedes are more likely to invite new acquaintances for dinner than people in other European countries, but their behavior will be very formal.

• Be punctual for a dinner invitation.

• Don't be surprised if there is no cocktail hour preceding dinner. Before-dinner drinks, when offered, are usually either Renat (vodka), scotch, brandy or wine.

• Don't expect a husband and wife to sit together at dinner. A man traditionally takes charge of the woman seated to his right for the evening. The male guest of honor sits to the left of the hostess, the female to the left of the host.

• Eat with the knife in the right hand and the fork in the left to avoid being seen as rude by Swedes, who regard the American style of eating as "shoveling" food into our mouths.

• At a formal meal, don't use your dinner knife for butter. There will be butter knives on the table.

• Help yourself to food as it is passed around the table. It's polite to try everything.

• Begin that unique Scandinavian meal, *smörgasbord,* by sampling herring, eaten with boiled potatoes and sour cream. Get a clean plate and try the other fish dishes. Get still another new plate and sample the cold meats and salads, then follow with the hot meat dishes.

• Don't be concerned that you will be pressed to drink if you don't care for alcohol. Swedes will not question your preference in this respect.

• To toast, look into the eyes of the person being toasted and say *"Skoal."* Bow your head slightly and take the drink in one gulp. Before putting the glass back on the table, meet the other person's eyes again and nod.

• Expect the host to make a small speech and offer the first toast at a formal dinner party. Guests may then toast each other or simply drink up.

• Toast the hostess by saying "Thank you." However, don't toast the hostess when there are more than six people at the table. She must drink when toasted and would have to drink a great deal.

• Try *aquavit,* a spirit distilled from grain or potatoes and often flavored with caraway seed. It is served so cold that the outside of the glass mists.

• Remember that when the meal ends, the male guest of honor thanks the hostess on behalf of all the guests, and the female guest of honor thanks the host. The thanks begin with the tapping of a knife on a glass.

• When invited to dinner, leave no later than 11:00 p.m. in the winter and 1:00 a.m. in the summer.

• It's very important to call the next day and thank your host and hostess for the meal.

Places to Eat

• Look to see what an eating place is called to get an idea of what kind of food will be served there.

Cafes serve sandwiches, hot and cold lunches, and wine.

Cafeterias in Sweden are self-service, but the food is cooked to order.

Källare are formal restaurants.

Konditori are a good bet for quick lunches, pastries and coffee.

• Because liquor is so expensive in restaurants, many people have a drink or two at home before going out to dinner.

• Take note that liquor is not

served in bars and restaurants till noon.

• If you want ice water, you must ask for it, since it is not usually served at a restaurant.

• In a restaurant, never yell to a waiter or snap your fingers to attract his attention. Saying "Sir" in English should get his attention quickly.

• Remember you can be thrown out of a restaurant for excessive noise or drunkenness.

Specialties

• Swedish cooking is famous for its open-faced sandwiches and the *smörgasbord.* Other special Swedish foods are *gravlax* (salmon cured with dill); *Janssons frestelse* (a casserole of sprouts, potatoes, cream and onions); *lütfisk* (lye-treated dried codfish, soaked and boiled, and served at Christmas with cream sauce, boiled potatoes and peas); reindeer meat; and Swedish cloudberries.

• At the end of August, people from northern Sweden enjoy *surströmming*—sour, rotten herring—eaten with thin bread, potatoes and strong cheese.

• The traditional meal on winter Thursdays is *ärter med fläsk* (pea soup and a platter of small, thin pancakes served with lingonberry jam).

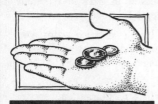

TIPPING

• Restaurants: Don't leave a tip on the table, as the tip is usually added to the check. If you do wish to leave an extra tip anyway, give it to the head waiter.

• Taxis: Tip drivers 20%.

• Porters: Give porters a total of 5 kroner.

PRIVATE HOMES

• Don't presume that an evening invitation to a Swedish home includes dinner, unless it is specified.

Gifts: When invited for a meal, bring unwrapped flowers or a bottle of wine or liquor. Liquor is an appreciated gift, as it is extremely expensive in Sweden. You may also bring candy, but don't bring any other kind of food.

If you're invited to stay, consider bringing books, rec-

ords or cassettes from the U.S. If you're visiting a family you know well, bring blue jeans. Don't bring crystal or other things for which Sweden is famous.

BUSINESS

Hours

Business hours: 9:00 a.m. to 5:00 p.m., Monday through Friday.

Bank hours: 9:00 a.m. to 4:00 p.m., Monday through Friday, and 9:00 a.m. to noon on Saturday. Electronic banking is available 24 hours a day.

Shop hours: 9:30 a.m. to 5:00 or 6:00 p.m., Monday through Saturday. In cities, each neighborhood has one night when shops stay open until 8:00 p.m. In Stockholm, some large supermarkets and stores are open evenings and on Sundays.

Business Practices

• Always be very punctual for any appointment.

• Be aware that the pace of business in Sweden is much more relaxed than in the U.S. Swedes feel that breaks are essential for their well-being, and they may take very long coffee breaks and lunch hours. Don't rush people, even if you have to stay beyond normal working hours to accomplish your business.

• Avoid planning business meetings for the popular vacation months of June, July and August. Also avoid February 20th through March 1, which is school vacation time. Note that all Swedes take at least five weeks of vacation a year.

• You don't need a letter of introduction to do business with a firm in Sweden.

• Keep in mind that Swedish business people are very serious and may seem stiff when you first meet them.

• Keep gestures to a minimum if you're asked to speak to a group. Don't talk with your hands.

• Make reservations in au vance for business lunches and dinners, both popular in Sweden. Spouses should be included at dinners. The formal restaurants, *Källare,* are a good choice for these occasions.

• You can presume the person with an expense account will take responsibility for the check. Businesswomen will encounter no resistance if they wish to pay.

Gifts: Bring American liquor or wine.

HOLIDAYS AND SPECIAL OCCASIONS

Holidays: New Year's Day (January 1), Epiphany (January 6), Good Friday, Holy Saturday, Easter Monday, Labor Day (May 1), Ascension Day (five weeks after Easter), Whit Monday (eight weeks after Easter Monday), Midsummer weekend (the weekend preceding June 24), Christmas Eve and Day (December 24-25).

• Enjoy Midsummer (June 21) along with the Swedes. People build Maypoles in their yards, and children make wreaths of flowers. The night is filled with dancing and singing, as well as feasts of shrimp, beer and wine. The usually reserved Swedes celebrate this occasion with exuberance.

• Whit Sunday (or Pentecost) is traditionally a day for picnicking. Many young people are confirmed in the Lutheran faith on this day, and it is also the most popular day for weddings.

TRANSPORTATION

Public Transportation

• Pay when you enter a bus or subway according to the number of zones you will travel through.

Driving

• Be sure to fasten seat belts. It's mandatory.

• Do not drink and drive. The penalties are severe and can include having your driver's license revoked for a year. (This penalty applies to foreigners as well.) Sometimes one person in a group volunteers to refrain from alcohol in order to drive the others home.

• Drive with headlights on, both day and night.

LEGAL MATTERS AND SAFETY

• If you wish to stay for more than three months, obtain permission from the passport police.

• Women can feel safe to walk alone at night or eat alone in a restaurant without being bothered. In fact, Swedish men won't approach you at all unless you give some sign of encouragement. Be aware, however, that going out alone to one of the restaurants featuring dancing is a signal that you would like to meet someone.

• Be at ease with Swedish police, who are polite and helpful. In Stockholm, most police speak English.

• You must pay a value-added tax on purchases. If you buy something and take it with you, show the receipt at the airport and get a refund. (But remember to allow extra time at the airport.) If you have something shipped from a store, the V.A.T is deducted.

KEY PHRASES

English	Swedish	Pronunciation
Good morning	God morgon	Goad móhr-rohn
Good afternoon	God afton	goad áhf-tohn
Please	Var vänlig	vahr-váhn-leeg
Thank you	Tack så mycket	tahk-seh míck-yeh
You're welcome	Var så god	bar so goad
Yes	Ja	yah
No	Nej	nay
Sir, Mr.	Herr	hair
Madam, Mrs.	Fru	frew
Miss	Fröken	frur-ken
Excuse me	Ursäkta mig	oó-er-séct-uh may
Good-bye	Adjo	ad-yóu-uh
I don't understand.	Jag forstar inte.	Yáh for-stóre ín-teh
I don't speak Swedish.	Jag talar inte Svenska	Yáh teh-lehr éen-teh svéhn-skah
Does anyone here speak English?	Finns dar nagon som talar engelska?	Finns darc no-gon som teh-lehr en-gels-skah

CHAPTER TWENTY-TWO

SWITZERLAND

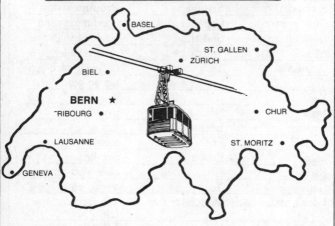

A trip to Switzerland is a real three-for-the-price-of-one bargain. Without leaving the country, you can visit France, Germany and Italy. In each of the three sections, the people's language and habits are those of the corresponding country.

Switzerland is justly famous for its beautiful mountain scenery. It should be equally famous for its cleanliness: stay in the cheapest hotel in the country, and you could still probably eat off the floor.

The Swiss are also extremely honest: one traveler went to a cafe for lunch and realized about half an hour after she walked out that she had left her brand new $300 camera on a chair there. She went back, and at the sight of her worried face, a young man picked the camera out of the drawer and said "Your camera, madame?"

GREETINGS

• Rise and shake hands when introduced. At parties, wait to be introduced. Children should also be encouraged to shake hands.

• Wait for the host or hostess to introduce you at parties, rather than introducing yourself.

• Notice that in the French part of the country, women friends embrace and kiss twice on each cheek, while in the Italian region women friends embrace but don't kiss when they meet. In both the French and Italian regions, when two male friends haven't seen each other for a long time, they sometimes embrace.

The German region tends to be more reserved, and only women embrace or kiss, and then only if they have been apart for a long period.

CONVERSATION

• Use last names when addressing people.

• Don't expect people to be convivial and friendly immediately. The Swiss take a very long time to establish a relationship. But when you do make a friend in Switzerland, that person will be loyal for life.

• Good topics of conversation: participatory sports such as sailing, hiking and skiing; spectator sports such as soccer and bicycle racing; what you like about Switzerland; and your travels in general.

• Topics to avoid: questions about someone's age, family, personal life or profession.

• Be prepared for serious political discussions, even at parties.

• Realize that people are passionate in their opinions about military service. Discussing it could lead to a major argument.

TELEPHONES

• Call from a public phone by depositing 40 centimes and then dialing. A tone sounds when the time expires, so deposit more money if you wish to continue the call.

• Make long-distance calls from the post office, airport or railroad station, and pay when the call is finished; or call from a public phone, and deposit money as you talk.

• Expect to hear various responses when people answer the phone. In the French section, people say *"Allô"*; in the

Italian section, people say *"Pronto";* and in the German section, people answer with their name.

PUBLIC MANNERS

• Stop and shake hands when you meet an acquaintance on the street. It is customary to shake hands when you depart from one another as well.

If you see a person on the other side of the street, simply call out "Hello" without stopping for a chat.

• In the German section, men should tip their hats when they see someone they know on the street.

• Sit up straight in public, as the Swiss consider sloppy posture rude.

• Be on time for all social and business engagements. The Swiss are extremely punctual and think it is insulting to be late. In fact, they pride themselves on the punctuality of all forms of transportation in the country.

• Help an elderly person getting on or off a bus or carrying heavy bags. Stand and give your seats to the elderly on public transportation as well.

• Expect some pushing and shoving in lines for buses, ski lifts and cinemas. To get a place, you may have to do likewise.

• Never throw a cigarette package, a gum wrapper or any form of litter on the street, or the people nearby may rebuke you severely.

• Say "Hello" to the clerk when you enter a shop.

• Don't try to bargain in any Swiss store, shop or market.

• Understand that even though the Swiss franc is the national monetary unit, in the German section, a franc is divided into 100 rappen, while in the Italian and French sections, a franc is divided into 100 centimes.

DRESS

• Shorts and jeans are fine for casual wear in the countryside, but don't wear shorts in cities.

• For business meetings, men wear suits and ties, and women wear dresses or suits. Women can wear pants if they're elegant.

• When invited to dinner at someone's home, men should wear trousers, shirts and sweaters, and women should wear skirts or elegant pants.

• Wear formal clothes for balls, openings of theater or opera, formal weddings or any other time the invitation specifies formal wear. This means tuxedos for men and long dresses for women.

MEALS

Hours and Foods

• The names for the following meals vary according to the region of the country. See the chapters on France, Italy and Germany. Also see these chapters for more specifics on foods served.

Breakfast: 7:00 a.m. This is a sit-down meal with the entire family present. A typical meal is cheese, bread, butter, jam and coffee with milk.

Lunch: Noon. Usually the main meal of the day, lunch begins with soup. The main course consists of meat, vegetables, potatoes, and green salad. Wine or beer, and mineral water are generally served with the meal. Fruit is the usual dessert except on Sunday, when cake, pastries or pudding are served. Bread usually comes with the main meal in restaurants only.

Dinner: 6:00 to 7:00 p.m. This is a light meal consisting of soup, followed by bread with cheese, ham or salami; or salad and eggs.

If it's a dinner party, the meal will usually start about 7:00 or 8:00 p.m. with before-dinner drinks such as wine, beer, Campari, Cynar (made from artichokes), *blanc-cassis* (white wine with a blackberry liqueur) or Pastis (anise liqueur). The meal may begin with soup, followed by the main course: meat (a pot roast, a pork roast, roasted or stewed venison or veal), vegetables, potatoes or rice, and a green salad. The meal ends with fruit and cheese, and/or cake or pudding. Espresso follows, along with after-dinner drinks such as *grappa* (brandy made from grape skins), cognac, kirsch or *pflümwasser* (plum brandy).

Table Manners

• Consider it a compliment to be invited to a dinner party. The Swiss are very private and don't often open their homes to strangers.

• Expect the party to be a small one if you're invited for cocktails or dinner, since space in houses and apartments is limited.

• If you're a guest of honor, sit in the middle of the side (not head) of the table.

• Keep your wrists on the table when you're not eating. Never put either hand in your lap.

• Don't drink the wine until the host has proposed the toast. Then look the host in the eye and say "To your health" in the language appropriate to the region. Clink glasses with everyone at the table.

• Help yourself to the food passed around the table on platters. You are expected to finish everything you put on your plate, so if you're not sure whether you'll like something, take a very small portion. Also take a small serving of something you know you won't like, to be polite.

• Notice that forks are set to the left of the plate and knives and soup spoon to the right. The dessert spoon will be above the plate.

• Eat as the Swiss do, with the fork in the left hand and the knife in the right. Use the knife to push food onto the back of the fork.

• Indicate you're waiting for a second helping by crossing the fork over the knife. The fork should point diagonally to the left, and knife to the right.

To show that you have finished, place the knife and fork horizontally across the plate, both pointing to the right.

• Break bread and rolls with your hands, rather than cutting them with a knife.

• If you're served fondue, eat it in the following way. In the center of the table will be a chafing dish with the fondue. Take the long fork beside your plate and spear a cube of bread. Dip the bread into the fondue and twist your fork to break the cheese strand as you pull the bread out. Tradition says that if the bread slips off the fork and falls into the fondue, you must buy a bottle of white wine for the group.

• Don't smoke between courses.

• Avoid mentioning diets or weight control when dining in a Swiss home.

• Stay until about midnight after a dinner party. If there are other guests, take your lead from them but don't leave much later than midnight.

Places to Eat

• Note that in the following list of eating places, the first word is French, the second is Italian and the third is German.

A *bar* (in all three languages) has tables and a counter and offers sandwiches and alcoholic drinks.

A *café/caffe/kafe* serves sandwiches, croissants, coffee, soft drinks and one daily special. A typical special would be bratwurst and potato salad, or stew with potatoes.

A *pâtisserie/pasticceria/ bäckerei* serves coffee, tea, soft drinks and pastries, but no alcoholic beverages.

A *restaurant/locanda/ wirtshaus* is a country restaurant, usually offering typically Swiss dishes and drinks.

• Know that country restaurants offer hearty meals at very reasonable prices. In the cities, most restaurants are German, French or Italian. Few other nationalities are represented.

• Check on available dishes and prices in restaurants by looking for the menu posted outside. Menus are displayed at all but the fanciest places.

• Seat yourself in all but the finer restaurants. When in doubt, ask a waiter if you should pick your own table or should wait to be seated.

• Don't be surprised in a small restaurant or cafe if someone sits at your table when there is a shortage of free tables. In the same way, feel free to join a stranger at a table where there's an available

place. Diners don't usually strike up conversations, so if you feel uncomfortable eating in silence, bring a book or a magazine with you.

• Be aware that the Swiss seldom order drinks before the meal.

Specialties

• Specialties throughout Switzerland are *fondue* (cheese, usually Emmentaler or Gruyère, melted with white wine, a touch of garlic, flour and *kirsch*, cherry liqueur); and *raclette bagnes* (cheese that has been grilled until it has melted and become crispy, served with cocktail onions and small boiled potatoes).

• In French Switzerland, try *croûtes aux morilles* (mushrooms served on toast); *choucroute garnie* (sauerkraut with ham, sausages and boiled potatoes); and *friture de perchettes* (fried fillets of fresh lake perch).

• In Italian Switzerland, try *busecca* (vegetable and tripe soup); *lumache* (snails served with walnut paste); *zampone* and *coppa* (sausages); *risotto con funghi* (rice with mushrooms); and *ravioli al pomodoro* (ravioli with tomato sauce).

• In German Switzerland, try *leberspiessli* (calves liver and bacon); *geschnetzeltes* (minced veal in a thick cream sauce); *bündnerfleisch* (air-dried beef cut into paper-thin slices and served with grated pepper as an appetizer); *bernerplatte* (sauerkraut with smoked pork chops or bacon, or sausages and boiled potatoes); and *rösti* (grated parboiled potatoes fried in butter).

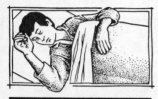

HOTELS

• Show your passport when you arrive at the hotel, but don't leave it at the desk.

• Keep your room key when you go out, rather than drop it at the front desk.

• In the room of a better hotel, don't be surprised to find a refrigerator stocked with champagne, white wine and soft drinks. Check off each drink you have on the slip attached to the refrigerator. The maid will check the list when you leave, and you'll pay when checking out.

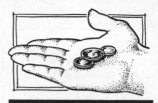

TIPPING

• Restaurants: Don't leave anything extra, as the tip is included in the bill.

• Washroom and cloakroom attendants: Give 50 rappen (or centimes).

• Taxis: Tip 10%.

• Porters: Tip one franc per bag.

• Gas station attendants: Give 10% of the gas charge.

• Ushers: Don't tip.

PRIVATE HOMES

• Call in advance and ask if it is convenient to visit. Never drop in on people.

• Keep in mind that no special times or days are set aside for visiting.

• If you're a house guest, be exceptionally neat and tidy. Make your bed immediately after getting up. The Swiss are very clean and tidy and never leave clothes on the bed or chairs.

• Offer to help, even though your offer probably will be refused.

• If you stay with a Swiss family for a couple of days, you won't get a clean napkin at each meal. Instead, store your napkin in the napkin ring provided.

• Ask if it's convenient for you to have a bath. Water often has to be heated.

Gifts: Bring flowers or chocolates when invited to dinner. Remember, however, that red roses and carnations are expressions of romantic love, and chrysanthemums and white asters are reserved for funerals. A huge bouquet is not necessary; three flowers or a flowering branch are sufficient. You can send flowers the next day if you're invited to someone's home and have no time to shop in advance.

You can also bring candy as a gift, but make sure it's the best quality and attractively packaged.

If you're a house guest, bring gifts from the U.S., such as bath towels, records, whiskey or handmade crafts from your home region. Give chocolates to the children in the family.

Realize that huge gifts are considered vulgar and ostentatious.

BUSINESS

Hours

Business Hours: 8:00 a.m. to noon and 2:00 p.m. to 6:00 p.m., Monday through Friday.

Bank hours: 8:30 a.m. to 4:30 p.m., Monday through Friday.

Shop hours: 8:00 a.m. to 12:15 p.m. and 1:30 to 6:30 p.m., Monday through Friday and 9:00 a.m. to 4:00 p.m. on Saturday. In larger cities, some shops don't close during lunchtime.

Business Practices

• Though you may be writing to a specific person at a company, address the envelope of a business letter to the company, not the individual. Letters addressed to an individual won't be opened if the person is away, and there may be a long delay in accomplishing your business. Do address the letter itself to the individual.

• Avoid making appointments during July and August, the traditional vacation period.

• Schedule appointments for the morning, any time after 9:00 a.m.

• Call for an appointment three or four days ahead if you're in continental Europe. When you telephone or telex from the U.S., allow about the same amount of time. If you're writing, allow a minimum of two to two and one half weeks to set up an appointment.

• Be assured that English is widely understood and spoken in all three sections of Switzerland, so language is usually no problem in business dealings.

• Bring business cards. If your company is very old, have the year of its founding printed on your card to impress the Swiss, who respect age.

• Hand your business card to the receptionist, even if you've arranged an appointment in advance. Also give a card to the person you're meeting.

• Expect people to come right to the point, without any initial small talk, in the German section. Business people in the French and Italian sections probably will be slower and more casual. Anticipate some opening small talk about your trip to Switzerland, where you are staying, and the like.

• Realize that Swiss business people are very conservative. Be patient, as they proceed in a very deliberate manner to a decision. Avoid high-pressure selling techniques. Once a decision has been made, the Swiss are extremely reliable.

• Note that business dinners are more common than business lunches. When lunching with a business person, it is common to be taken to the cafeteria at the work place.

• Bear in mind that you are more likely to be entertained in a restaurant than invited to someone's house.

• Include spouses in dinner invitations unless the sole purpose of the meal is to discuss business.

Gifts: Give a good bottle of whiskey or cognac.

HOLIDAYS AND SPECIAL OCCASIONS

Holidays: New Year's Day (January 1), January 2, Good Friday, Easter Monday, Ascension Day (five weeks after Easter), Whit Monday (eight weeks after Easter), Independence Day (August 1), Christmas (December 25), December 26.

• On Independence Day, expect to see fires everywhere. People collect pieces of kindling and bring them to the highest place in their neighborhoods. At night, there are huge bonfires and children carry lanterns with candles in them. People have picnics, which usually include cooking sausages. If you're staying with someone, offer to help build the fire or do the cooking.

TRANSPORTATION

Public Transportation

• Look for automatic ticket-dispensing machines at bus and streetcar stops (there are no subways in Switzerland). The machines have instructions in English. Note that you need exact change.

• Keep the ticket to present to any inspector who boards the vehicle.

• Phone for a taxi or look for a taxi stand near railroad stations, bus stations, airports and major places of business.

Driving

• Wear a seat belt in the car and make sure other passengers do likewise. Children under 12 aren't allowed to sit in the front seat.

• Always obey the rules of the road, even when you see Swiss drivers traveling very fast. If you switch lanes quickly without signaling, or violate other rules, nearby drivers are likely to yell at you.

• Be aware of these right of way regulations: vehicles approaching an intersection from the right have right of way. When main highways and secondary roads intersect, the main highway has priority. On mountain roads, ascending vehicles have priority over those descending. Pedestrians have the right of way at street crossings.

• Be cautious about driving in the mountains during winter. Always check weather conditions in advance and be sure that your car has the necessary equipment for winter driving.

• Respect police officers in Switzerland and don't argue with them if you are stopped for a traffic violation. You'll have to pay a fine on the spot for most violations, usually about 100 Swiss francs.

• Don't drink and drive. If you're caught, you could go to prison.

LEGAL MATTERS AND SAFETY

• Note that Switzerland has a very low crime rate, and it is generally safe for anyone to go out alone at any hour of the day or night.

• Don't drink if you're under 20, the legal drinking age. There are no restrictions on when you can drink in a bar or restaurant.

• Note that the price of all goods in Switzerland includes a value-added tax. If you buy something for 500 or more Swiss francs, you can get this tax refunded. Some shops make refunds on the spot, but in others you must get a form and have it stamped by a customs official when you leave the country. Your refund will be mailed to you.

KEY PHRASES

See Germany, France, Italy

CHAPTER TWENTY-THREE

TURKEY

ISTANBUL
BURSA
ESKIŞEHIR
★ ANKARA
IZMIR
KONYA
GAZIANTEP

What will surprise you most about Turkey is that it doesn't surprise you—at first. In large cities, people look and dress like Western Europeans, and the street signs are written in familiar Roman letters.

The initial shock may come at sunrise on your first morning. You will hear, amplified by loud speakers, the sound of a man, the *muezzin*, calling people to the mosques for prayer. You'll hear this five times a day, and religious Moslems will respond each time.

While Americans are accustomed both to giving and receiving insincere invitations ("Do drop in when you're in the neighborhood" or "We must have lunch some time"), Turks are not. Their warmth and offers of hospitality are real and sincere.

In small villages, a visitor is such a rarity that people will offer to put you up and feed you within minutes after meeting you. Travelers should feel free to accept such invitations, without worrying about obligations. It's a wonderful way to experience a rich new culture.

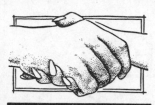

GREETINGS

• Shake hands when introduced, using a firm handshake.

• If you enter a room in which there is a group, greet each person, beginning with elders, and shake hands. You need not shake hands with each person when you leave.

• Show respect to elders by rising to greet them when they enter a room.

• Keep in mind that the Turkish people traditionally use first names when addressing each other. To follow the traditional method, use a man's first name followed by *"bey"*; with a women use her first name followed by *"hanim."* Use this with older people in particular.

The more modern form of address is *"Bay"* followed by the man's last name; for a woman use *"Bayam"* followed by her last name. Use this with most business and social contacts.

• Address professionals by occupational title alone (in other words don't use the last name after the title). For ex-

ample, address a lawyer as *"Avukat."*

If you're speaking to a woman, use the same title but add the word *"Bayan"* after it (for example, *"Avukat Bayan")*.

CONVERSATION

• Good topics of conversation: families, professions, personal hobbies and interests, and non-controversial international affairs.

• Topics to avoid: communism and the Cyprus-Greece conflict. Don't take sides in discussing any aspect of Turkish politics.

• Never argue with elders or speak to them in a loud voice.

• Don't cross your arms while facing someone; it's considered rude.

• Don't put your hands in your pockets when speaking to someone; it's a sign of disrespect.

• Always keep both feet flat on the ground when seated. Crossing your legs or showing the soles of your shoes or feet is discourteous.

• To summon someone, wave

your hand up and down (not from one side to another).

• To indicate that something is nice or delicious, use a Turkish gesture: open your hand palm up and gradually move your fingers up to touch them to your thumb. Move your hand towards you and away from you in this position.

• If someone raises his chin, shuts his eyes and tilts his head back, realize that he is saying "No."

TELEPHONES

• Buy the tokens needed for public phones at a post office. You can talk as long as you want on one token if the call is local.

• When answering the phone, say "Hello."

• Be prepared to wait several hours for the call to go through if you make international phone calls from a post office. If time is more important to you than money, make the call from your hotel room, where the charge will be considerably higher.

PUBLIC MANNERS

• Don't kiss, hold hands or otherwise show affection in public with a member of the opposite sex.

• If a man wants to speak to a Turkish woman, he must be formally introduced. Be aware that very few Turkish women will go out on dates unless accompanied by a sister or friend.

• Remember that women seldom go out alone in Turkey. If you are a woman, arrange to eat out or sightsee with a friend to avoid unwelcome attention.

• When the national anthem is played (before soccer games or national holiday activities), stand quietly. Don't move or chew gum. Bear in mind that people will be very offended if you don't stand up.

• If you visit a mosque, remove your shoes. Pay the attendant outside 50 Turkish lira for the use of slippers.

• When you're staying someplace without a bath—or if you would like to try something a little different—visit a *hamam* (public bath).

There are separate baths for men and women: small boys usually go to the women's section with their mothers.

There is usually a large, central bathing area with marble steps, but more modern public baths have private tubs. You'll get a towel when you pay your fee. If there's a central bathing area, soap yourself at a stone sink and use a special flat cup to pour water over yourself. Then go and soak in the water. If you pay extra, someone will wash and dry you.

• Bargain when shopping, especially in bazaars and markets, but don't underbid grossly. Start by offering 25% less than the posted price and negotiate from there. If you're interested in a large item, be prepared to take coffee or tea with the shopkeeper. If you leave without making your purchase, the shopkeeper may run after you and agree to your price.

• Be aware that it is against the Moslem religion to reproduce the human image. Therefore, when you go into smaller towns or villages, always ask permission before you photograph anyone.

• Ask permission before you take pictures in a mosque. You may be allowed to take pictures of the building but not of people.

• Don't photograph military installations.

DRESS

• For casual dress, men wear shirts and pants, and women wear pants or skirts. Don't wear shorts unless you're at a seaside resort.

• Women should avoid wearing short skirts or low-cut blouses, as Turkey is a Moslem country and women are expected to dress modestly.

• When visiting mosques, women should cover their heads and wear long sleeves, and pants or skirts.

• Men wear conservative suits for business. In very hot weather, men may go without jackets or even ties. Businesswomen should wear suits and heels.

• Bring formal dress (dark suits for men and long dresses for women) if you plan to attend the balls held at New Year's and at the Turkish National Holiday (October 29).

MEALS

Hours and Foods

Breakfast (*kahvalti*): 7:30 or 8:00 a.m. Expect to be offered hard-boiled eggs, olives, feta cheese, breads, rosewater, eggplant or fig marmalade, and tea. (Coffee is served before breakfast.)

Lunch (*öğle yemeği*): Noon. Plan to eat soup, salad, a vegetable dish and bread.

Dinner (*aksam yemeği*): 7:00 p.m. Before dinner you'll probably be offered *raki* (an anise liqueur), wine or beer, and appetizers. The evening meal consists of soup, a course of beans and meat, salad, yogurt, fruit, dessert and coffee. Bread is available throughout the meal. With dinner, people usually drink water, *ayran* (a drink made from yogurt, water and salt), beer or wine.

Table Manners

• Outside large cities, drink only bottled water.

• Be punctual for dinner invitations. However, it's fine to be a few minutes late for a large gathering, such as a cocktail party.

• Be aware that religious families never drink or serve alcohol.

• When you sit down to eat, expect your host to say *"Buyrun,"* which means "Here, I am extending this to you."

• The hostess will serve or will ask someone else at the table to serve. Note that as a guest you'll be served first, followed by the elderly and children.

• To adopt the Turkish eating style, keep the fork in your left hand and the knife in your right. Use the knife to push food onto the back of your fork.

• When eating soup, tip the spoon toward you. For the last drops, tip the bowl toward you.

• Never eat with your fingers.

• Expect your hosts to insist that you eat a great deal. They'll be offended if you don't.

• People usually smoke between courses, but ask permission and conform to what others at the table do.

• When you're offered a toothpick after dessert, use it at the table, covering your mouth with your hand.

• When you're offered Turkish coffee after dinner, specify if you want it sweet, medium or without sugar.

• After the meal, say to your hostess, *"Ziyade olsun,"* which means "Thank you for the energy you've spent."

• Don't get up from the table until everyone has finished.

Places to Eat

• Look for the following eating places:

Kahve hane are coffeehouses offering pastries, coffee, tea and liquor, but no meals. They are frequented mostly by men, who go to listen to music on the radio, talk and play backgammon. Bear in mind that Turkish women don't go to coffeehouses, except in large cities, and a women who goes into one alone may be harassed.

At a *kebabei* you can get different kinds of kebabs cooked on a grill: *döner* (lamb cooked on a vertical spit); *kofte* (long hamburger patties with spices cooked on a spit); and *kebab* şiş (lamb and vegetables cooked on a skewer).

Pasta hane are pastry shops serving coffee, tea and pastries. Feel free to sit and chat for as long as you want.

A *restoran* or a *lokanta* is a Turkish full-service restaurant.

• Don't expect to find bars except in deluxe hotels.

• Look for excellent fish restaurants, especially along the coast. Ask the price before you order. The waiter will ask you to choose the method of cooking: broiled, fried or baked.

• Note that service in Turkish restaurants is extremely fast. If the waiter seems to be rushing you, remember that he or she is just being professional.

• If you don't understand the menu in a restaurant, go into the kitchen to choose your meal or check the counter to see if there is a display of the dishes offered. Since Turkey is a Moslem country, you won't be able to order pork.

• If you suggest to someone that you have a meal together, plan to pay the entire check. Pay no attention to arguments and attempts to grab the check. The "Dutch treat" doesn't exist in Turkey. If you are invited to a meal, you won't be allowed to pay any part of the check.

Specialties

• Sample these special foods of Turkey: *börek* (cheese- or meat-filled pastries); *patlican salatasi* (eggplant salad—eggplant, roasted, pureed and mixed with yogurt and lemon); *imam bayildi* (eggplant stuffed with tomatoes and onions and baked in oil); *kebab* (chunks of lamb cooked on a spit).

HOTELS

• Make hotel reservations as soon as you decide to go to Turkey. First-class hotels are scarce.

• Note that most hotels below first class don't have shutters or shades. Noise, sunlight and sign lights will penetrate most rooms. If you will be staying in a hotel that isn't first class, it may be wise to bring an eye mask and ear plugs.

• Before you register, inspect the room assigned to you. If you don't like it, look at several until you find one that pleases you. Avoid rooms facing the street where you may be bothered by noise from traffic and cafes. Be sure to check lights, door locks, shower and toilet to see that they all work.

• If you feel that the price is excessive, try bargaining with the clerk. Don't attempt to bargain in large hotels.

• Don't expect room service except in first-class hotels.

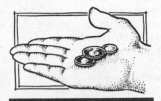

TIPPING

• Restaurants: Leave 15% if the tip is not included in the bill.

• Taxis: Tip 15% of the fare.

• Ushers in theaters and cinemas: Tip 25% of the ticket price.

• Cloakroom attendants: Give 20 Turkish lire.

• If you visit a cemetery, tip the attendant 50 Turkish lire.

• If you take a moist, perfumed towel in a public washroom, leave 25 lire in the plate next to them.

PRIVATE HOMES

• Don't be surprised if you're invited to stay in a private home for several days. In fact, people you meet casually on a train or boat may want you to come to stay for a week. Turks feel very warm towards Americans and are curious about life in America. If you want to refuse an invitation, say that you have arranged to stay with someone else or that you'll be leaving the country.

• Call the people you would like to visit and ask if they will be in. The customary time for visiting is about 9:00 p.m.

• In private homes or in offices, expect your host to offer you cologne to refresh yourself. Pour the cologne into your hands and rub it on your face and hands.

• Offer to help with the cleaning and dishes. If you're staying for a few days, your offer will probably be refused. If you're staying a week or more, insist on sharing the household chores.

• Ask permission to take a bath, so that water can be heated if necessary.

• Don't plan to make long-distance calls from phones in private homes. The family will think it inhospitable to accept payment, and they will be stuck with the bill.

Gifts: If you're invited to dinner, bring flowers (roses or carnations), candy or pastries. If you know that the

family serves liquor, you could also bring wine. Glassware, such as water goblets or a vase, are good gifts for a special occasion.

When visiting a family with children, bring them chocolates or small toys.

If you're staying with a family, bring records or books in English, which are very hard to find.

Don't insist that your hostess open a gift in front of you. Opening the gift would be considered rude because it would take her attention away from her guest and direct it toward the gift.

BUSINESS

Hours

Bank and business hours: 9:00 a.m. to noon, and 2:00 to 5:00 p.m., Monday through Friday. Executives usually arrive at their offices between 9:30 and 10:00 a.m. and return from lunch about 2:30 p.m.

Store hours: 9:00 a.m. to 1:00 p.m., and 2:30 to 7:00 p.m., Monday through Friday; and 9:00 a.m. to noon, and 1:30 to 8:00 p.m. on

Saturday.

Business Practices

• Don't plan a business trip to Turkey in June, July or August; most business people vacation during those months.

• Write business letters in English. Companies dealing with foreign firms will always have someone who understands English.

• Note that most Turkish business people speak English. If you take the trouble to learn a few words of Turkish, they will be both surprised and pleased. Business can also be conducted in French or German.

• Bring business cards. You don't have to have special ones printed in Turkish. When you go to an office, give one to the receptionist, one to the person you are meeting with, and one to anyone else you're introduced to.

• Try to arrange a personal introduction or bring a letter of introduction from a Turk; it will help ensure your acceptance.

• Be punctual for all business appointments.

• Before a meeting gets down to business, expect to spend a long time in small talk. You may be asked about your background, education and work. If you ask Turkish men about their sons, they will be very pleased; they enjoy talking about their sons' accomplishments.

• When you visit a factory, shake hands with the workers when you arrive and again when you leave.

• Don't expect a Turkish business person to invite you to dinner in his or her home. Most business entertainment takes place in restaurants.

• If you have met the spouse of a business colleague, include both in a dinner invitation.

Gifts: Bring a good bottle of liqueur or whiskey, if you know your colleague drinks.

HOLIDAYS AND SPECIAL OCCASIONS

Holidays: National Sovereignty and Children's Day (April 23), Spring Day (May 1), Youth and Sports Day (May 19), Freedom and Constitution Days (May 27 and May 28), Victory Day (August 30), Anniversary of the Declaration of the Republic (October 29 and 30).

• Realize that it's customary for people to take off the

afternoon preceding a public holiday. Expect some offices and stores to be closed.

• Youth Day (May 19) is a major national holiday. Mustafa Kemal Pasha (known as Ataturk) began the struggle for the liberation of Turkey. As first President of the Republic, he stressed the importance of young people to the nation. There are celebrations, sports events and special radio broadcasts. Anticipate student speeches on radio and television, and at ceremonies in schools and public squares.

• An important Moslem holiday is *Kurban Bayram* (Feast of the Sacrifice), a four-day feast scheduled on different dates each year. Depending on their wealth, people sacrifice a sheep, a goat, a cow or a camel and distribute the meat to family, to friends and relatives, and to the poor. (The origin of this tradition is the Abraham/Isaac story.)

• The holiest time in the Moslem year is *Ramadan*, which lasts for 30 days. The date changes each year, since it is based on a 13-month lunar calendar. Check with the Turkish consulate or embassy to find out when it occurs each year.

During the day people spend time in mosques praying and reading the *Koran*. It is customary not to eat, drink or smoke from dawn until sunset. If you hear a cannon, don't panic. It announces sunrise and sunset.

Observance of the fast is no longer a universal custom. But to be considerate, don't eat, drink or smoke in front of people during the daylight hours. If you're staying with a family that is keeping the holiday, observe the fast with the family or eat in your room, unless they tell you that it isn't necessary. Buy food for your own use at food stores, which remain open during the day.

In major cities, you can expect some restaurants to be open at lunchtime—especially in tourist areas and hotels—but you won't find any open in small towns. (The owners would be stoned if they remained open.)

• When *Ramadan* ends, there is a three-day festival called *Sugar Bayram*. People spend time visiting family, then neighbors, then friends. Anticipate being served coffee, tea and sweets.

TRANSPORTATION

Public Transportation

• Note that cities have bus and trolley service. On main routes service is every two to five minutes until 11:00 p.m. or midnight.

• Buy tickets at the bus stop or at some banks before you get on. You pay one fare no matter how far you travel.

• Look for a vehicle with a black-and-yellow checkered band when you want a taxi.

• Be sure to find out the fare before you get in, since taxi meters are not used. You should bargain with the driver.

• Realize that the driver will charge you more if you get your taxi near a large hotel. Also expect to pay extra for a taxi on weekends.

• Look for a *dolmuş,* or shared cab, along specified routes, usually main bus routes. They aren't easy to identify, especially at night. Some have a solid yellow band around them, some have no band, and others are mini-buses.

A *dolmuş* will stop anywhere along the route. You need not talk to your fellow passengers, and you need not tip the driver.

Driving

• Allow more time than you think you'll need to get anywhere. Major traffic jams are frequent.

• Seat belts are not compulsory.

• Watch carefully for bikes and carts; they sometimes go against the traffic so that the drivers can see better. In the countryside, watch out for animals, such as sheep, crossing the road.

• Don't assume that there are rules about who has the right of way. It's established by physical presence: whoever gets to a spot first has right of way.

• Try to avoid driving at night; it's very hazardous because many cars have badly adjusted headlights or don't have them at all.

• Parking is chaotic. Park where you can—even on the sidewalk.

• Be aware that if you're involved in an accident, you may have to pay a great deal because you're a foreigner. Insurance involves many conditions and delays. For these and other reasons, some foreign companies don't allow their business people to drive in Turkey. If you can afford the expense, hire a car and chauffeur instead of driving yourself.

LEGAL MATTERS AND SAFETY

• Remember that there are severe penalties for taking antiques or antiquities out of the country without authorization.

• Don't try to bring weapons or ammunition into the country or take them out.

• Never have anything to do with drugs, unless you fancy life in a Turkish prison. If you're with someone who is carrying drugs, you can be arrested, whether or not you knew about the drugs. For this reason avoid coming into Turkey in the car or van of someone you don't know and trust.

• Keep receipts from your money-changing in Turkey. You will need those receipts to change Turkish money into another currency at the border.

• Be alert to prevent being pickpocketed. Often a group of women and children begin a fight, with a tourist trapped in the middle. Then someone else picks your pocket.

• Turkish women almost never travel alone, so be especially careful outside major tourist areas if you are a woman traveling by yourself. Don't accept invitations from men, but do make friends with women and with families.

• Women can go to restaurants alone during daylight hours and until early evening (8:00 p.m.). Either have an early supper or plan to eat in a major hotel and take a taxi home. Even two or three women should not walk alone at night. Choose any form of transportation rather than walking, but taxis are best.

KEY PHRASES

English	Turkish	Pronunciation
Good morning	Günaydin	Gewn-áhy-din
Good evening	Iyi akşamlar	Ée-yee áhk-shahm-lahr
Please	Lütfen	Léwt-fen
Thank you	Teşekkür	Teh-sheh-kéwr
You're welcome	Hoş geldiniz	Hosh géhl-din-iz
Yes	Evet	Éh-vet
No	Hayır	Hire
Sir	Bay + last name	Buy
Madam, Mrs., Miss	Bayam + last name	Buy-yahm
Excuse me	Affedersiniz	Ah-feh-déhr-sin-iz
Good-bye (said by one who's leaving)	Allah ısmarladık	Ah-láhs-mahr-lah-dik
Good-bye (said by one who's staying)	Güle Güle	Gew-léh Gew-léh
I don't understand.	Anlamıyorum.	Án-lah-mee-yo-room
I don't speak Turkish.	Turkçe bilmem.	Turk-jeh beel-mem
Is there anyone who speaks English?	Ingilizçe bilen varmı?	Een-geel-eez-jéh bee-lén váhr-meh

CHAPTER TWENTY-FOUR

YUGOSLAVIA

ZAGREB

FIUME (RIJEKA)

OSIJEK   NOVI SAD

BANJA LUKA   **BELGRADE** ★

SARAJEVO
SPLIT

DUBROVNIK

Yugoslavia, with its six republics, four languages, three religions, and two alphabets, is a country of great diversity.

It is also a major contrast to other communist countries in Eastern Europe. There is little of the rigidity about rules or scarcity of consumer items you'll find in other Eastern bloc countries. In Yugoslavia, you can bring in a small amount (500 dinars) of currency, you can find consumer goods without problem, and you can even go to a nude beach.

You'll also find Yogoslavs much more open in expressing political opinions than residents of other communist countries, and you may even find them openly disagreeing with government policies. Because they are free to travel abroad, the Yogoslavs you meet may have a very sophisticated, first-hand knowledge of Western Europe and America.

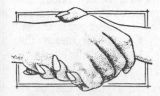

GREETINGS

• When greeting or leaving someone, shake hands. Men should wait for women to extend their hands first.

• Expect to be embraced and kissed on the cheek when you meet friends.

• If you go to a large party, speak to each person individually as you are introduced. As a foreigner, prepare to be the center of attention.

• At business meetings, shake hands with each person present as you arrive and depart.

• If you know someone's professional title, use it in addressing her or him (e.g., *Doktor Radovanovitch*).

CONVERSATION

• Begin to call someone by their first name only after he or she uses your first name. This usually occurs after a very short time.

• Good topics of conversation: what life is like in the U.S.; your family and your town (you might bring along a few photos); and shopping in the U.S., what's available and how much it costs.

• Expect Yugoslavs to ask personal questions, such as "Are you married?" or "What kind of work do you do?" very soon after meeting you. Feel free to ask them the same types of questions.

• Topics to avoid: religion (most religions are freely practiced, but many young people advocate atheism), the pros and cons of communism, or any other sensitive political issue.

TELEPHONES

• To make a local call from a public phone, deposit 2 dinar and dial. For long-distance calls and telegrams, go to the post office, where calls are less expensive than from a private or pay phone. Expect to wait in line, because many people don't have telephones.

- Answer the telephone by saying *"Sdravo."*

PUBLIC MANNERS

- Attempt to bargain at outdoor stands where merchandise and produce are sold, but never in government-owned stores.

- Join the Yugoslavs in *orzo* (evening promenade) between 5:00 and 8:00 p.m. People of all ages stroll up and down the main street of the town, gossiping and meeting friends. They often go into bars or pastry shops for a snack and then return home for supper at 9:00 p.m.

- If you visit Sarajevo, the area where the Moslem population lives, and go into a mosque, leave your shoes outside.

- Request permission to take photographs in museum or church interiors. Don't photograph anyone in uniform (e.g., soldiers, police) or peasants without their permission. Also don't photograph Moslems, as it is against their religion to reproduce the human image.

Don't photograph military or naval installations, or you may have your camera confiscated. Before taking any picture, look for a sign showing a camera with an "x" over it, which means that photography is forbidden.

- If you decide to go to one of the gambling casinos restricted to foreigners, bring your passport.

DRESS

- Don't wear shorts except at a lake or at the seaside.

- Although jeans are considered a status symbol among students, keep in mind that they commonly are not worn by anyone over 30.

- Dress modestly if you are a woman.

- In towns, wear dressier clothing, not casual wear. Women usually wear skirts or dresses.

- If you visit someone at home in the late afternoon, don't be surprised to find men in undershirts and women in bathrobes. Don't be embarrassed; you haven't intruded at the wrong time. There's still a tradition of taking a nap in the afternoon, and people often don't dress in street clothes afterwards.

• Note that for business, men wear suits and ties. In hot weather, men remove jackets and ties, but keep your jacket on until others remove theirs.

• Be aware that Yugoslav businesswomen wear very dressy clothes. They also wear a great deal of makeup and jewelry.

• For formal dress occasions, such as official receptions and weddings, men wear dark suits and ties, and women wear long dresses.

• Men should wear long trousers, and women should wear skirts and should have their arms covered when visiting all churches and monasteries.

MEALS

Hours and Foods

Breakfast *(doručak):* 8:00 a.m. The usual meal is bread, cheese, eggs, salami, fruit and warm milk with coffee, or artificial coffee made from carob beans. As a guest, you may be offered a shot of *rakia,* a homemade liqueur made from plums or other fruits.

Lunch *(ručak):* 2:00 p.m. Often the main meal of the day, lunch may begin with soup, then salad, followed by a main course of meat with potatoes, beans or rice, and a vegetable. In the south, the main course is usually a mixture of vegetables and potatoes without meat. Wine or beer will be served with the meal. Dessert and Turkish coffee, if it's available, follow.

If it's a formal meal, lunch will begin with a distilled spirit: *lovogaca* (grape brandy), *slivovitz* (plum brandy) or sherry. Cheese and slices of *prosciutto* (thin, salty ham) are often served before the soup course. Salad follows, then the meat course. A typical dish would be hamburger kabobs or steak with French fries and peas. Dessert could be ice cream or cream cakes, followed by Turkish coffee and brandy or *Ferret* (a digestive with a somewhat bitter taste).

Supper *(večera):* 9:00 p.m. Expect leftovers from lunch, cold foods, fish and hard-boiled eggs. If it's a social occasion, it will follow the courses of a formal noon meal.

Table Manners

• When pressed to drink alcoholic beverages, don't refuse without some explanation. There is also usually a carafe of water on the table, but people will think it's odd if you drink only water with a meal.

• Eat with the fork in the left hand and the knife in the right. When you're not eating, place your knife and fork with the handles resting on the table and the tines and point on the plate. To show that you've finished eating, put both knife and fork completely on the plate.

• Serve yourself from platters of food passed around the table family-style. As the guest at a meal, you'll be given the platters first.

• At a dinner party, be prepared for a great deal of food, including several desserts. Your hosts will probably press you to eat more and more. Try to pace yourself and take small portions at first, so that you can taste everything. Be sure to allow adequate time for eating, since large quantities of food are served at most meals.

Places to Eat

• Look for these alternatives to formal restaurants:

Cafes serve drinks and sometimes food. Don't be surprised if service is slow. If pressed for time, pay when you're served. "Toast" on a cafe menu means grilled ham or grilled cheese sandwiches.

A *cevabdzinica* serves only grilled meat, so don't go expecting a full meal.

Express are fast-food restaurants, which often serve food cafeteria-style. Most have counters for eating; some also have tables.

A *pasticceria* in the south, and a *slasticarna* in the north, are pastry shops that serve ice cream (by the scoop) and pastries. Don't ask for coffee or tea to accompany your pastry, except in the very best shops. The common beverage offered is lemonade or, sometimes, *boza*— a thick, cold semi-fermented drink made of grain, which people either love or hate. Fill up on pastries; the usual order is three or four per person.

• Don't assume that all the items on the menu are available. Ask the waiter what the restaurant has and also what local specialties are featured.

• If you want to treat someone to a meal in a restaurant, be sure to tell him or her in advance. Otherwise you'll never be allowed to pay.

• Remember that if you go to a restaurant with a group, only one person pays the check. It's understood that the next time the group goes out, someone else will pay.

• If you are a woman alone and go to a cafe, bring along something to do—postcards to write, a book to read—as a sign that you're not there to be picked up. To avoid harassment, don't make eye contact with men.

Specialties

• Yugoslavia has several regions, each with a distinctive character and special foods.

• In Serbia, try *sarma* (grape or cabbage leaves stuffed with meat and rice) and *gibanica* (a pastry made of phyllo, cream cheese and eggs, and served with fruits or preserves).

• In Croatia, look for *knedla od zemicke* (steamed dumplings, which are sliced and served with butter and sour cream) and *zdenka* (cheese served as a dessert).

• In Slovenia (where no meal is complete without soup), taste *vipavska čorba* (a thick soup with sauerkraut, pork, potatoes, and beans, served with sour cream) and *potica* (layered coffee cake with nuts).

• In Bosnia-Herzegovina (where the general way of life is Turkish, so there's no pork), eat *bosanke cufte* (baked meatballs topped with a custard made of eggs and yogurt) and *lokum* (Turkish Delight, a jelly candy rolled in powdered sugar).

• In Montenegro, sample lamb, corn pudding, yogurt and *kajmak* (a cream cheese).

• In Macedonia (where food tends to be very spicy), try yogurt, feta cheese and *tarana*, a rice-like pasta, used in soups and casseroles.

• Unless you thrive on exotic foods, don't order *beli bubrezi* (pigs' testicles, which are marinated for several days in wine, vinegar and onions, and are then grilled).

HOTELS

• When you check in, present your passport and expect it to be retained overnight.

• Be sure to leave your key at the desk when you go out.

• Keep in mind that at most hotels you may not bring guests into your room.

• Hotel maids usually begin working at about 6:00 a.m. If you don't want to be disturbed this early, be sure to put the "Do Not Disturb" sign on your door.

• People often breakfast very early, so you won't have to skip your morning meal if you have a very early plane or train. Plan to eat as early as 5:30 or 6:00 a.m.

• Remember that the hot water in hotels is often turned off in the afternoon.

• Inquire about rooms in private homes through the Tourist Bureau. You will also find people waiting at the bus station, offering a room in their home. Feel free to check your luggage and look at the room before making your decision.

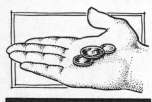

TIPPING

• Restaurants: The check usually includes a 10% service charge, but give the waiter an extra 5%.

• Porters: Tip 10 dinar per bag.

• Taxis: Tip 10% of the fare.

• Cloakroom attendants: Give 3 dinar.

PRIVATE HOMES

• Call on people around 5:00 p.m., the usual visiting hour.

If the people you plan to visit have a phone, call to find out if it's convenient for you to come.

• If your hosts serve preserved fruits in a thick sugar syrup, along with a glass of water, eat a spoonful of the fruit and then drink the water. When you're finished, put the spoon in the glass. You will then be offered Turkish coffee and a liqueur (often plum brandy). Accept one or both; otherwise, you will offend your hosts.

Your host will keep refilling your glass with brandy. If you would prefer not to drink more, leave some brandy in your glass.

• When visiting the region called Dalmatia, expect refreshments to be brandy with dried figs on a bed of bay leaves.

• Should you call on several people in a single afternoon, plan to eat a small amount at each stop. You will offend your hosts if you refuse to accept something.

• If you stay with a family, shake hands when you get up in the morning and before going to bed at night.

• Offer to help with small chores but do not insist on helping if your offer is refused. Even women who work outside of the home insist on doing all the housework and cooking themselves; it's a source of pride for them. Keep your hostess company in the kitchen while she's working but don't expect to be allowed to do anything.

• Always ask permission to use the phone in a private home and always offer to pay for your calls.

• Feel free to bathe daily, but don't wash your hair as often. Yugoslavs consider such frequent washing unnecessary and even harmful.

Gifts: Bring flowers (an odd number but never thirteen) or wine to dinner. If you're coming from outside the country, bring chocolates, which are difficult to obtain in Yugoslavia; Western whiskey, which is very expensive; or coffee beans (Yugoslavs love coffee, but prices are very high and it's often unavailable).

If you stay with a family, bring special gifts from the U.S. such as American cigarettes, shirts, sunglasses, perfume and blue jeans for teenagers.

BUSINESS

Hours

Business and government office hours: 7:00 a.m. to 2:00 p.m., daily except Sunday.

Bank hours: 7:00 to 11:00 a.m. and 5:00 to 8:00 p.m. in the summer, and 8:00 a.m. to noon and 4:00 to 7:00 p.m. in the winter, every day except Sunday and national holidays.

Shop hours: 7:00 or 7:30 a.m. to noon and 5:00 to 8:00 p.m. in the summer, and 8:00 a.m. to 1:00 p.m. and 4:00 to 7:00 p.m. in the winter, Monday through Saturday.

Business Practices

• Most Yugoslavs vacation during July and August, so try not to plan a business trip during that time.

• Check with the Yugoslav National Tourist Office about the many local holidays when businesses will be closed.

• If you make appointments by letter or telephone from the U.S., be sure to confirm them when you arrive in Yugoslavia.

• At a business meeting, expect to be offered juice, coffee and brandy. To be polite, have at least one of them.

• Don't give a direct order about how you want something done. Explain carefully why you believe it is advisable to take the course of action you propose.

Gifts: Give business associates something with your company name on it.

HOLIDAYS AND SPECIAL OCCASIONS

Holidays: New Year's celebration (January 1 and 2), Labor Day (May 1 and 2), Partisan Day (July 4), Republic Day (November 29 and 30).

• Marshal Tito's birthday (March 25) is celebrated as the Day of Youth. About two weeks before, runners set out from remote villages bringing messages to Belgrade. The celebration includes cultural events, sports and folk dances throughout the country.

• Note that some 42% of the population is Eastern Orthodox and therefore celebrates religious holidays in accordance with the Greek Orthodox calendar. Christmas and Easter usually come later than they do on a Western calendar. These days are not official holidays, however.

• If you happen to visit during Ramadan (a 30-day holy period, which varies according to the Arab calendar), be sensitive to the Moslems' religious feelings. Moslems must fast from sunrise to sunset, and they also refrain from smoking. When visiting during this time, don't smoke or eat in front of other people. Note that many restaurants will be closed until after sundown.

TRANSPORTATION

Public Transportation

• You'll find that most cities have bus and streetcar lines that are efficient and inexpensive. They're also well used, since only 10% of the population own cars.

• Buy tickets for the bus and streetcars at kiosks. Before you board, put your ticket into a machine and have it stamped according to how far you are going. Keep your stamped ticket in case of inspection.

• Hail taxis on the street or go to taxi stands, which are often found near bus stops or train stations.

Driving

• To drive in Yugoslavia, obtain a blue or green insurance card at the border or from Yugoslav insurance agencies.

• If you're going to be driving around the country, bring road maps with you if possible, as they are difficult to obtain in Yugoslavia.

• Gas is rationed for Yugoslavs, but as a foreigner, you can buy gas coupons at the border or at large travel agencies.

• If you're going to be driving in a city or town between 5:00 and 8:00 p.m., try to find out in advance where *orzo* (evening promenade) is held, since that street is usually closed to traffic during those hours.

• Be very careful driving along the Adriatic coast during or after rain. Oil and gasoline on the roads—and heavy traffic—make them very treacherous.

• Avoid heavy truck traffic by staying off the main highways through Yugoslavia. Parallel roads are much safer.

• Remember that seat belts are mandatory.

• If you are stopped for a traffic violation, expect the police to ask you to pay the fine (usually $5-$6) on the spot.

LEGAL MATTERS AND SAFETY

• Obtain a visa to enter Yugoslavia or simply pay a symbolic visa fee at the border if you are a U.S. citizen.

• Customs officials tend to be very lenient with tourists, but be aware that merchandise brought in should be for your personal use.

• Don't bring more than two pounds of coffee into the country.

• When you change dollars into dinars, ask for government checks. These give you a 10% discount at all hotels and shops and for all services. Also, if you have some of these checks left over when you leave the country, you can change them back into dollars. If you have dinars in cash left over, you cannot change them into dollars.

• Never exchange currency on the street or with an individual who suggests doing so. You could be arrested for dealing in the black market.

• Feel safe in walking after dark if you know exactly where you are going. If you are a woman and encounter verbal harassment, don't make eye contact and don't smile. When visiting friends, you can expect them to escort you back to your hotel if you leave after dark.

KEY PHRASES

English	Yugoslavian	Pronunciation
Good morning	Dobro jutro	Dó-bro yóotro
Good afternoon	Dobar dan	Dó-bar dáhn
Good evening	Dobro veče	Dó-bro váy-chay
Good night	Laku noć	Láh-koo notch
Please	Molim	Mó-leem
Thank you	Hvala	Chváh-lah
You're welcome	Molim	Mó-leem
Yes	Da	Dah
No	Ne	Nay
Sir, Mr.	Gospodine	Gos-pó-dee-nay
Mrs. Madame	Gospodjo	Gó-spod-yo
Miss	Gospodjice (On the Adriatic coast, Signorina)	Gos-pó-jee-tsay
Excuse me	Izvinite	Eez-vée-nee-tay
I don't understand.	Ne razumem.	Náy rah-zóo-mehm
I don't speak Yugoslavian.	Ne govorim srpsko-hrvatski.	Neh góv-o-reem sérp-sko-hér-vaht-ski
Does anyone here speak English?	Govori li neko ovde engleski?	Go-vó-ree lee náy-ko óv-dch en-gláy-skee

The Traveler's Guide to Asian Customs and Manners
by Kevin Chambers

A quick-reading, easy-reference book of travel etiquette to help you avoid feeling uncomfortable in unfamiliar surroundings. It includes fourteen Asian countries plus Australia and New Zealand.

Order #5090

Best European Travel Tips, 7th Edition

by John Whitman

2001 tips for saving money, time and trouble in Europe. A "how to" guide to European travel that's the best-selling book of its kind.

Order #5070

Order Form

Qty	Title	Author	Order No.	Unit Cost	Total
	The Travelers' Guide to European Customs & Manners	Braganti/Devine	5080	$7.95	
	The Travelers' Guide to Asian Customs & Manners	Chambers, K.	5090	$8.95	
	Best European Travel Tips	Whitman, J.	5070	$7.95	
				Subtotal	
				Shipping and Handling (see below)	
				MN residents add 6% sales tax	
				Total	

YES, please send me the books indicated above. Add $1.25 shipping and handling for the first book and $.50 for each additional book. Add $2.00 to total for books shipped to Canada. Overseas postage will be billed. Allow up to 4 weeks for delivery. Send check or money order payable to Meadowbrook Press. No cash or C.O.D.'s please. Quantity discounts available upon request.

Send book(s) to:

Name _____

Address _____

City _____ State _____ Zip _____

☐ Check enclosed for $_____, payable to Meadowbrook Press

☐ Charge to my credit card (for purchases of $10.00 or more only)

☐ Phone Orders call: (800)338-2232 (for purchases of $10.00 or more only)

Account # _____ ☐ Visa ☐ MasterCard

Signature _____ Exp. date _____

Meadowbrook Press,
18318 Minnetonka Boulevard, Deephaven, MN 55391
(612) 473-5400   Toll free (800) 338-2232

Meadowbrook Press